# TWENTIETH CENTURY VIEWS

The aim of this series is to present the best in contemporary critical opinion on major authors, providing a twentieth century perspective on their changing status in an era of profound revaluation.

Maynard Mack, *Series Editor*
Yale University

# CHARLES DICKENS

## NEW PERSPECTIVES

Edited by
*Wendell Stacy Johnson*

*Prentice-Hall, Inc.*  A SPECTRUM BOOK *Englewood Cliffs, N.J.*

*Library of Congress Cataloging in Publication Data*
Main entry under title:

Charles Dickens, new perspectives.

(Twentieth century views) (A Spectrum Book)
Bibliography: p.
Includes index.
1. Dickens, Charles, 1812–1870—Criticism and
interpretation—Addresses, essays, lectures.
I. Johnson, Wendell Stacy    II. Series.
PR4588.C36      823'.8        82-440
                                    AACR2

ISBN 0-13-128157-7

ISBN 0-13-128140-2 {PBK.}

Editorial/production supervision by Alberta Boddy
Woodcut illustration by Vivian Berger © 1982
Manufacturing buyer: Barbara A. Frick

The essay *Our Mutual Friend*: A Rhetorical Approach to the First
Number, which appears on p. 159 of this volume, is from *Dickens
Studies Annual*, 3 (1974), 198–213. Copyright © by Southern Illinois
University Press; 1980 by AMS Press, Inc. Reprinted by permission of
the publishers.

10  9  8  7  6  5  4  3  2  1

PRENTICE-HALL INTERNATIONAL, INC. *(London)*
PRENTICE-HALL OF AUSTRALIA PTY. LIMITED *(Sydney)*
PRENTICE-HALL OF CANADA, LTD. *(Toronto)*
PRENTICE-HALL OF INDIA PRIVATE LIMITED *(New Delhi)*
PRENTICE-HALL OF JAPAN, INC. *(Tokyo)*
PRENTICE-HALL OF SOUTHEAST ASIA PTE. LTD. *(Singapore)*
WHITEHALL BOOKS LIMITED *(Wellington, New Zealand)*

*For Richard Katz*

# Contents

*vii*

# Introduction

*by Wendell Stacy Johnson*

Asked to name the foremost English novelist, most moderately well-educated readers today will probably say Dickens. If we consider what the novel is, we can agree. Jane Austen displays more worldly wit, George Eliot more apparent moral and intellectual consistency, Henry James a finer narrative concentration. Charles Dickens, sometimes heavy-handed if not morally inconsistent, sometimes diffuse, nevertheless retains his preeminence in the art of English fiction.

This judgment on Dickens is a comment on the mixed nature of the genre itself, for the novel, especially as it has developed in English, is an impure form. It can be repertorial and fanciful both, social in subject and popular in appeal but personal in mode of vision—any or all of these.

Dickens is the essential novelist, the *ur*-novelist; he is himself a mixture, writing in a mixed form. He is both a reporter and a playwright of sorts. A journalist at the end of his career as at its beginning, he was always something of a dramatist (or maker of melodramas) and something of a player or speaker (a ham, a rhetorician)—with a need to communicate vocally. In stories he records the oddities along with the plain, hard facts of his times, and he reflects them to give these facts a mythic form, thus dramatizing himself as the teller, teacher, and the tale itself.

The recent criticism of his fiction, much of it, has emphasized his artist's imagination as deriving from the interplay of a journalist's desire to communicate to his audience with a rhetorical lyricist's desire to reveal himself in dramatic speech and gesture.

Two closely related ways in which such an interplay can be worked out are the fairy tale or traditional story, with the teller as father-figure to his audience, both passing on lore and reliving his childhood; and the highly rhetorical speech or attempt persuasively to communicate—sometimes stuttering in the process—with the

*1*

rhetorician either failing to establish kinship through communication or succeeding as he masters his art and speaks in his true voice.

Myth, self-revelation, and reflection upon kinship in the human family, all of these matters and the very idea of language as mythic expression, intrinsically human in nature, are involved in current criticism of the novel, whether the criticism is called psychological, linguistic, structuralist (or even poststructuralist). All are centrally involved in the criticism of Dickens, most central of our novelists.

Not that the more frequent concerns of earlier critics are now rejected: that concern, especially, with that great novelistic as well as Aristotelian question of the relationship between plot and character. Readers from Dickens's own contemporaries to the present-day student have raised questions about the use of coincidence in his plots and the extravagant portrayal of his characters. But criticism now is likely to find his fictional coincidence an expression of the socially complex nature that makes up the life of his work because it makes up the life his work represents. The apparently various and contrasting levels, aspects, human beings and their origins all do in the human order coincide; all are apparent orphans, all are members of one family. Modern criticism is likely to perceive the eccentric character or type not just as flat and comic, presented as a means to satirize or entertain, but also as one facet of the full human character, often one among several refractions of a complicated psychological whole—the whole person, in a psychoanalytical reading, who is the artist. And for a critic now, assuming and accepting Dickens's complicated plot structures and his simplified characters, the problem of plot and character means more yet.

It means, first, not merely which is the more important, but how plot and character reinforce each other or fail to do so. In a sense this is the matter Vande Kieft and Levine consider when they write about communicating in *Great Expectations*. Do the protagonist and those who should make up his family, if the theme of the novel is a fulfillment of expectations unexpected by the would-be gentleman, fully communicate at last? Is the kinship of common humanity altogether sustained in Pip's and others' actions and speech?

It means too—and this question is related to that—the problem whether Dickens's rhetoric bears out the spiritual or "inner" life which is his own so that plots and characters emerge by being authentically one, David Copperfield adequately telling his story, Esther Summerson hers, and Charles Dickens *his*.

## II

In such discussions, the critics tend still to stress mythic plotting and personae, in particular the myths of generation and the generations: the generating father, author, teller of tales, who is also the liar, who poses and distorts by limiting his potential and his child's, who must be forgiven as the failed fathers in Dickens stories—and the father of his own imprisoned childhood, himself imprisoned—must be forgiven. Sometimes the failure of the parent is simply in leaving, leaving the child an orphan. Sometimes, again, the children of Dickens's world may only seem to be orphans.

Pip is literally an orphan, one who needs to find a brother—Joe, literally his brother-in-law—and to find a sort of father, too, the initially threatening convict Magwitch—who becomes his father in law in the legal sense of adopting him and giving him an inheritance, just as Estella has been adopted.

Oliver Twist, however, in a story potentially more cheerful but actually one with darker ogres that are not so easily exorcised, is a child outlawed, the illegitimate son. He is one version of the foundling who must apparently "make good" on his own, as Colby's study shows; yet, in truth, in his outlawing world of outlaws he cannot make himself or be good. He is not only an orphan because he has no legal father but is also the orphan of, the illegitimate or nonmember of, a whole social order, one in which exploitation of the vulnerable often masks itself as charity and the crime of being a rejected child is likely to be followed by a criminal life rather than the "parish boy's progress" upward. For only a Carlylean ideal orphan can, heroically, transcend time, place, and percentage. Oliver must have a benefactor come to his aid, an apparently surrogate parent. Otherwise, as Dickens demonstrates but perhaps never quite fully recognizes, Carlyle's self-sufficiency cannot be heroic enough in the hard world—not without a supporting family of humankind. The orphan who, transcendentally or as in popular fiction sentimentally, so prides himself on being self-made is, in spite of all the Teufelsdröckhs and Cheerybles and, finally, the Bounderbys, a fraud. He is not an authentic character who can be sustained in that pride through the plots of an authentic fictive word, the world of Dickens's own hard times, real times; this is not Carlyle's timeless never-nowhere-land, but the England of really or partly orphaned sons, Pip and Oliver and Nicholas Nickleby, Barnaby Rudge, Martin

Chuzzlewit, and of psychologically orphaned daughters as well, Florence Dombey, Sissy Jupe, Louisa Gradgrind.

Those who should serve as his parents and mentors, both wicked uncle and stupidly cruel teacher, betray Nicholas Nickleby. But if the corruption of Dotheboys Hall is unmanning, the alternative suggested by the Cheeryble brothers (with a pragmatism from Samuel Smiles glossing over their failure to grow up, their generative and thus sexual retardation which is disturbingly suggestive of the twins Balin and Balan in Tennyson's *Idylls*) is even more so, being as unreal as the sickly candied part of a childhood fairy-tale. These are no fathers, and their story is a tidied-up version of myth, a wishful and willfully blinded account of the greedy world it apologizes for. The plot in which they fleetingly live exists as if that world of time had no existence, had no plot, no plotting.

There is plotting of the most sinister kind in *Barnaby Rudge* and *Martin Chuzzlewit*, and vicious betrayal. The former presents, like *King Lear*, parallel relationships of child and parent, with power at dispute between son and father in each filial—or, rather, unfilial—pair; so Steven Marcus observes in his chapter "Sons and Fathers," adding that these rivalries display a radical distortion, a challenge to parental authority, that can result in "social suicide." Or, as Edgar Johnson puts it, the betrayal of the bastard Hugh by his father Sir John Chester epitomizes "a society that denies its children," thus its future. *Martin Chuzzlewit* exposes again what Barickman's essay here calls the corrupt and corrupting patriarchal system with its translating of sexual generation and the generations into the false value of brute dominance.

Within this dark scheme of values that Dickens illuminates, parents can deny and betray children—as Dombey denies his daughter—and children can betray by denying parents. The denial of parentage is an act of the "self-made man" who is a grim version of Carlyle's Hero. He becomes the parody of Teufelsdröckh, the counterfeit orphan: the mechanized Bradley Headstone of *Our Mutual Friend*, the grim Josiah Bounderby of *Hard Times*.


## III


*Hard Times* shows the range of possible relationships between parent and child and what each implies. Bounderby, who pretends to be self-generated and without a filial obligation, is the heartless husband and master. Gradgrind is the father who fails, not heartless but foolish, and his failure blights the life of a daughter as it virtually destroys the son's. Jupe, too, is a failure, but once again the forgiving child becomes a surrogate parent, and Sissy Jupe sustains Louisa as she remains loyal to her parentage. Each character can be judged according to her or his acceptance of a family relationship; Sissy, the moral touchstone of the novel, is, as her nickname implies, a sister because she is a daughter; she can be like a mother, as well, because she can be a child.

True social relations in the novel are family relations—as in Sleary's circus, one family teeming with life, with babies and babylike people—and false ones are social impositions, Louisa's marriage to Bounderby which follows from blighted childhood affections, Stephen's disastrous marriage which blights his love for Rachel.

Hard times, hard facts: this is what Dickens reports. He also reports what he remembers and imagines, and that means childhood memories taking the form of myth, of tales from the childhood of humanity. He persuades us that plotted coincidence, what Jung calls synchronicity, and personality caricatured, as in the melodrama, are forms, too, of truth. In fantasy he may seem to escape the prison of Gradgrind's facts, but the result is not simply escapism: as Robert Garis comments in *The Dickens Theatre*, his actor's rhetoric and playing of roles, his disguising and refracting of personality, constitute an untranslatable dramatic reality—personal, psychological, ultimately moral. Or, in Garrett Stewart's words, Dickens is a "dramatic symbolist" with "lyric inwardness of style."

He can, like the most richly realized of his people, play the roles of child and parent, of storyteller and storybook character, because he is identified with his own fiction—that is to say, he is identified as one in the family of human kind. So he was for his generation, so he is for ours.

The essays selected for this book concern Dickens as a reporter and social critic and, at the same time, as an imaginative genius. Most of them were written during the past two decades. Chosen as representative and exemplary pieces of criticism, they vary in degree of complexity, of difficulty, and in method: their several emphases are historical, thematic, mythic, psychoanalytical, structural, rhetorical, biographical. These should suggest the variety of modes that characterizes modern critical work on the novels, even when—as here—the work tends to follow some common lines of interest. Finally, most of these essays are not easily available as chapters of books or in other collections.

# Oliver Twist:
# The Fortunate Foundling

*by Robert A. Colby*

Oliver Twist announces his entrance into life with a lusty cry. As Dickens says, had little Oliver known what awaited him, he would have cried louder. Without the social status of Edward Waverley, or the family connections of Fanny Price, "he was badged and ticketed, and fell into his place at once—a parish child—the orphan of a work-house—the humble, half-starved drudge—to be cuffed and buffeted through the world—despised by all, and pitied by none." Despite his low status, however, he is subjected no less than Fanny Price to educational schemes: "a systematic course of treachery and decep-tion" at the parish workhouse, the "parental superintendance" of that efficient domestic economist Mrs. Mann; the "experimental philosophy" tried out by the board of the "brick and mortar elysium" which serves Oliver, for lack of better, as his nursery and elementary school. Because of Oliver's peculiar circumstances, his formal education is brief, perfunctory, and rather hit-or-miss, but he somehow manages to acquire perfect manners and faultless grammar.

In Jane Austen's time, as we have observed, bluestockings like Hannah More, Laetitia Matilda Hawkins, and Elizabeth Hamilton dedicated their pens to the cause of the education of the poor, but by the 1830's the issue was being debated in the halls of Parliament. The New Poor Law, a familiar part of the background of *Oliver Twist*, raised the nagging problem of the schooling of workhouse wards.[1] By now the need for educating the children of paupers and abandoned

[1] The background information supplied by Humphry House in *The Dickens World* (London, 1960) is supplemented by Edgar Johnson, *Charles Dickens: His Tragedy and Triumph* (New York, 1952), I, 275.

or orphaned children was widely recognized, but there was no agreement as to who was responsible for it. The farming-out system
employed for Little Oliver and his fellow inmates was certainly
obsolete by this time. Dickens, a legislative reporter, was undoubtedly aware of the bill proposed by John Arthur Roebuck in
1833 calling for the establishment of an infant school in every
parish.[2] But this was before the concept of state education had taken
root, and Roebuck's scheme came to naught. In May 1835 Lord
Brougham, addressing the House of Lords, declared it inexpedient
to establish parish schools; he suggested instead "voluntary effort"
by the philanthropic and civic-minded.[3] It may have been he whom
Dickens lampooned a few years later in a sketch as "the Radical . . . of
the utilitarian school . . . having many ingenious remarks to offer
upon the voluntary principle and various cheerful disquisitions
connected with the population of the country."[4] Most of Dickens'
examples of volunteer educators in *Oliver Twist*, at any rate, are far
from heartening. Mrs. Mann is one. Fagin is another, offering to
Oliver the seminary for youth where he is such an inept pupil. Oliver
eventually proves more fortunate than Fagin's other pupils by falling
in with Mr. Brownlow, who furnishes the home-school so congenial
to Dickens' ideals of education. But first he—and the reader—
undergo the rigorous regimen of the streets.

Oliver Twist is not only tossed between the Old Poor Law and the
New Poor Law, but bandied about from guardian to guardian. Nor
does there seem to have been much agreement as to what waifs
thrown on "the tender mercies of churchwardens and overseers"
were supposed to learn. The red-faced "philosopher" in the white
waistcoat who interviews Oliver in the workhouse assumes that he is
to be "taught a useful trade," but depends on unsupervised volunteers to carry out the program. Evidence from other sources indicates
that vigorous efforts were being made during these years to protect
helpless boys from the real-life Gamfields and Sowerberrys. Barbara
Hofland, a popular children's writer, pointed to her native Sheffield
as a model for the administration of poor relief. In this large
manufacturing town, she proudly proclaimed, even though the poor
are numerous, funds are ample and the overseers are "men of

[2]Summarized by John Manning in *Dickens on Education* (Toronto, 1959), pp. 17–
18, p. 150.
[3]Ibid., p. 18.
[4]"The Political Young Gentleman," *Sketches of Young Gentlemen*, Standard Library
Edition (Boston, 1894), XXVIII, 243. *Sketches of Young Gentlemen* was first published
by Chapman and Hall in 1838.

property and benevolence, alike liberal and conscientious"—more like Mr. Brownlow, one supposes, than Mr. Bumble. She contrasts the wealthy city with "petty villages" where "the poor are at the mercy of the mean and tyrannical who conceive that they oblige their neighbours by curtailing the comforts of the poor."[5] Among Oliver Twist's misfortunes is being born in the "petty village" of Mudfog.

Bill Sikes, of all people, is our source of information about another institution that was trying to ease the "parish boy's progress." The master thief complains that the Juvenile Delinquent Society is encroaching on his "occupation" when it takes a vagrant boy in hand, "teaches him to read and write, and in time makes a 'prentice of him." But things could be worse. "If they'd got money enough (which it's a Providence they have not), we shouldn't have half a dozen boys left in the whole trade, in a year or two" (CH. XIX). That threat seems indefinitely averted. Dickens had, however, a more encouraging example before him in the Foundling Hospital, located in Great Coram Field near Doughty Street, where he lived while he was writing *Oliver Twist*. He took an active interest in this institution, regularly attending chapel there during the few years that he lived in the neighborhood, and in this connection became acquainted with a namesake of Oliver's benefactor—John Brownlow.[6] At the time when Dickens met him, Brownlow was in charge of the placement of boys and had succeeded in reforming the policy of the Foundling Hospital with regard to apprenticeship after bringing to light cases of cruelty by masters. In other respects too Brownlow showed up the "experimental philosophers" of Mudfog, effecting improvements in the physical care and the diet of the inmates of the Foundling Hospital.[7] Brownlow himself was living proof of the benefits of this institution; he had originally entered it himself as a charity boy. As will be shown later, Dickens' association with this asylum, rooted in eighteenth-century paternalism and hallowed by missionary zeal, is closely linked to the theme and tone of *Oliver Twist*.

To its first readers, *Oliver Twist* had the glare of an exposé. Serial

---

[5]Preface to *Elizabeth and Her Three Beggar Boys* (1830).

[6]The Foundling Hospital owns an unpublished letter dated February 26, 1840 from Dickens to Brownlow apologizing for not having given notice of change of residence and relinquishing his pew in the chapel. By now the prosperous author had moved from Doughty Street to Regent's Park.

[7]In connection with Oliver's famous asking for more, it might be noted that after 1840 the allowance of meat, potatoes, bread and butter was increased, and the oatmeal was discontinued altogether (R. H. Nichols and F. A. Wray, *The History of the Foundling Hospital* [London, 1935], pp. 227–78).

publication allied it with topical journalism; Cruikshank's illustrations made the characters leer, simper, glower, and beam right out of its pages. In the playbill of a "serio-comic burletta" hacked out of the tale while the press ink was hardly dry, the author was applauded for " 'Holding the mirror up to nature' albeit in its worst light." Dickens, according to this playsmith, was "opening one of the darkest volumes of life, and revealing facts that must startle the more strongly, from the previous total ignorance of their existence, even by those persons residing in the very heart of the scenes in which they are daily and nightly passing."[8] Dickens was not, of course, introducing his readers to the seamy side of London life for the first time. Some of the *Sketches by Boz Illustrative of Every-Day Life and Every-Day People*, which first appeared in newspapers, germinated characters and episodes in *Oliver Twist*. The first of the sketches, "The Parish," begins ominously: "How much is conveyed in those two short words—'The Parish.' And with how many tales of distress and misery, of broken fortune, and ruined hopes, too often of unrelieved wretchedness and successful knavery are they associated." Bumble is anticipated in the portrait that follows of the Beadle "in his state-coat and cocked hat with a large-headed staff for show in his left hand, and a small cane for use in his right" officiously marshaling the urchins in his charge. The master of the workhouse and the parish schoolmaster are among others sketched. "A Visit to Newgate" takes in juvenile delinquents and a school for pickpockets. Among the "Scenes" transferred in part to *Oliver Twist* are "The Streets—Morning," "The Streets—Nights," "Gin-Shops," "Criminal Courts," "The Prisoners' Van," and "The Drunkard's Death." In Dickens' first book, parish boys, charity schools, apprenticeship, and crime are brought together between covers but not yet amalgamated into a novel.

In the Preface to the Second Edition of the *Sketches*, the youthful "Boz," pleased with the success of his "pilot balloon," promises his

---

[8]Although the serialization of *Oliver Twist* in *Bentley's Miscellany*, which began in February, 1837, extended to April, 1839, its first edition in book form appeared on November 9, 1838. This burletta by George Almar, staged just ten days later at the Royal Surrey Theatre, has the dubious distinction of being the first to be based on the entire novel. At least three earlier dramatizations were on the boards during the previous spring, before Dickens had even completed the writing of the story. (For the stage record, see Forster's *Life of Dickens*, ed. J. W. T. Ley [London, 1928], p. 129.) According to Kathleen Tillotson ("Oliver Twist," *Essays and Studies*, 1959, pp. 87–88), Dickens had finished only two-thirds of the novel by mid-July, 1838. Almar's version, which had a revival as late as 1893, is reprinted in Lacy's *Acting Edition of Plays*, Vol. 33, No. 494 (1858).

faithful readers "fresh sketches, and even connected works of fiction of a higher grade, [for which] they have only themselves to blame." Connection, indeed, is what he particularly insists upon in many of the chapter headings of his first plotted novel: "Treats of a very poor Subject. But is a short one; and may be found of some Importance in this History" (CH. XXIV—the death of the hag who stole the locket from Oliver's mother); "In which a mysterious Character [Monks] appears upon the Scene; and many things inseparable from this History are done and performed" (CH. XXVI); "Is a very short one, and may appear of no great importance in its Place, but it should be read notwithstanding, as a Sequel to the last, and a Key to one that will follow when its Time arrives (CH. XXXVI—the parting of Rose Maylie and Harry). His description of his new book as a "history" in itself stresses causal sequence. Dickens was struggling against the serial publication of the story, its picaresque tendency and particularly the association of his name in readers' minds with trivial comedies and ephemeral journalism. His problem was complicated by the concurrent appearance of *Pickwick Papers* and the reissue of *Sketches by Boz* in monthly parts.[9] Probably, however, Dickens was most concerned about his reputation with critics who had questioned his ability to sustain a long narrative and were already predicting the exhaustion of his sparkling vein.[10] The highly cultivated

[9]The name given in the serial version to the village where Oliver was born—Mudfog—suggested a continuation of *The Mudfog Papers*, another set of pieces that Dickens contributed to *Bentley's Miscellany*. In subsequent editions the place is referred to merely as "a certain town, which for many reasons it will be prudent to refrain from mentioning and to which I will assign no fictitious name."

Apart from his sketch writing, Dickens had some theatrical reputation at this time as collaborator with John Hullah of a musical farce, *The Village Coquettes*, and sole author of a burletta, *The Strange Gentleman*. Many years later he requested that the composer leave his name off a republication of *The Village Coquettes*. (See *Dickens' Correspondence with John Hullah* [Printed by Walter Dexter for His Friends, September, 1933], p. 19.)

[10]The critic for the *London and Westminster Review* admired the *Sketches by Boz* for their wit, humor, and keen observation, but thought they tended toward monotony because of their slightness and repetitiousness. He observed of the *Pickwick Papers* that while the author hits off "little traits of conduct" and describes "the more obvious peculiarities of mind and person" nicely, "he does not appear to appreciate the minute shades of characters; and, above all, he shows no particular skill in developing character in action" (July, 1837, pp. 198–99). However, this reviewer detected signs of maturity in *Oliver Twist*, which he found "indeed remarkable, as a specimen of a style rather more serious and pathetic than any other of the author's longer works" (p. 213). The critic for the *Quarterly Review*, having feared on the basis of a "decline visible in the later number of Pickwick" that Boz' talent was in danger

style of the book, which contributes to its satirical effect, also indicates, together with his self-conscious exposure of his artistry, that
he was trying to convince the snobbish gentlemen of the press that he
was something more than "the literary Teniers of the metropolis."[11]
Dickens, moreover, was making a bid for consideration as an
interpreter of life, not merely a reporter of it. The playbill of the
burletta that was the first of numerous efforts to extend his message
to the semiliterate who attended the theatre hailed the author of
*Oliver Twist* as a "Hogarth [who] has raised a beacon on the basis of
truth to warn the erring, guide the inexperienced, instruct the
ignorant to avoid the shoals by which they are surrounded." Dickens'
tale was reduced here to "a great moral lesson" proving that vice is
eventually punished and virtue rewarded. Dickens himself, though
disavowing this dramatization,[12] echoed its program note in his first
public pronouncement on his first novel, the Preface to the Third
Edition of 1841, where he invoked the spirit of Hogarth, "the
moralist and censor of his age."[13] Too many readers, to Dickens'
annoyance, had become so engrossed in the low life of his novel that
they had missed its high purpose. The Princess Victoria for one,
reading it in *Bentley's Miscellany*, confided to her mother that she
found it "too interesting" and was promptly scolded for indulging in
light literature.[14] Thackeray, his greatest rival, while ridiculing *Oliver
Twist* in his mock-novel *Catherine*, admitted that "the reader at once
becomes [Dickens'] captive, and must follow him whithersoever he
leads."[15] But Thackeray did not like where he was being led. Against
critics who had condemned *Oliver Twist* as salacious and immoral,
Dickens felt compelled to defend his choice of characters, "from the
most criminal and degraded of London's population." "I have yet to

of running into the ground, was pleased to find that in the first numbers of *Oliver Twist* "there is a sustained power, a range of observation, and a continuity of interest in this series, which we seek in vain in any other of his works" (October, 1837, p. 518).
[11]So called by the critic for the *London and Westminster Review* (cited in note 10 above).
[12]According to Forster, he lay on the floor of his box practically throughout the performance that he attended. (See *The Life of Charles Dickens*, ed. Ley, p. 125.)
[13]Dickens defends himself here against periodical reviewers who, unlike the writer of the playbill quoted above, had denounced *Oliver Twist* as vicious and obscene. See particularly *Atlas*, November 17, 1838; *Spectator*, November 24, 1838; and *Quarterly Review*, June 1839.
[14]Elizabeth Longford, *Queen Victoria: Born to Succeed* (New York, 1964), p. 90.
[15]Oxford Thackeray, ed. George Saintsbury (London, 1908), III, 185.

learn," he continues, "that a lesson of the purest good may not be drawn from the vilest evil." Out of Oliver's adventures in the underworld he extracted a fable of incorruptible innocence, as wholesome as *Sandford and Merton* or *The Shepherd of Salisbury Plain:* "The principle of Good surviving through every adverse circumstance, and triumphing at last."

The serial publication of *Oliver Twist* tended to leave the outcome of "the principle of Good" in suspense as Oliver was shunted between malefactors and benefactors. The three-volume publication, which antedated the conclusion of the serial, also left the survival of innocence in doubt, since the first volume ended with Fagin's turning over Oliver to Bill Sikes, and the second with the rendezvous between Oliver's evil half-brother Monks and the corruptible Bumble. But Dickens' intention was finally fixed indelibly in the readers' minds with the edition in numbers which, contrary to normal practice, came out five years after the three-decker.[16] Here the front wrapper designed by Cruikshank sets out in a series of panels Dickens' conception of Oliver's "progress" as a modern morality—at the top Oliver embracing a benign lady inside a cottage, at the bottom Fagin shivering in his cell, while flanked on the right and left between "heaven and hell" are Oliver's tormentors and tempters. To us, the survival of Good "through every adverse circumstance" seems a matter of Oliver's being in the right place at the right time, but we need to put ourselves in the frame of mind of Dickens' generation, who more readily assumed that God helps the helpless. Many years later, in a letter to Wilkie Collins, Dickens expressed his own conviction as to "the ways of Providence, of which all art is but a little imitation."[17]

In his 1841 Preface Dickens emphasizes the pathos of his tale, for the benefit of children and his more delicate adult readers. A careful reading of his pronouncement prepares one for the full blend of sensation, satire, and sentiment that he was working up into his formula, but he shrewdly understates the first two elements. During the serial publication of *Oliver Twist* and afterward, he was plagued by invidious comparisons with the so-called "Newgate" school of fiction. The coupling of his novel with *Jack Sheppard* was inevitable, since

---

[16]For the best account to date, admittedly tentative, of its tangled textual history, see Kathleen Tillotson, *"Oliver Twist* in Three Volumes," *The Library*, 5th Series, XVIII (1963), 113–32.

[17]October 6, 1859, from Gad's Hill Place. *Letters of Charles Dickens to Wilkie Collins, 1851–1870*, ed. Laurence Hutton (London, 1892), p. 104.

the Ainsworth melodrama also appeared in *Bentley's Miscellany* (under Dickens' editorship) and was illustrated by Cruikshank. A reviewer of *Jack Sheppard* recognized the essential moral seriousness of Dickens' story but candidly added, "We are certain that it is far less the undercurrent of philosophy which has sold his book, than the strong flavour of the medium, in which he has disguised the bitterness of its taste."[18] Thackeray, despite a "sneaking kindness" for the book, lumped it—largely on the basis of the sentimental treatment of Nancy—with Ainsworth's stories and with Bulwer's *Paul Clifford* and *Eugene Aram* in his parody *Catherine*, where he denounced the glorifying of crime. Dickens does his best to dissociate himself from this company, writing in the Preface: "Here are no canterings on moonlit heaths, no merry-makings in the snuggest of all possible caverns, none of the attractions of dress, no embroidery, no lace, no jackboots, no crimson coats and ruffles, none of the dash and freedom with which 'the road' has been, time out of mind, invested." Instead, like Cervantes, he attempts "to dim the false glitter surrounding something which really did exist, by showing it in its unattractive and repulsive truth." So his criminals are city thieves and murderers, not glamorous highwaymen, wear greasy flannel, frayed velveteen, soiled breeches, and disport themselves in dark, filthy taverns. Little Oliver, no more attracted by crime in literature than in life, flings away the lurid history of the lives and trials of great criminals that Fagin gives him, just as readers are supposed to do.

The pumped-up Gothic atmosphere of some scenes in *Oliver Twist* suggests a lingering memory of Dickens' childhood reading in other crime fiction. Old Sally, the midwife who attends Oliver's mother, is a stereotype of the literary witch: "Her body was bent by age, her limbs trembled with palsy, and her face distorted into a mumbling leer" (CH. XXIV). As Dickens admits, she "resembled more the grotesque shaping of some wild pencil than the work of Nature's hand," perhaps a concession that he got her out of an illustration from a penny dreadful. Oliver's elder brother, with his "dark figure," "trembling hands," "grim laughs," "excited imagination," and obsession with demons is straight out of the literature of "the awful and the terrific." The nocturnal meeting between this villain and the Bumbles takes place in a noisome swamp near the river, amidst a cluster of abandoned huts and a dilapidated old factory where they are interrupted occasionally, and predictably, by peals of thunder

---

[18]*Athenaeum*, October 26, 1839, p. 804.

and flashes of lightning. Here Dickens transforms the props of the Gothic romances—ruined castles, abbeys, murky tarns, and crashing storms—to suit a modern urban setting. His giving the nickname Monks to his malevolent schemer is a lame joke that has generally gone unappreciated.

His true wit comes out in his handling of a more contemporaneous realistic genre. A contemporary of Dickens, accounting for the success of *Oliver Twist*, recalled that "he arose at a time when the novels of England were both vicious and snobbish, when one set of writers was producing the Satanic school of literature, and another, like those poor things whom we name to forget, the Countess of Blessington and Lady Charlotte Bury, was cultivating what was appropriately called the silver-fork school."[19] In "London Recreations," one of the *Sketches by Boz*, Dickens pokes gentle fun at "the small gentility—the would be aristocrats—of the middle classes, . . . tradesmen and clerks, with fashionable, novel reading families." One of the early reviewers of *Oliver Twist* was pleased that its author took the novel out of the drawing room into the streets. Dickens' popularity, he observes, "has been fairly earned without resorting to any of the means by which most other writers have succeeded in attracting the attention of their contemporaries. He has flattered no popular prejudices and profited by no passing folly; he has attempted no caricature sketches of the manner or conversation of the aristocracy; and there are few political or personal allusions in his works."[20] Dickens himself declared in his 1841 Preface:

> I saw no reason, when I wrote this book, why the dregs of life, so long as their speech did not offend the ear, should not serve the purpose of a moral, at least as well as its froth and cream. Nor did I doubt that there lay festering in Saint Giles's as good materials towards the truth as any to be found in Saint James's.

These words have usually been taken at their face value, but the alert reader can catch the sly author winking between the lines. Such a reader is best able to savor the irony of Dickens' description of the infant Oliver in his swaddling clothes: "What an excellent example of

---

[19]J. Hain Friswell, "Mr. Charles Dickens," *Modern Men of Letters Honestly Criticised* (London, 1870), pp. 133–34.
[20]*Quarterly Review*, p. 484. This reviewer affirms that "the portrait of the author of 'Pelham' or 'Crichton' was scraped down or pasted over to make room for that of the new popular favourite in the omnibuses." However, the advent of Dickens hardly ended the vogue of Ainsworth and Bulwer.

the power of dress, young Oliver Twist was! Wrapped in the blanket which had hitherto formed his only covering, he might have been the child of a nobleman or a beggar; it would have been hard for the haughtiest stranger to have assigned him his proper station in society" (CH. I). Dickens does not mean here merely to anticipate Oliver's refined parentage. The barbed chapter headings scattered through the novel suggest that, but for the grace of God, Oliver "might have been" the hero of a "Silver Fork" novel. His apprenticeship in particular suggests an unlike likeness with the career of the dandy. Chapter III, which introduces Gamfield, "Relates How Oliver Twist was very near getting a Place, which would not have been a Sinecure"—like a seat in the House of Lords or a commission. Oliver's situation at this point could also have been contrasted with that of the hero of another Bentley novel advertised in the first edition—*Melton de Mowbray; or, The Banker's Son*.[21] The next chapter, where Oliver meets Sowerberry, headed "Oliver, being offered another Place, makes his first Entry into public Life," suggests the fortunes of Disraeli's Young Duke. This vein is sustained by ambiguous chapter summaries that ape the *ton*: "How Oliver passed his Time in the improving Society of his reputable Friends" [Jack Dawkins and Charlie Bates]; "Atones for the Unpoliteness of a former Chapter; which deserted a Lady [Mrs. Corney] most unceremoniously"; "An old acquaintance of Oliver's [Noah Claypole], exhibiting decided Marks of Genius, becomes a public Character in the Metropolis"; "Comprehending a Proposal of Marriage [Harry and Rose Maylie] with no Word of Settlement or Pin-money."[22]

Through Noah Claypole in particular Dickens parodies the peacocks who strut through *Almacks* and *The Exclusives*. As a charity-boy, Noah is one rung up the social ladder from Oliver, a mere workhouse orphan: "No chance-child was he, for he could trace his genealogy all the way back to his parents, who lived hard by; his mother being a washerwoman, and his father a drunken soldier."

[21]CH. IV begins: "In great families, when an advantageous place cannot be obtained, either in possession, reversion, remainder, or expectancy, for the young man who is growing up, it is a very general custom to send him to sea. The board, in imitation of so wise and salutary an example, took counsel together on the expediency of shipping over Oliver Twist in some small trading vessel bound to a good unhealthy port. . . ." Advertisements of such novels as Captain Glascock's *Land Sharks and Sea Gulls*, Cooper's *Homeward Bound*, and Captain Chamier's *Life of a Sailor* and *Ben Brace* formed a fitting backdrop to this passage.

[22]Quite possibly an allusion to Mrs. Gore's *Pin Money* (1831).

Noah, himself derided by the shop-boys, follows the pecking ord by abusing Oliver, "now that fortune had cast in his way a nameless orphan, at whom the meanest could point the finger of scorn." Among other things, Dickens is writing the poor man's *Book of Snobs*. As he observes of the relationship between Noah and Oliver: "It shows us what a beautiful thing human nature is, and how impartially the same amiable qualities are developed in the finest lord and the dirtiest charity-boy" (CH. V).

Bill Sikes, hiding out in a dingy tenement after an unsuccessful "expedition" to Chertsey, bears a faint resemblance to Beau Brummell: "The house-breaker was lying on the bed, wrapped in his white greatcoat by way of a dressing gown"; "Nor were there wanting other indications of the good gentleman's having gone down in the world of late, for a great scarcity of furniture, and total absence of comfort, together with the disappearance of all such small movables as spare clothes and linen, bespoke a state of extreme poverty" (CH. XXXIX). Bill's overdressed accomplice Toby Crackit, with his "smartly cut snuff-colored coat, with large brass buttons; an orange neckerchief," and his red-dyed hair "tortured into long corkscrew curls," is a grotesque version of a Regency fop, and at the same time neatly hits off Bulwer's gentleman thieves (CH. XXII). His speech also is pseudo-Holland House: "I can't talk about business until I've eat and drank; so produce the sustainance, and let's have a quiet fill-out for the first time these three days!" (CH. XXV).[23] Dickens has indeed kept his promise to his readers not to "offend the ear." Crackit is ashamed to be seen playing cribbage with Tom Chitling, "a gentleman so much his inferior in station and mental endowments," but is pleased to take the easy money. Chitling is too much dazzled by Crackit's gentility to care about his loss. Their creator cannot help interposing that "there are a great number of spirited young bloods upon town who pay a much higher price than Mr. Chitling for being seen in good society, and a great number of fine gentlemen (composing the good society aforesaid) who establish their reputation upon very much the same footing as flash Toby Crackit" (CH. XXXIX). He depicts two such, Lord Frederick Verisopht and Sir Mulberry Hawk, in his next novel, *Nicholas Nickleby*.

In "London Recreations" Dickens had observed: "The wish of

---

[23]He progressively combed out "damns" and other oaths, even references to profanity, from his manuscript and the serial version as he revised it for subsequent editions. (See Tillotson, "Oliver Twist," *Essays and Studies*, p. 100.)

persons in the humbler classes of life to ape the manner and customs of those whom fortune has placed above them is often the subject of remark, and most frequently of complaint." He furnishes plenty of examples among Oliver's "improving friends." The Artful Dodger, Jack Dawkins, a "young gentleman," introduces Oliver to Fagin, a " 'spectable old gentleman." Fagin lives up to the role. When Oliver first meets him, "the Jew grinned; and making a low obeisance . . . took him by the hand, and hoped he should have the honour of his intimate acquaintance" (CH. VIII). Everybody to him is "my dear"; Oliver is taught manners ("Make 'em your models, my dear—make 'em your models . . . do everything they bid you, and take their advice in all matters—especially the Dodger's, my dear. He'll be a great man himself, and will make you one, if you take pattern by him"); he is avuncular toward Nancy ("Why . . . you're more clever than ever tonight. Ha! Ha! my dear, you are acting beautifully [giving her a basket]. Carry that in one hand, it looks more respectable, my dear"); he attempts to polish her uncouth companion ("Come, come, Sikes . . . We must have civil words—civil words, Bill."). Bill proves somewhat refractory, but Nancy knows how to lay out "tea things" in the garret after he has finished a bout of debauchery, and Oliver takes time out for "making his toilet" before accompanying him on a predawn burglary expedition.

But Dickens' satire is double-edged. Most of the episodes involving Fagin, Bill Sikes, their "associates" and their "protégés" have their counterparts in the "Exclusivism, fashionable novelism, Nashism, and fifty other fribbleisms of the West-end" recalled by one of Mrs. Gore's retired gentlemen.[24] For the schools of deportment and the dancing academies, substitute the public house in Saffron Hill where Fagin puts his "dear boys" through their paces. For the faro and gaming tables, substitute the whist matches of the Artful Dodger, Toby, and Tom. In Fagin's household the magazine is not the *Journal des Modes* but the *Hue and Cry*. In place of the elegant shopping districts of Bond Street and Regent Street, readers are escorted to Field Lane, the "dismal alley" leading to Saffron Hill, in whose "filthy shops are exposed for sale huge bunches of second-hand silk handkerchiefs, of all sizes and patterns; for here reside the traders who purchase them from pickpockets," and are invited to peer inside warehouses where "stores of old iron and bones, and

[24]*Cecil the Peer*, I, CH.II.

heaps of mildewy fragments of woollen-stuff and linen, rust and rot in the grimy cellars" (CH. XXVI).

Among their other "London Recreations" Dickens' would-be aristocrats of the lower classes like to "get up tavern assemblies in humble imitation of Almack's and promenade the dingy 'large room' of some second-rate hotel with as much complacency as the enviable few who are privileged to exhibit their magnificence in that exclusive haunt of fashion and foolery." Peer, parvenu, and poor come together in that low-life Almack's, the Three Cripples Inn. This euphemistically styled, smoke-laden "establishment" has its "chairman with a hammer of office in his hand" and its exclusive membership like "a professional gentleman, with a bluish nose and his face tied up for the benefit of the toothache, [who] presided at a jingling piano in a remote corner." Soon the distinguished company joins voices in a ribald ballad. A few years earlier, Bulwer had proclaimed proudly in *England and the English* that the clubs which "form a main feature of the social system of the richer classes of the metropolis" were no longer "merely the resort of gamblers, politicians or bon vivants." He ventured to predict, completely without tongue in cheek, that these institutions would infiltrate the lower levels of society, for their atmosphere of "moral dignity" and "intellectual relaxation" "contain the germ of a mighty improvement in the condition of the humbler classes."[25] This improvement obviously has not reached that hideout, the Three Cripples, to judge by the music of the establishment and the conversation, which turns mainly on such topics of the day as police news and the affairs of Fagin, Sikes, and Company. The membership as a whole has reached this stage of enlightenment: "Cunning, ferocity and drunkenness in all its stages were there, in their strongest aspects . . . presenting but one loathsome blank of profligacy and crime."

One has the feeling that in this Hogarthian scene Dickens was not merely exposing his more privileged readers to the cesspools of London but showing them their own reflections there. Certainly the society mirrored in some of the novels of the day was not the shining example visualized by Bulwer. The hero of the anonymous *Russell; or, The Reign of Fashion* shuns "that too numerous class of idle, useless, worthless fools of fashion, whose studies and anxieties are devoted to cravat-tying, whisker-pruning, opera-lounging, actress-hunting,

[25]Book II, CH. I ("Society and Manners"), pp. 97–98.

dinner-eating, tobacco-smoking, prize-fighting, billiard-playing."
Another disenchanted member of the Silver-Fork set recalls a
Grosvenor Street soirée where "I, of course, met with some of my
Oxford contemporaries, of whom I recognized some dandies and
dissipated idlers transformed into legislators and official personages;
others sustaining their original characters, and matured into gamblers, jockeys, patrons of tailors, and opera-girls—in a word, men of
fashion."[26] Dickens, it appears, had not really separated the "dregs"
of society from its "froth and cream," but homogenized them. His
fictitious inhabitants of St. Giles could just as well be the inhabitants
of St. James in masquerade. When all is said and done, both groups
are engaged in the same occupations—drinking, gambling, idling,
and whoring. Presumably the criminal poor of *Oliver Twist* are no
more parasitic either than the wastrels of high society. Of all the early
reviews of *Oliver Twist*, the youthful Dickens must have been particularly gratified by one which compared it with *The Beggar's Opera* and
*Jonathan Wild* for "the boldness with which the writers have stripped
society of its disguises, and exhibited the shallowness of those
conventionalities which varnish the vices of fashionable life, the
falsehood of its pretences, the hypocrisy of its assumptions of decency and propriety."[27]

A modern reader of *Oliver Twist* might prefer the bitter without
the sweet, but the story was undoubtedly most palatable to its first
audience as the *Parish Boy's Progress*, promised by its original label.
The universal appeal of the orphan in fiction, the topicality of the
workhouse and private charity, along with Dickens' own identification with the plight of oppressed children—these suggested to

[26]W. Massie, *Sydenham; or, Memoirs of a Man of the World*, CH. VI.

[27]*Athenaeum*, October 26, 1839, p. 804. Thackeray, ridiculing *Oliver Twist* among
other "Newgate novels" in his mock-novel *Catherine*, seems not to have recognized
that Dickens' book was related in genre to his own. Both authors were making an
analogy between society and criminal life, in imitation of *The Beggar's Opera*.

Early in his career the writer with whom Dickens was most frequently associated
was Theodore Hook. Hook preceded Dickens as a chronicler of town life, and his
popularity as a humorist grew out of various devices that we now associate with
Dickens, such as the clumping of quaint detail, whimsical "humours" characters,
and the exposure of fraud and humbug. A typical butt of ridicule for Hook was the
middle-class parvenu, such as Gervase Skinner, Peregrine Bunce, Jack Brag, and
young Danvers. Dickens extended this line of satire down to the lower depths. For
detailed parallels between Hook and Dickens, see Myron F. Brightfield, *Theodore
Hook and His Novels* (Cambridge, Mass., 1928), pp. 313–31.

him the foundling story as a vehicle for his parable of society. The
tradition of the orphan eventually rescued from poverty by revelation of his respectable birth extends well back into the eighteenth
century. Its central theme is announced in the title of Eliza Hay-
wood's once popular *The Fortunate Foundlings* (1744). Literary his-
torians customarily trace Oliver Twist back to *Tom Jones* and *Humphry
Clinker*, which are among the books read by young David Copperfield. However, waifs and strays abounded in the early nineteenth
century—Charlotte Brooke's *Emma; or, The Foundling of the Wood*
(1803); the anonymous *Amasina; or, The American Foundling* (1804);
Elizabeth Somerville's *Aurora and Maria; or, The Advantages of Adversity*
(1809); Mary Pilkington's *Sinclair; or, The Mysterious Orphan* (1809);
Charles Lucas' *Gwelygordd; or, The Child of Sin* (1820); Dorothy Kilner's
*Edward Neville; or, The Memoirs of an Orphan* (1823); and the perennial
and much pirated *Fatherless Fanny; or, A Young Lady's First Entrance into
Life*.

A foundling story in vogue during Dickens' childhood, Agnes
Maria Bennett's frequently reprinted *The Beggar Girl and Her Benefactors* (1797), may be taken as seminal in its mixture of philanthropy
with picaresque adventure.[28] Mrs. Bennett apologizes, exactly forty
years before Dickens, to her "polite readers, supposing she should be
honoured with any such," for "the vulgar people and low scenes to
which perforce the memoirs of a beggar must introduce them" (I, CH.
VI). With gentle mockery she twists humility into subtle indignation:

> But notwithstanding no creature living has a more due and profound
> respect for the higher order of society which all ranks know they merit
> . . . yes, as, to the eternal disgrace of the police, which, to be sure,
> should order these things better, there are such things as little folk,
> who have the presumption to breathe the same atmosphere with the
> greatest of the great, and by the up and down jumble of chance, not
> only mingle their paltry interests in the grand movement of high life,
> but sometimes actually swim on the surface, like common oil on the
> richest wines. . . .

[28]*The Beggar Girl*, Mrs. Bennett's fifth novel, first published in 1797 by the Minerva
Press, reached a third edition in 1813, five years after the author's death. Although it
does not appear on Mudie's lists, it is reported late in the century that it was at that
time "still a popular 'number' book and shares the pantry shelf with *Pamela,
Fatherless Fanny*, and a host of similar rubbish" (*Notes and Queries*, 4th Series, VIII
[December 9, 1871], 348).

Presumably, the fact that Mrs. Bennett's beggar girl Rosa Wilkins turns out, like Oliver Twist, to be derived from rich wine rather than common oil does not negate her egalitarian philosophy.

*The Beggar Girl and Her Benefactors* probably did much to fix in the minds of early nineteeth-century readers the stereotypes of the outcast waif and benevolent gentleman. The ingredients of Dickens' fable are laid out here: the specter of the parish workhouse (Rosa is rescued from its jaws by the wealthy Colonel Buhanun, who takes her to live with him), the career of persecution and exploitation, the flight to the city, the long-delayed reunion (Rosa proved to be not the daughter of a prostitute, as was supposed, but the natural daughter of her benefactor). There is also satire, if somewhat crude, of the world of fashion through such figures as Mrs. Modely, Lady Gauntley, and Mrs. Wouldby, with whom little Rosa gets involved during her London adventures.

The prestige of a commendation from Coleridge in one of his rare remarks on the fiction of his times has kept the name of Mrs. Bennett flickeringly alive. "*The Beggar Girl* is the best novel, *me judice*, since Fielding," he scribbled on the flyleaf of one of his books. "I should like, therefore, to read the others."[29] At a time when the ranks of female novelists were headed not by Jane Austen but by Jane West, such a remark may not have seemed outlandish. Agnes Maria Bennett might be described as a self-taught writer, but she schooled herself in masters. Such figures as the semiliterate maid Betty Brown, whom Coleridge enjoyed, the tenderhearted hypochondriac Colonel Buhanun, and the scoundrelly Sir Solomon Mushroom bear the stamp of Smollett; elsewhere she echoes Fielding's banter. Her loosely woven tale is eked out with much padding (she was paid by the volume and had a large family to support by her pen), but its

[29]Written on the flyleaf of his copy of *Conciones ad Populum* (1795). (See Blakey, *The Minerva Press*, p. 54.) In a letter of April 8, 1820 to his friend Thomas Allsop, Coleridge placed her in distinguished company by affirming that he never found in all of Scott "a character that approaches Parson Adams, Blifil, Strap, Lieutenant Bowling, Mr. Shandy, Uncle Toby, Trim, Lovelace, Miss Byron, Clementina, Emily or Betty in Mrs. Bennett's Beggar Girl" (*Letters, Conversations and Recollections*, ed. Thomas Allsop [New York, 1836], p. 40). In *Table Talk* he spoke in similar glowing terms of Rosa's benefactor Colonel Buhanun, and, according to his nephew, "the character was frequently a subject of pleasant description and enlargement with Mr. Coleridge and he generally passed from it to a high commendation of Miss Austen's novels" (Coleridge, *Complete Works*, ed. Shedd [New York, 1854], VI, 305).

good spirits and warm humanity carry one over dull stretches.[30] Whether Dickens knew it directly or not is uncertain, but he was acquainted with many a tale influenced by it. In "Astley's," one of the *Sketches by Boz*, he chafes at the popularity of estranged fathers and children in the theatre:

> By the way, talking of fathers, we should very much like to see some piece in which all the dramatis personae were orphans. Fathers are invariably great nuisances on the stage, and always have to give the hero or heroine a long explanation of what was done before the curtain rose. . . . Or else they have to discover, all of a sudden, that somebody whom they have been in constant communication with, during three long acts, without the slightest suspicion, is their own child, in which case they exclaim, "Ah! What do I see! This bracelet! That smile! These documents! Those eyes! Can I believe my senses?—It must be!—Yes—it is—it is—my child!" "My father!" exclaims the child, and they fall into each other's arms, and look over each other's shoulders; and the audience give three rounds of applause.

He followed through with a piece in which virtually "all the dramatis personae were orphans," but he was not above bringing in his own variant of a stage father to effect a happy ending.

The 1830's in particular saw a proliferation of orphan tales, bounded at one end of the decade by *Elizabeth and Her Three Beggar Boys* and *The Stolen Boy; An Indian Tale*, at the other end *Oliver Twiss*, a parody-sequel of Dickens' novel by a hack named Thomas P. Prest, who signed himself "Bos." In the year when *Oliver Twist* was being serialized in *Bentley's Miscellany*, there appeared one of the numerous reprints of *Fatherless Fanny*. Again, that enterprising hawker of literary wares, Newman, points to an important vogue. It is significant that after 1820, "Minerva Press," with which he had long been associated from his partnership with William Lane, was dropped from his imprints and his catalogues began to feature very prominently "Juvenile and Prize Books." Some of these were of the fanciful and

[30]Some years later, Miss Mitford, author of *Our Village*, wrote to her friend Barbara Hofland: "The prodigious quantity of invention, the identity of the characters, particularly a certain Mrs. Feversham and Betty Brown, and above all a total absence of moral maxims of the do-me-good air which one expects to find in Miss Edgeworth gives a certain freshness and truth to the *Beggar Girl*, which I never found in any fiction except that of Miss Austen" (*Letters*, ed. Henry Chorley [London, 1872], I, 68).

pretty sort, such as *Angelina; or, Conversations of a Little Girl with her Doll* and Miss Selwyn's *Fairy Tales*, but his staple was the true adventure story. Superseding the romantic, didactic fables of the last century— such as Fénelon's *Télémaque*, Lucy Peacock's *The Adventures of the Six Princesses of Babylon in Their Travel to the Temple of Virtue*, and the twice-told ancient legends that were supposed to edify Sandford and Merton—were the pious, polemical tales of the times toward which Hannah More had led the way. One of the most popular and fertile producers of this "improving" fiction for youth during the 1820's and 1830's, and one of Newman's stars, was the "amiable and ingenious writer of tales for young and old alike," Mrs. Barbara Hofland. Her titles bristle with the moral virtues—*Decision, Energy, Self-Denial, Fortitude, Patience,* and virtually all of them, like *Young Crusoe; or, The Shipwrecked Boy*, follow the tribulations of young vagabonds whose characters are strengthened rather than toughened by the buffets of the cruel world.

One of Mrs. Hofland's fiction-sermons, *Elizabeth and Her Three Beggar Boys* (ca. 1830), adapted from her earlier *Tales of the Priory* (1820),[31] attaches the foundling tale to the social agitation that preceded the enactment of the New Poor Law. Like many of Mrs. Hofland's books, this is a "Tale Founded on Fact." It concerns the progress of a parish boy, William Warren, from rags to riches, as he passes from the workhouse into the rough hands of a cruel farmer, thence into the kinder hands of a religious farmer's wife. She has him apprenticed to a pottery manufacturer, who makes him a partner. The fact is based on the career of the charitable Elizabeth Linley, a cottager's wife from Wakefield, who, despite her poverty, devoted her life to the care of homeless children. The purpose is made explicit in the preface:

> To shew the poor, that even in their poverty they may do much good, and to prove to the rich, that the poor are capable of displaying those virtues which circumstances render extremely difficult, and thus to bring both parties into that contact which their common nature admits, and the religion they alike profess insists upon, wherever faith or morals are concerned, is the especial object of the writer. In her own opinion she has never offered to the world a narrative more true to nature, or better calculated to move the rich to benevolence, and the poor to exertion; and this belief must be her apology for rewriting and re-offering to the young and amiable a "twice-told tale."

[31]In its first appearance the story was entitled "Elizabeth and Her Boys, or, The Beggar's Story."

Mrs. Hofland defines here the role of emissary of good will among the classes that was being amused by some of the more social-minded writers at this time. The humbler format of this new condensed version of her tale is an emblem of her humanitarianism— stately half-calf giving way to paper wrappers in order to insure it wider circulation. She reaches simultaneously up and down, involving high and low in a sense of mutual obligation, anticipating Dickens' moral scheme in *Oliver Twist*. In other ways too Mrs. Hofland's tale for her times prepares us for Dickens' fable. Both their parish boys are miraculously preserved from sickness and starvation, despite the workhouse, are saved from criminal careers, are brought up on the New Testament, *The Pilgrim's Progress*, and hymn books. With Mrs. Hofland, as with Dickens, Good Works is the hero and Public Charity the villain. With both authors the pastoral scene is sentimentalized and sacramentalized. Oliver inherits wealth, unlike William Warren, but like William he becomes the benefactor of the next generation of poor. Sympathy and benevolence lubricate the wheels of society.[32]

Another tale of the day, although it is placed in the previous century, is *Hans Sloane: A Tale Illustrating the History of the Foundling Hospital* (1831), written by Dickens' friend John Brownlow. Brownlow's sole venture into fiction rather awkwardly interweaves a rudimentary tale of a fortunate foundling with a memorial to Captain Coram, the founder of the hospital that employed Brownlow. *Hans Sloane* went generally unnoticed in its time, but there is every evidence that Dickens was familiar with it. Brownlow's story, with its lurid intrigue joined to sentimental humanitarianism, seems to have influenced *Oliver Twist* even more than his real-life career.

*Hans Sloane* begins in the summer of 1740, about a year after Captain Coram's establishment of the Foundling Hospital. The young hero is legitimate and of a well-to-do family, but becoming orphaned at birth, he falls into the hands of an unscrupulous uncle. The uncle, now sole heir to the strictly entailed family estate, is worried about the eventual claim of his brother's surviving child. He refuses to adopt the infant, as his wife wishes. Refraining from murdering him only out of fear of the law, he orders his wife to leave

[32]In the longer version that appears in *Tales of the Priory* are two comic characters who prefigure Mr. Bumble and Mrs. Corney—the mean and avaricious parish beadle Mr. Gunner and his shrewish wife. Like Dickens' officious beadle, Gunner suffers so from the nagging of his Xantippe that he takes it out on the poor boys under his supervision.

the child at the newly established Foundling Hospital, where it can be brought up in ignorance of its birth. Reluctantly she brings the infant to the home in the dead of night, concealing her own identity. But, contrary to her husband's instructions, she ties around the baby's neck an amulet containing a miniature portrait of his mother. Here is the germ of the much deplored Monks' plot of *Oliver Twist*, which Dickens complicated by making his infant illegitimate, the villainous relative a half-brother instead of an uncle (though preserving his motivation), and by having him seek out the child and rather implausibly plan its moral destruction. Above all, Dickens conceals the whole relationship from the reader until the end to invest the story with an air of mystery.

To return to the misadventures of little Hans Sloane—he is named by the nurses at the hospital after one of its great benefactors, the distinguished Chelsea doctor who also endowed the British Museum.[33] After baptism, little Hans is sent out to be reared by cottagers and then comes back to the hospital, where he spends his childhood. Despite the constricted spiritual and physical fare of this institution, Hans, like Oliver, grows into a sprightly, alert lad. He is, however, spared one of Oliver's ordeals. As a "private" child he remains up to the age of twelve under the protection of the hospital instead of being sent out to work. It is then his good fortune to be adopted by a kindly childless couple, the Reverend Mr. Humphries and his wife. By a contrived quirk of destiny the miniature portrait around his neck is recognized by Mrs. Humphries as that of her dead sister. All comes to light when Mr. Humphries attends the death bed of a strange woman at an inn; she proves, of course, to be Hans' aunt, who had deposited him at the Foundling Hospital years before. Upon seeing the amulet she confesses all and dies; and the unscrupulous uncle, his treachery now discovered, commits suicide, leaving the family estate clear for Hans. The Humphries feel thankful "for the miraculous interposition by which they were restored to a relative of whom they had every reason to be proud," and young Hans is determined to use his new-found wealth for the benefit of less fortunate orphans.

---

[33]The only copy of *Hans Sloane* that I have been able to locate is, appropriately, in the British Museum. The sketch of Brownlow in Nichols and Wray's *The History of the Foundling Hospital* (pp. 277–78) refers to this book mistakenly as a biography of Sir Hans Sloane. Brownlow subsequently expanded the historical sections of his book in *Memoranda; or, Chronicles of the Foundling Hospital, Including Memoirs of Captain Coram* (London, 1847), and *The History and Design of the Foundling Hospital* (1858; four editions by 1881), but the fictitious interlude concerned with the orphan Hans was dropped.

Allowing for additional complications introduced by Dickens to unravel his more whorled plot, the conclusion of this crude fable anticipates the dénouement of *Oliver Twist*, with the function of Mr. and Mrs. Humphries dispersed among Mr. Brownlow, Dr. Losberne, Rose Maylie, and her adopted mother. *Hans Sloane* is basically a prose hymn of praise to the Foundling Hospital and to its benefactors. In *Oliver Twist* Dickens retains the eighteenth-century moral atmosphere—faith in human benevolence and divine providence (the key, probably, to his much denounced sentimentalism and "outrageous" use of coincidence), along with the assumption of the original virtue and innocence of children. But he updates his story to bring it into line with then current interests in the New Poor Law and juvenile crime.

The historical essays and lay sermons that interlard Brownlow's desultory tale concern perils that Little Hans escapes, but to which Little Oliver is exposed. The initial situation of *Oliver Twist*, for example, may well have been suggested by the account of Captain Coram's encounter with a victim of seduction who had abandoned her infant, an experience which led him to establish the hospital. Brownlow's animadversions on the education of foundlings in the last century prefigure, in turn, the "school" for thieves. He relates that Doctor Johnson, horrified during a visit to the Foundling Hospital to discover that the inmates were not receiving religious instruction, exclaimed: "To breed children in this manner is to rescue them from an early grave, that they may find employment for the gibbet; from dying in innocence that they may perish by their crimes." With his particular interest in apprenticeship, Brownlow denounces the bonus system introduced by Parliament during Captain Coram's time to induce employees to take on homeless boys and relieve the towns of the burden of rearing them. He cites good as well as bad examples, but leaves the impression that Gamfield and Sowerberry were more typical than the unnamed farmer who supervises the regeneration of Charley Bates. All of these issues are revived by Dickens in contemporary settings. The Reverend Mr. Growler, the cynical friend of Mr. Humphries, who predicts a bad end for little Hans, has his counterpart in Mr. Grimwig, the friend of Oliver's benefactor, Mr. Brownlow. Another parallel is Paul Pipkin, an unscrupulous tavern keeper of Eastcheap, whom Bill Sikes resembles.

Dickens' imagination seems particularly to have been stirred by one of Brownlow's moral digressions in which he pleads for sympathy for the unwed mother, urging his readers to abandon their smugness in favor of "a compassionate estimate of the weaknesses of humanity, and a just measure of relief to voluntary repentance":

> This lesson of mercy was eminently taught by the Founder of Christianity Himself, when he bade the Jew who was without sin cast the first stone at the repentant adultress, and then calmly dismissed her with the charge to *sin no more*. It was not that her crime was venial, but He who desired not the death of a sinner, but rather that she should repent and live, saw perhaps in this wretched criminal sufficient of remorse to be the object of a lesson to mankind—that the rigor of human law should not be exercised without a human regard to the circumstances under which the crime may have been committed, and the sincerity which may have followed. (CH. X)

For the character of Fagin, Dickens is now believed to have drawn upon a notorious Jew named Ikey Solomon, a fence and a seducer of boys into crime. His "fallen woman," Nancy, presumably could have been based on numerous Cheapside prostitutes. But Brownlow's allusion suggests the biblical analogy that Dickens intended the Fagin-Nancy relationship to convey. Fagin, forgetting that he is responsible for her downfall, flings stones at Nancy for her profession, as the unenlightened reader might also be disposed to do. Dickens' frequent reference to Fagin by the generic term "the Jew" indicates that he may have conceived him in the image of the sanctimonious Pharisee of the New Testament. Certainly Nancy is a modern incarnation of the penitent Magdalen, the aspect of her character that Dickens emphasizes in her meeting with the innocent Rose Maylie (CH. XL), and reiterates with scriptural eloquence in his preface to the 1841 edition, where he felt called upon to defend her portrayal:

> IT IS TRUE. Every man who has watched these melancholy shades of life, knows it to be so. . . . It is emphatically God's truth, for it is the truth He leaves in such depraved and miserable breasts; the hope yet lingering behind; the last fair drop of water at the bottom of the dried up, weed-choked well. It involves the best and worst shades of our common nature; much of its ugliest hues, and something of its most beautiful; it is a contradiction, an anomaly, an apparent impossibility; but it is a truth.

In naming Oliver's benefactor Mr. Brownlow, Dickens seems to have been paying an early tribute to one of the most dedicated social servants of his age.[34] John Brownlow must be counted among Dickens' unsung progenitors, but it is probable that a far more distinguished foundling than Hans Sloane is to be included among Oliver's literary brothers—Professor Diogenes Teufelsdröckh. Among the first critics of *Oliver Twist*, the young George Henry Lewes was virtually alone in noting that Dickens' works "are volumes of human nature, that have a deep and subtle philosophy in them, which those who read only to laugh may not discover."[35] As early as *Oliver Twist* we may discern the allegorizing tendency of Dickens' imagination, particularly in his attempts to invest his sordid characters with moral—even biblical—significance. But the moral that draws together all his characters—genteel and pseudo-genteel—grows out of the initial episode where Little Oliver, "enveloped in the old calico robes which had grown yellow in the same service . . . was badged and ticketed, and fell into his place at once—a parish child. . . ." The whole novel, as well as Oliver himself, is "an excellent example of the power of dress." Incongruities of wearing apparel, as we have seen, figure in the satire of the book—Fagin in his greasy coat teaching his ragamuffins how to filch silk handkerchiefs, the elaborate getup of the housebreaker Toby Crackit, Nancy's passing herself off as Oliver's mother by means of a shawl and basket. Dickens also uses the device seriously to connote characters. Bill Sikes' "black velveteen coat, very soiled drab breeches . . . dirty belcher handkerchief around his neck" are the fitting garments of his obscene soul, just as the "powdered head and gold spectacles . . . bottle-green coat with a black velvet collar, . . . white trousers, and . . . smart bamboo cane"

[34]Although Dickens left the neighborhood of the Foundling Hospital after *Oliver Twist* made him rich (see note 6 above), his interest in the institution did not cease. As late as *Little Dorrit* (1855) he has the Meagles change the name of Harriet Beadle to Tattycoram after the "blessed creature" who founded the home they took her from. Among the documents preserved at the hospital is a copy of a Christmas number of *All the Year Round* (December, 1868) inscribed by the editor. Brownlow rose to the position of Secretary of the Foundling Hospital in 1849, retaining this office until his retirement in 1872. On the occasion, the Governors, granting him a superannuation allowance, wished him "that full measure of ease and comfort which he has so well earned by a course of life singularly disinterested, benevolent and charitable" (Nichols and Wray, p. 278). He lived a year and a half beyond his retirement, surviving Dickens by three years.

[35]*National Magazine*, December, 1837, pp. 445–46. This was the most enthusiastic of the early reviews. It is assigned to Lewes in *The Letters of Charles Dickens* (Pilgrim Edition), I, 403, n. 5.

appropriately deck out Mr. Brownlow's fairy-godfather elegance of character.

However, the idea Dickens wished to convey in his novel was that clothes do not really make the man except in the eyes of the beholder. So he hints in his pointed Preface of 1841, when he defends his choice of characters from St. Giles to his more squeamish readers:

> But there are people of so refined and delicate a nature, that they cannot bear the contemplation of these horrors. Not that they turn instinctively from crime; but that criminal characters, to suit them, must be, like their meat, in delicate disguise. A Massaroni in green velvet is an enchanting creature; but a Sikes in fustian is insupportable. A Mrs. Massaroni, being a lady in short petticoats and a fancy dress, is a thing to imitate in tableaux and have in lithograph on pretty songs; but a Nancy, being a creature in a cotton gown and cheap shawl, is not to be thought of. It is wonderful how Virtue turns from dirty stockings; and how Vice, married to ribbons and a little gay attire, changes her name, as wedded ladies do, and becomes Romance.

Accordingly, in the novel itself he scrambles clothes and characters to illustrate the arbitrariness of distinctions based on dress. Rags cover Nancy as well as Bill Sikes and Fagin. Bill Sikes and Mr. Brownlow both wear black velvet. To outward seeming, Monks and Mr. Brownlow are both gentlemen. Oliver changes clothes as he moves from thieves' den to country cottage and back again, but he does not change character. A facetious illustration of the accidents of attire is Bumble's fall from beadledom after his marriage to Mrs. Corney:

> The laced coat, and the cocked hat, where were they? He still wore knee-breeches, and dark cotton stockings on his nether limbs; but they were not *the* breeches. The coat was wide-skirted, and in that respect like *the* coat; but, oh, how different! The mighty cocked-hat was replaced by a modest round one. Mr. Bumble was no longer a beadle.

Bumble's downfall leads Dickens to philosophize on mankind in general:

> There are some promotions in life, which, independent of the more substantial rewards they offer, acquire peculiar value and dignity from the coats and waistcoats connected with them. A field-marshal has his uniform, a bishop his silk apron, a counsellor his silk gown, a beadle his cocked hat. Strip the bishop of his apron, or the beadle of his hat and lace; what are they? Men. Mere Men. Dignity, and even

holiness, too, sometimes, are more questions of coat and waistcoat than some people imagine. (CH. XXXVII)

These observations were not new. A few years before, some, at least, of the first readers of *Oliver Twist* had been startled also by passages like:

> Has not your Red hanging-individual a horsehair wig, squirrel-skins, and a plush-gown; whereby all mortals know that he is a JUDGE?— Society, which the more I think of it astonishes me the more, is founded upon Cloth.
>
> Aprons are Defenses; against injury to cleanliness, to safety, to modesty, sometimes to roguery. . . . How much has been concealed, how much has been defended in Aprons! Nay, rightly considered, what is your whole Military and Police Establishment, charged at uncalculated millions, but a huge scarlet-coloured, iron-fastened Apron, wherein Society works (uneasily enough). . . . But of all Aprons the most puzzling to me hitherto has been the Episcopal or Cassock. Wherein consists the usefulness of this Apron? The Overseer (*Episcopus*) of Souls, I notice, has tucked-in the corner of it, as if his day's work were done: what does he shadow forth thereby?
>
> Lives the man that can figure a naked Duke of Windlestraw addressing a naked House of Lords? Imagination, choked as in mephitic air, recoils on itself, and will not forward with the picture. The Woolsack, the Ministerial, the Opposition Benches?—*infandum! infandum!* And yet why is the thing impossible? Was not every soul, or rather every body, of these Guardians of our Liberties, naked, or nearly so, last night; 'a forked Radish with a Head fantastically carved'? And why might he not, did our stern fate so order it, walk out to St. Stephens's, as well into bed in that no-fashion; and there, with other similar Radishes, hold a Bed of Justice?

Thomas Carlyle's Professor Diogenes Teufelsdröckh was, of course, after bigger game than parish beadles, but his caustic wisdom encompasses Mudfog. The life and opinions of this abandoned waif, who grew up to occupy the Chair of Things-in-General at the University of Weissnichtwo, appeared in book form in 1838, while *Oliver Twist* was still running serially, but they had burst forth five years earlier in the pages of *Fraser's Magazine*. Dickens' long-lived (and generally unrequited) adulation of Carlyle's writings apparently began even earlier than *The French Revolution.*[36] *Oliver Twist* takes over

[36]Among critics who have traced Carlylean ideas and imagery in Dickens' novels are: Arthur A. Adrian, "Dickens on American Slavery: A Carlylean Slant," PMLA, LXVII (June, 1952), 315–29; Kathleen Tillotson, *"Barnaby Rudge,"* *Dickens at Work*

from *Sartor Resartus* not only Professor Teufelsdröckh's Philosophy of Clothes, but his scorn for the dismal science of political economy as well. Herr Teufelsdröckh's "Liberals, Economists, Utilitarians . . . European Mechinisers" are Dickens' "experimenters" and "well-fed philosophers" anonymously and mysteriously responsible for Oliver's plight. Carlyle, in addition, overtly denounces what Dickens implicitly parodies—the "buck, or Blood, or Macaroni, or Incroyable, or Dandy."[37]

Of all Dickens' immediate contemporaries it was Carlyle who raised the orphan tale to the level of metaphysical and moral fantasy. *Oliver Twist* echoes the transcendentalism as well as the satire of *Sartor Resartus*. Entepfühl embraces Eastcheap, particularly in Teufelsdröckh's recollection of his obscure origins, as recorded in the chapter pointedly entitled "Genesis":

> Ever, in my distress and my loneliness, has Fantasy turned, full of longing, to that unknown Father, who perhaps far from me, perhaps near; either way invisible, might have taken me to his paternal bosom, there to lie screened from many a woe. . . .
>
> And yet, O Man born of Woman . . . wherein is my case peculiar? . . . The Andreas and Gretchen, or the Adam and Eve, who led thee into Life, and for a time suckled and pap-fed thee there, whom thou namest Father and Mother; these were, like mine, but thy nursing-father and nursing-mother; thy true Beginning and Father is in Heaven, whom with the bodily eye thou shalt never behold, but only with the spiritual.

So Dickens reminds us about his orphan hero. In one of the more

---

(London, 1958), p. 84; John Butt, "The Topicality of *Bleak House*," *Dickens at Work*, p. 178.

[37]Carlyle describes the very section of London in which CH. XXVI of *Oliver Twist* takes place, even anticipating Dickens' detail about the goods on display: "Field Lane, with its long fluttering rows of yellow handkerchiefs . . . where, in stifled jarring hubbub, we hear the Indictment which Poverty and Vice bring against lazy Wealth, that it has left them there cast-out and trodden under foot of Want, Darkness and the Devil. . . ." ("Old Clothes"). Cf. Dickens' description, quoted above, where Carlyle's "rag-fair" is depicted literally.

Thackeray's *Catherine* and *Oliver Twist* also have in common the influence of *Sartor Resartus*. Thackeray illustrates the idea that "Society is founded upon Cloth" through the ease with which his criminals are able to simulate class by simply disguising themselves. He goes so far as to introduce as a character in his mock-novel a tailor named Beinkleider, "a German . . . skilful in his trade (after the manner of his nation, which in breeches and metaphysics—in inexpressibles and incomprehensibles—may instruct all Europe)."

sentimental episodes he shows us Little Oliver, after suffering in silence from the corporal punishment of Mr. Sowerberry and the brutal taunts of Noah, finally giving vent to his repressed emotion: "But now when there were none to see or hear him, he fell upon his knees on the floor, and hiding his face in his hands, wept such tears as, God send for the credit of our nature, few so young may ever have cause to pour out before Him!" (CH. VII). This cloys because we feel removed from the situation and flatter ourselves that we don't need to be reminded, as Dickens assumed that his first readers needed to be, that the high and the humble have a common origin. Oliver's angelic appearance, his preternatural virtue and piety, his general aura of "clouds of glory" are all intended to recall his eternal home.

At a remove of more than a century we are especially likely to squirm over Oliver's farewell to the dying orphan Dick:

> "Yes, yes I will [stop] to say good-bye to you," replied Oliver. "I shall see you again, Dick, I know I shall! You will be well and happy!"
> "I hope so," replied the child. "After I am dead, but not before. I know the doctor must be right, Oliver, because I dream so much of Heaven, and Angels, and kind faces that I never see when I am awake. Kiss me," said the child, climbing up the low gate, and flinging his arms round Oliver's neck. "Good-bye, dear! God bless you!"
> The blessing was from a young child's lips, but it was the first that Oliver had ever heard invoked upon his head; and through the struggles and sufferings and troubles and changes of his after life, he never once forgot it. (CH. VII)

But no reader of Wordsworth had difficulty believing in children who see angels. A reader of Carlyle besides, like Dickens, could see the orphan as representative of man's estrangement from his creator—Diogenes Teufelsdröckh's vision of the human condition. Little Oliver and Little Dick are best regarded not as real children but as symbolic children moving in a world that seems real but is reality transfigured.

Dickens provided a kind of postscript to *Oliver Twist* in his letter, "Crime and Education," contributed to the *Daily News* several years after the novel was first published.[38] Here he comments on the Ragged Schools he had visited, charity schools where overworked volunteers attempted to teach the poor, children and adults, "and show them

---

[38]February 4, 1846. Reprinted in *Works*, Gadshill Edition (London, 1908), XXXV, 25–29.

some sympathy and stretch a hand out, which is not the iron hand of Law, for their correction." He conveys a lesson he carried away from a fetid classroom in Saffron Hill, where *Oliver Twist* takes place:

> This, Reader, was one room as full as it could hold; but these were only grains in sample of a Multitude that are perpetually sifting through these schools; in sample of a Multitude who had within them once, and perhaps have now, the elements of men as good as you or I, and maybe infinitely better; in sample of a Multitude among whose doomed and sinful ranks (oh, think of this, and think of them!) the child of any man upon this earth, however lofty his degree, must, as by Destiny and Fate, be found, if, at its birth, it were consigned to such an infancy and nurture, as these fallen creatures had!

Such a "fallen creature" is Oliver Twist, who "might have been the child of a nobleman or a beggar." Unlike Nancy and Little Dick, he is rescued from this multitude because Dickens has singled him out for a special mission. Dickens was critical of the Ragged Schools, particularly of their overemphasis on religious mysteries beyond the comprehension of their pupils, but he urges his readers to support them. He would especially like to see funds that have been contributed by the wealthy toward the building of new churches diverted to these impoverished classrooms, "as an appropriate means of illustrating the Christian Religion." He suggests, moreover, that they do not remain aloof, but "go themselves into the Prisons and the Ragged Schools, and form their own conclusions." Through Oliver Twist, in effect, he enables his readers to be reborn. With Oliver they live among the "doomed and sinful ranks," the Ragged Schools writ large in the dens of Eastcheap. They even descend with him into the cells of the condemned. What we might have expected to be a shattering, traumatic experience for Little Oliver—his witnessing of Fagin's last night alive—instead brings out the depth of his human sympathy. "Oh! God forgive this wretched man!" are his words as his most fiendish tormentor is led to the gallows. So high and low, old and young, virtuous and villainous, are brought together in a common bond.[39]

Sensationalism, satire, and sentiment—those disparate and sometimes discordant elements of Dickens' genius—tend toward the same goal—to make humanity recognize what they have in common.

[39]J. Hain Friswell wrote of *Oliver Twist* that "amidst vice, depravity, cunning, theft, and murder, the author treads firmly and cleanly, and teaches us that best of lessons—to pity the guilty while we hate the guilt. . . ." (*Modern Men of Letters Honestly Criticised*, p. 14).

Depending on Dickens' mood, all men are crim
As early as *Oliver Twist* we recognize a tension
minded and the tough-minded Dickens. "Mer
and their fellow men, and cry that all is dark a
right," he observes halfway through his st
colours are reflections from their own jaundic
real hues are delicate and need a clearer vision
seems to see more powerfully out of his "jaunuicu ⌐,
his "clearer vision." In *Oliver Twist* his "sombre colours," the murky
city scenes, somehow impress themselves on our memory, while the
"delicate hues," the idyllic country scenes, remain a roseate blur.
The vividness that Dickens gives to the world of darkness has led
Graham Greene mistakenly to call him a Manichean. Dickens really
means for "the principle of Good" to survive, but the principle of
Evil engaged both his imagination and his sense of humor more.
Whereas his irony and caustic wit come into play in his treatment of
the thieves, he leaned on stock associations of the good, the beautiful, and the pathetic in representing Rose Maylie and her family.[40]
His own representation of humanity, therefore, may seem out of
focus; but a balanced picture, he reiterates in his various prefaces to
*Oliver Twist*, includes "the best and worst shades of our nature; much
of its ugliest hues, and something of its most beautiful."

Although we tend to think of *Oliver Twist* as a novel about the poor,
it really contains in essence the novel of society that Dickens developed with great amplitude in *Bleak House, Little Dorrit,* and *Our Mutual
Friend*, where all classes are reciprocally involved not merely symbolically but literally. The pattern of the well-born descending to the
lower depths tends to reverse itself in the mature novels, with the
low-born moving up and discovering their new-found wealth to be a
curse rather than a blessing. With his growing cynicism Dickens
also was to stress the acquisitiveness rather than the kindliness of the
wealthy. But he continued to lodge his faith in the hearts of men
rather than in institutions. The motiveless benignity of a Mr.
Brownlow and the Cheeryble Brothers counted for more than a
parish workhouse, a Bible Institute, or organized philanthropy as
represented by Mrs. Jellyby and Mrs. Pardiggle. If distrust of institutions accounts for some of his most effective satire, trust in
man accounts for some of his most mawkish sentimentality. At the

[40]It is now generally assumed that through Rose Maylie, Dickens was in part
releasing his sorrow over the untimely death of Mary Hogarth, which occurred while
he was writing *Oliver Twist*.

of his career he could glance back nostalgically at an ideal
th-century vision of the benevolent gentleman carrying on
work in the world. This is the tradition inherited by Oliver
st and Rose Maylie, who—temporarily fallen from their true
aces—are restored to them; "tried by adversity, [they] remembered
its lessons in mercy to others, and mutual love and fervent thanks to
Him who had protected and preserved them." Humanity is joined
in a circle of empathy and an apostolic succession of benevolence.

Of all the popular types of fiction that Dickens wove into this
children's story for adults, he had a special affinity, in these early
years, for the foundling tale. A true story that his first readers did not
know—as remarkable in its way as the Parish Boy's Progress—was his
own progress from Baynham Street and Camden Town to Regent's
Park. *Oliver Twist* was the first of what was to be a series of projections
of his own situation as the *arriviste*. It is not a mere accidental detail,
surely, that Oliver sees his gentleman-savior for the first time in
front of a bookstall. It was, after all, to literature that Dickens owed
his own "rescue" from obscurity. Mr. Brownlow's library plays as
important a part in Oliver's rehabilitation as the village church.
Oliver rejects the crime thrillers of Fagin in favor of the Bible, *The
Pilgrim's Progress*, and those numerous unnamed books given him by
Mr. Brownlow, at the time when Dickens was leaving behind mere
amusement and entertainment and dedicating himself to "improving" literature. Mr. Brownlow, in a way, stands for the reading public
that made possible Dickens' rise from reporter to novelist-prince.
This public Dickens was later to visualize as Abel Magwitch, in terms
of Frankenstein's monster pursuing his creator—but that, of course,
is another story.

# The Subversive Methods of Dickens' Early Fiction: *Martin Chuzzlewit*

*by Richard Barickman*

In the later novels—roughly, from *Dombey and Son* onward—Dickens develops remarkably elaborate structures of romantic motifs that penetrate the mimetic structures of the narratives but remain distinct and, in some ways, separable. ("Mimesis" signifies, in this context, a network of causal influences that arise from particular social circumstances and exert a primary influence over the formation of characters' personalities and behavior.[1])

In *Great Expectations*, for example, Orlick is both a powerful direct influence on Mrs. Joe and a fictional device to expose the unacknowledged psychological forces that motivate her behavior. He helps develop our understanding of her character through a series of hostile interchanges between them; and he helps to place her in the novel's primary network of relationships between aggressors and victims.[2] Orlick does not, however, constitute an inseparable element of her psychological life. When she had no Orlick, she invented one—two, in fact. She treats Joe and Pip as the vicious malefactors Orlick actually turns out to be. And Orlick has his own plausible history of psychological motivation, which he spews out to Pip at the end of the novel.

The seething hostilities that agitate Mrs. Joe's behavior and trouble the lives of her victims have a direct, though indirectly revealed, source in the social circumstances that make up the village environ-

---

"*Martin Chuzzlewit* and the Methods of Dickens' Early Fiction" by Richard Barickman. This essay is published here for the first time.
[1] For a perceptive discussion of the nature of romance and mimetic modes in fiction, see Patrick Brantlinger, "Romances, Novels, and Psychoanalysis," *Criticism* 17 (1975): 15–40.
[2] See J. Hillis Miller, *Charles Dickens: The World of His Novels* (Cambridge, Mass., 1958), pp. 254–61.

ient. Mrs. Joe is not, as she pretends, tyrannized by Pip or Joe or even by hard household labor. But she is subjected to the subtler and more devastating constraints of a society that offers no satisfying course for a woman as shrewd and intelligent as Mrs. Joe, as energetic, and as poor, isolated, and uninformed. Frustrated by this most elusive of oppressors, she understandably rages against a marriage and a child virtually forced upon her, against a husband who seems, by her standards, her inferior in every way except gender, and against the domestic conditions that constrain her life into the narrowest scope. So Mrs. Joe, like all the other characters in the novel, can be understood in exclusively mimetic terms, even though these terms can give only a limited sense of her significance in the novel.[3] The novel works vigorously against this limited reading; it attempts to fuse mimetic and romance modes, as it progressively enlarges the range of symbolic analogies among characters and events and alerts us to psychological states that seem to surpass or lag behind mimetic causation (Pip's sudden "irrational" sense that he has struck down his sister, for instance).

The earlier novels have a substantially different design and method. There the mimetic patterns peter out into inconsequential denouements or, more typically, become entangled in such contradictions and anomalies that we are turned toward the much more powerful and expressive romance patterns—not as an extension or enrichment of mimetic substance but as an alternative to it. Heroic and villainous, ordinary and eccentric, passive and frenetic characters enact extremes of mental life intelligible as parts of a system of symbolic relationships coextensive with plot, narrative commentary, and action.

The earlier novels are often as subtle and penetrating as the later, and as intent on revealing the forms of mental life that help shape the whole culture's modes of thought and behavior. But they are much more systemic in showing the individual's place within the cultural patterns. Characters like Quilp and Nell are so interdependent and so little explicable in terms of a particular social environment that they are likely to seem histrionic fabrications rather than extreme expressions of actual psychological life, if they are treated in isolation

[3]The distinct character of mimetic and romance modes allows, and perhaps even prompts, such diverse and perceptive readings of Dickens' novels as G. Robert Stange's "Expectations Well Lost," *CE* 16 (October 1954): 9–17 and Julian Moynahan's "The Hero's Guilt," *Essays in Criticism* 10 (January 1960): 60–79.

from each other. The behavior of such characters is intriguing precisely when it becomes anomalous, when it departs from the norms of their social world and the norms of our expectations about mimetic fiction. Why does Rose Maylie suddenly abandon her pious rejection of Harry Maylie just after her encounter with the prostitute Mary? What causes Grandfather Trent's compulsion to gamble? Such behavior resists comprehension and invites the catchall rationale of simple melodramatic suspense if we approach it only through the social and psychological circumstances that work on the characters directly—that is, through the mimetic dimension of the novel.

Quilp does not embody and act out the secret lusts of Nell in the way that Orlick does represent a version, however exaggerated, of the inner lives of both Mrs. Joe and Pip. The possible interior life of a Nell, and of Quilp himself, is sealed off from our direct scrutiny by Dickens' fictional methods; our attention is diverted instead to symbolic patterns that reveal the mental life playing through the whole fictional society. The forces of the private unconscious break through in dispersed and fragmented forms; the interior self is externalized; and characters exist in inseparable psychic tandems, and more complex sets, that are absurd by mimetic standards and wholly true to experience. For this method is no less "realistic" than the methods of mimesis. It expresses in a coherent, consistent, and subtly elaborated form a sense that individual character is a function of a comprehensive and mysterious system. This sense is particularly disturbing, even terrifying, in modern culture, where hidden systems seem to proliferate outside any supernatural control or intelligible human purpose; but it is a sense that all cultures seem to have shared, in some form, as a fundamental part of their reality.

In both early and late novels of Dickens, then, the manifest social roles the characters perform and their conscious reflections on their roles do not give the sole or even the primary coherence to the structures of action and theme. This circumstance has been the source of perplexity and dissatisfaction to "realists" from Lewes to Orwell to Robert Garis.[4] Orwell puts the general objection, as usual, in succinct and persuasive form:

> Dickens sees human beings with the most intense vividness ... [but] as soon as he tries to bring his characters into action the melodrama

[4]George Henry Lewes, "Dickens in Relation to Criticism," *Fortnightly Review* 17 (1872); George Orwell, "Charles Dickens," *Dickens, Dali, and Others* (New York, 1946); Robert Garis, *The Dickens Theatre* (Oxford, 1965).

begins. He cannot make the action revolve around their ordinary occupations; hence the crossword puzzle of coincidences, intrigues, murders, disguises, buried wills, long-lost brothers, etc. etc.[5]

Orwell's description is shrewd and accurate so far as it goes. But his common-sense version of the social world, where manifest social roles define the scope of the action, gives way *by design* in Dickens' novels to a world of mysterious interconnection and hidden relationships. The characters do not act as "functional members of society" if we assume that society functions as it professes to. But this assumption is the major target of Dickens' social satire from the first novel to the last. The ordinary business of society, and the expectations of many readers, are frustrated precisely as Orwell complains; but as this level of action falls to pieces, as characters seem not so much static as paralyzed in their overt social roles, another dimension of the action takes shape. The intensely vivid details that seemed like a "confusion of gargoyles" to Orwell cohere in an "interior" social system whose interrelations are established largely through symbolic analogies. The melodrama of the direct narrative expresses the bizarre nature of this hidden social world far more powerfully and accurately than any action based on common-sense ideas of probability could do. It is precisely such notions of probability that Dickens challenges—like most writers in the romance mode—seeking to reveal them as protective illusions that disguise the real business of society, the hidden motives that shape and drive both individual people and the institutions and rituals they develop.

There is abundant evidence that Dickens did not conceive his novels in these terms, that his conscious intentions were far more commonplace than his actual creations turned out to be. *Martin Chuzzlewit*, for instance, the first novel to assail Victorian family values directly and savagely, was designed by Dickens as an assault instead on selfishness. Once the actual process of composition began, however, the intuitive design, the real theme and target of the novel, had become clearer to Dickens. He planned to print on the title page the motto: "Your homes the scene, yourselves the actors, here." Though the motto was suppressed on the advice of Forster, who feared that readers would be offended, the satiric purpose was not. And Forster proved to be right. The novel caused the first real breach between Dickens and his middle-class audience, who bought fewer than one-half the numbers *Pickwick Papers* and *Nicholas Nickleby* had

[5]Orwell, pp. 89–90.

sold, and less than one-fifth of the highest sales of the *Old Curiosity Shop*.

Though Dickens clearly became aware of his real preoccupations in this novel, they continue to spring from intuitive rather than analytical perceptions. He always relied on intuition, visual imagination, on all the resources of nonanalytic perception for his most brilliant effects. He had extraordinary access through these methods to the processes of his unconscious mind (and to the unconscious lives of his audience, as the extreme reactions of adoration and loathing suggest).

One of Dickens' most revealing references to this most powerful and basic method of his imagination appears in response to a passage in *Oliver Twist*: "I scarcely know what answer I can give you," he wrote to G. H. Lewes. "I thought the passage a good one *when* I wrote it, certainly, and I felt it strongly (as I do almost every word I put on paper) *while* I wrote it, but how it came I can't tell. It came like all my other ideas . . . ready made to the point of the pen and down it went." So also, in reference to Pecksniff and Sairey Gamp—two of the least "functional" characters in *Martin Chuzzlewit* in Orwell's terms, two of the most functional in Dickens' symbolic vision of social and psychological life—Dickens wrote: "as to the way in which these characters have opened out, that is one of the most surprising processes of the mind in this sort of invention. Given what one knows, what one does not know springs up; and I am as absolutely certain of its being true, as I am of the law of gravitation—if such a thing be possible, more so."[6] As with the defense of his characterization of Nancy in *Oliver Twist* and of Krook's death by spontaneous combustion in *Bleak House*, Dickens asserts the truth of the romance mode in defiance of common-sense or rationalist probabilities. His imagination leaves conscious design and attitude ("what one knows") for intuitive perception ("what one does not know").

*Martin Chuzzlewit* exemplifies the purposes and methods of Dickens' early fiction and is a virtual mode of a persistent theme in his fiction: the systematic corruption of the family, women's roles, and the patriarchs themselves. The sense that the self is isolated, dispossessed, preyed on by interior motives and external pressures that seem to have little to do with ordinary assumptions about personality and social role inevitably comes to focus on the source

---

[6]John Forster, in *The Life of Charles Dickens*, ed. J. W. T. Ley (London, 1928), p. 311; quoted in Marcus, (New York, 1968): p. 222.

and site of the disorder: the system of sexual relations within the family. Though *Martin Chuzzlewit* presents the family as the source of both individual and social corruption with an intensity and directness new to his fiction, this has been the pattern for all the earlier novels.[7] And they have also dramatized, as *Martin Chuzzlewit* does, the sense that the family itself has been corrupted by a patriarchal system whose bizarre manipulations are thoroughly insidious, pervasive, and uncontrollable because they have broken free from conscious design and conscious recognition. Pecksniff and Old Martin Chuzzlewit are the primary false patriarchs in *Martin Chuzzlewit*. They dominate theme and action more directly than Grandfather Trent, Ralph Nickleby, and Fagin; and they are corrupt and vicious in themselves while Pickwick and Brownlow are benevolent and innocent of malice. But the most general implications about the patriarchal system of values are similar for all these novels. It is corrupt and corrupting in ways that supersede and even neutralize distinctions of moral character, temperament, and conscious motivation.

In one of the most profound ironies of Dickens' fiction—an irony that reflects not on Dickens, as many have assumed, but on the nature of the society he portrays—the condition of women can be approached accurately only by presenting them as objects manipulated in a continual struggle for power waged among men. The male characters in *Martin Chuzzlewit* are all compelled to act, constantly and obsessively, as son or father or some combination of the two roles. All of the other distinctions of social rank and social role they attempt to make (here, as elsewhere, Montague Tigg and Jonas Chuzzlewit are disturbingly close to young Martin Chuzzlewit) cannot disengage them from these primary family roles and this primal conflict. In a similar but still more radical process, the narrator's efforts to maintain sharp moral and sentimental distinctions among the female characters works in constant tension against the desire of the patriarchal system to use them as interchangeable sexual objects. Even the distinctions among mother and daughter and wife are

---

[7]*Pickwick Papers* seems the anomaly among the early novels, but its regenerative comedy evades rather than resolves the elements of social and psychological disorder that gather to a point of crisis in the Fleet episodes. Though *Pickwick* manages, as no other Dickens novel will, to sequester the forces of corruption within the Victorian system of sexual values, they assert their presence regularly throughout the novel—in the interpolated tales and in a variety of symbolic forms. See Marcus, pp. 41–44.

obliterated, as the anomalous circumstances of Mary Graham, the Pecksniff sisters, Ruth Pinch, and Mrs. Todgers all suggest at various times. Mrs. Lupin, for example, is flustered by her inability to determine Ruth's relationship to Old Martin, referring to her in quick, embarrassed succession as his granddaughter, daughter, and wife. (She finally suspects that Mary is his mistress.)

Although it is one of the most episodic and digressive of Dickens' novels in the direct formulation of plot and action, *Martin Chuzzlewit* is the most complex and systematic of the early novels in its presentation of sexual roles and sexual conflicts. The American episodes, which seem set up so that Dickens can vent his personal reactions to his American tour regardless of his original design for the novel, are symbolically integrated with the English episodes. They reveal that the promise of freedom and regeneration the United States offered meant only a more rampant, grotesque, and smugly hypocritical abuse of patriarchal power. Jefferson Brick, Colonel Scadder, and other jingoist bullies make the point in marvelously varied burlesques of masculine mannerisms. The diseased, starving, spiritless family Mark and Martin discover in Eden present the ultimate consequences of this abuse. This savage parody of family nurture reveals destitution more extreme than anywhere in the English episodes.

The novel maunders about in its direct development of the action—shunting Martin Jr. from the expected confrontation with his grandfather into the picaresque journey to America; undercutting the motif of Tom Pinch's victimization by setting him up in a mock-career provided by an unknown benefactor and a mock-marriage with his sister; concocting Old Martin's pretense of senility, whose primary result is to expose Ruth Pinch to Pecksniff's sexual assault. But this dereliction of the direct narrative—in plot, action, and moral commentary—allows the symbolic patterns of analogy and the thematic material they imply to emerge with greater force and clarity.

The image of the family the novel presents seemed to many of Dickens' contemporaries to be a grotesque distortion. It is actually a parody of the often grotesque psychic forces masked by habitual routines and idealized assumptions about domestic harmony. The typical comic plot of the English novel—the courtship and marriage of one or more young couples—is displaced to the periphery of *Martin Chuzzlewit*. It is supplanted by a complex of plots, all centering on the corruption spread throughout the social system by the abuse of masculine, specifically patriarchal, power. Old Martin Chuzzlewit and Pecksniff are the false patriarchs who control the main plot (though Pecksniff increasingly becomes the dupe and surrogate of Old Martin). Together they parody the benign control supposedly exercised by fathers, but actually cause most of the viciousness and misery in the English episodes. Jonas Chuzzlewit parodies the son corrupted by manipulative power; he attempts to murder his father, brutalizes the wife he has wrested from the patriarchy, and succeeds in murdering a caricature of masculine sexual prowess, Tigg Montague. Meanwhile two other parody sons, Young Martin and Mark Tapley, attempt to flee the patriarchal system (and the system of marriage which it controls) by immigrating to America. But when they finally set up house in the Eden settlement, in a masculine travesty of the first marriage relationship, they have merely arrived at the heart of the most grotesque and brutal parody of masculine power in the novel—a whole nation of bragging, braying, swindling, knife-, gun-, and slogan-wielding men, sons of England in perpetual rebellion against the parent they have disowned.

*Martin Chuzzlewit*'s female characters are generally reduced to virtually interchangeable symbols within this patriarchal system. Marriage becomes a male-dominated institution for conferring or withholding or extorting power. Jonas' marriage, for instance, is an economic transaction with Pecksniff; he easily substitutes Mercy for Charity Pecksniff at the last moment. Pecksniff in turn gladly abandons both daughters to pursue his own courtship; his assault on Mary Graham is consciously designed to ensure his power over Old Martin. Martin allows Pecksniff to pursue her as part of his own plans to entrap Pecksniff and use him to mortify the other Chuzzlewit relations. Mary is finally transferred to Young Martin, for whom she was originally intended by both Martin Chuzzlewits. Mercy Pecksniff is transferred from Jonas to Old Martin to replace Ruth Graham as his surrogate daughter, wife, and nurse. Meanwhile, Ruth Pinch has been shifted from her employer—another bullying patriarch—to her brother and finally to John Westlock. This charade within the novel's homeostatic system of male power relations would be simply farcical if it did not reflect, through parody, the actual treatment of women in marriage.

Courtship in this world is invariably a front for some ulterior purpose; and the purpose invariably has been shaped by the pressures and constraints of the patriarchal sexual system. As in so many of his hypocritical dealings, the mock-patriarch Pecksniff sets the pattern for the whole society in his courtship of Mary Graham. He is both fawning and coercive, mixing unctuous endearments with blackmail. His daughter Mercy accepts Jonas Chuzzlewit's proposal, even though she considers him a repulsive fool, in order to escape her father. Jonas himself is more intent on proving his masculinity to his father and to himself than in securing any erotic pleasure. Young Martin hardly gives a thought to Mary Graham; he seems more intent on fleeing all the pressures of social life in England, including the complexities of sexual relations.

All courtships that take place are tortuous and troubled by concealed anxieties and hostilities. Jonas tacks off at Charity Pecksniff in order to court her sister Mercy. And the real pleasure he takes in marriage is humiliating and abusing his wife as he has been humiliated by his father and by more stereotypically virile characters like Tigg Montague. Pecksniff fawns over Mary as a way of ingratiating himself with Old Martin. The mannerisms of the servile son, a kind of Ur-Heep, mingle horribly with the mannerisms of the benevolent father in Pecksniff's charade.

The persistent symbolic association of marriage with death and swindling provides a thematic matrix for the individual characters' fraudulent and oppressive dealings. The one cheerful, harmonious family in the novel literally thrives on death, the snug little "harem" of Mr. Mould, the undertaker. The only other family in the novel that has the ordinary complement of husband and wife is also the only family formed in the course of the novel, the wretched marriage of Mercy and Jonas. It is, appropriately, formed as a mutual swindle (like Jonas' partnership in the Anglo-Bengalee Life Assurance Association), and it serves as the primary emblem of what marriage and the family have become—the husband is master, the wife totally submissive, suffering his brutal treatment and being still. The grotesque courtship ritual—Mercy's shrill, affected coquetry and tormenting of Jason, Jason's shamefaced wheedling and bullying—is replaced by mutual contempt and hatred. The household functions as a sequestered society; the virtuous and sentimental characters do not interfere even though they are quite aware that Jonas beats and humiliates Mercy. There is even a parody child and nanny, the senile Chuffey and Sairey Gamp. And the family's chief moral and emotional dealings have shifted from greedy swindling to attempted patricide (just as the Anglo-Bengalee bases its swindles on death). In reaction to this pandemic sexual fraud, characters parody traditional sexual relations in bizarre ways. Some assail traditional taboos, desperate for freedom and revenge (Jonas' attempt to murder his father; the two Martin Chuzzlewits' struggle for possession of Mary Graham, only one generation away from incest). Others seem to be groping toward some substitute relationship that is less sterile and emotionally crippling than erotic pairings. Young Martin and Mark Tapley, Poll Sweedlepipe and Bailey Jr., Chevy Slyme and Tigg Montague, Jonas and Tigg, Pecksniff and Old Martin form masculine relationships of this sort—one or the other of the pair invariably making the intense emotional commitment we associate with romantic love. Cherry and Merry Pecksniff, the two sisters leagued with Mrs. Todgers, Sairey Gamp and Betsey Prig, Sairey and Mrs. Harris are the female counterparts.

There are any number of inversions and distortions of stereotypic sexual roles which proceed from the corruption of traditional roles. Betsey Prig is bearded; the preadolescent Bailey Jr. vaunts non-existent whiskers and suspects Mrs. Gamp of harboring a secret passion for him. Most of the traumatized individuals in Mrs. Gamp's chamber of childbirth horrors are expectant fathers. Mrs. Todgers is surrogate mother to a collection of commercial bachelors, a kind of lower-middle-class mercantile monastery. (It is curious that a number of critics, like Steven Marcus, have seen Todgers' as a model of humane civilization. Its harmony depends directly and obviously, like Pickwick's benevolent innocence, on the avoidance of any form of sexuality other than the sentimentally rhetorical.) Ruth Pinch plays at housekeeping for her brother; Mrs. Lupin professionalizes the housewife's role in her inn as she waits for Mark Tapley to propose. (His "humour," the idea that marriage to Mrs. Lupin would be so pleasant that he could take no credit for his cheerfulness, is another contrivance to avoid the perils of traditional sexual roles and rituals in this society.)

*Martin Chuzzlewit* presents a characteristic feature of Dickens' early fiction in its clearest form: given the thorough sterility, fraudulence, or corruption of manifest social and psychological processes, the novel's romance motifs tend toward pure parody. As the manifest categories of value in the narrative are subverted, it is fitting that the novel's viewpoint takes refuge in a character who seems, by mimetic standards, both peripheral and vicious.

In a novel full of parody figures, Sairey Gamp is the sole satirist. In a novel full of con-artists, she is the sole rival of her creator, an artist

who follows, in this way, the great tradition of Falstaff and the Wife of
Bath. In a novel full of female characters who have succumbed to the
stereotypic roles prescribed by their society, she is the only woman
who refuses to be subdued to what she works in.

Sairey Gamp is everything a Victorian wife should not be. First, she
is a widow—a widow, the narrator of *Martin Chuzzlewit* reports, of
"such uncommon fortitude . . . as to dispose of Mr. Gamp's remains
for the benefit of science." (We can assume this was before she
established her profitable connection with Mr. Mould, the undertaker.) And she was as uncommon a wife as she is a widow. The
Gamps had separated long before his death "on the ground of
incompatibility of temper in their drink." (We later learn that "incompatibility of temper" meant, among other things, that Gamp
knocked out four of her front teeth with one blow.) Unlike an Amelia
Sedley, a Dorothea Brooke, or Dickens' own Clara Cooperfield, she
has refused to subserve her husband alive or dead. Instead she has
surpassed Gamp in longevity, economic career, and both spiritual
and spirituous capacities.

Second, she has no discernible children. The son she mentions in
one of her anecdotes has apparently died or been fabricated. Third,
she is economically independent—and in a particularly vexing way
for the patriarchal social system that dominates the novel. She is a
midwife, who assists women when men seem as helpless and dis-
concerted as her own Mrs. Harris' husband: "Mr. Harris who was
dreadful timid went and stopped his ears in a empty dog-kennel, and
never took his hands away or come out once till he was showed the
baby, wen bein' took with fits, the doctor collared him an' laid him
on his back upon the airy stones, and she was told to ease her mind,
his 'owls was organs." The narrator himself cannot even call "childbirth" by its name, but instead, in a euphemism that reveals his own
anxiety, calls it the "curse of Adam."

Fourth, she is emotionally independent of men. Her one flesh-
and-blood friend is her apparent counterpart, Betsey Prig; but her
real capacities for love and friendship are invested in the woman of
her own creation, the famous Mrs. Harris. Betsey's vicious assault on
the reality of Mrs. Harris threatens the integrity and autonomy that
Sairey alone of all the female characters in the novel has wrested from
a hostile social world. But Sairey, though deeply shaken, defends
Mrs. Harris, repudiates Betsey, and exposes her as the Prig and
traitor she has been from the moment she appeared in the novel:

"Mrs. Prig was of the Gamp build, but not so fat; and her voice was deeper and more like a man's. She had a beard."

Fifth (and this is as telling in relation to Dickens the novelist as her other virtues are in relation to Dickens the husband and father), she is a creator who rivals her author and opposes the sexual values of his overt narrative structure—the only woman in Dickens' novels who has this double distinction.

Sairey professionalizes her confirming social roles; pretending to be all role, she is actually all self and thus triumphs over some of the most restrictive marital practices devised by man. This paradoxical wife is husbandless and childless because there is no available conception of marriage that equals her own imagination and capacities. She is, both by necessity and choice, an antiwife.

Given the supremacy of brutal masculine power in *Martin Chuzzlewit* and the corresponding victimization of the few female characters who still have some nominal status, Sairey Gamp's social role ought to restrict her severely. As a midwife, she is already a "female functionary," subordinated by sex and social function. But Sairey is not to be dominated, coerced, ignored, or, as she sums it up, "impoged upon." She refuses to be reduced to wife or midwife. In a novel filled with parody figures she is the sole consistent satirist and the novel's chief antagonist to the stereotypes of the wife. Her primary instrument of satire is the anecdote, which typically assails the values of the overt narrative while asserting its own shrewd alternatives. Thus, in one major example, the narrator's effusions over Ruth Pinch make Sairey's insidiously satiric response to her beauty all the more piquant and welcome:

> Now, ain't we rich in beauty this here joyful arternoon, I'm sure. I knows a lady, which her name, I'll not deceive you, Mrs. Chuzzlewit, is Harris, . . . and often have I said to Mrs. Harris, 'Oh, Mrs. Harris, ma'am! your countenance is quite a angel's!' Which, but for Pimples, it would be. 'No, Sairey Gamp,' says she, 'you best of hard-working and industrious creeturs as ever was underpaid at any price, which underpaid you are, quite diff'rent. Harris had it done afore marriage at ten and six,' she says, 'and wore it faithful next his heart 'till the colour run, when the money was declined to be give back, and no arrangement could be come to. But he never said it was a angel's, Sairey, wotever he might have thought.'

In this seemingly random and garbled patter, Sairey insinuates a number of the forces that work to transform the ersatz angel of courtship into the actual Victorian wife: pimples, multiple childbearing, the fading (and even the running) of sentiment, the grim permanence of marriage contracts, the economic forces that permeate the rituals of courtship and marriage, and the impossibility, for most wives, of escaping from even the worst of marriage bargains.

Sairey conflates Charity, Mercy, and Ruth into one "rich" image of female beauty, blithely overturning all the distinctions the narrator has tried to create among them. She catches him in his own contradictions; he has, in fact, persistently equated the good and desirable woman with a fragile stereotype of feminine beauty: "pretty little figure," "delicate waist," "tiny, precious, blessed little feet." Each epithet has deprived Ruth of a little more individuality, has objectified and diminished her a little more; each reveals less about the nature of women in Victorian society and more about the nature of male fantasies. The fantasy of a childlike, angelic, desexualized maiden of courtship is obviously the inverse of the aggressive sexuality that the masculine narrator has repressed and displaced onto Jonas Chuzzlewit.

So the narrator has foisted on the reader a portrait of the maiden as angel that is as shoddy as the miniature portrait foisted on Mr. Harris. The colors run at the touch of a little sweat, just as the confusion of erotic and spiritual desires in the image of the angel is exposed by Sairey and Mrs. Harris with the eruption of a few pimples.

It is in this same episode that Sairey casually comments on the loss of her teeth: "Gamp hisself . . . at one blow, bein' in liquor, struck out four, two single and two double, as was took by Mrs. Harris for a keepsake, and is carried in her pocket to this hour." Sairey leaves us with this comic, mordant double image: Mr. Harris with his portrait, an emblem of the masculine sentimentality that aggressively defaces the woman it supposedly enshrines; Mrs. Harris with Sairey's teeth, a relic of masculine brutality toward wives.

Only Sairey, of all the characters in *Martin Chuzzlewit*, can transcend this polarized image, which reflects two extreme projections of the same antifeminist attitudes. And, given the psychic and social conditions of the novel, she can do this only in her imagination, through the marriage of the marvelous Harris: "For if ever a woman lived as know'd not wot it was to form a wish to pizon them as had good looks, and had no reagion give her by the best of husbands, Mrs. Harris is that ev'nly dispogician." Mrs. Harris may bear no ill will; but Sairey, who directs this remark toward Ruth Pinch, does infiltrate her description of Mrs. Harris' heavenly disposition with the urge to poison the beautiful, brittle creatures of male desire. Because figures who dominate the world of Martin Chuzzlewit—the narrator as well as the characters—cannot even conceive the ideal of marriage created in the earthy heaven of Sairey's imagination, her doses of satiric aggression and satiric exposure are the best tonic for her imagination and for ours.

Thus *Martin Chuzzlewit* develops a theme that persists throughout Dickens' work: the crippling distortions of sexual and family roles by the oppressive patriarchal system and the extension of corrupted sexual patterns into every major institution of Victorian society. Through recurrent types of characters—the angel women, the masculinized shrews, the inadequate young men, the oppressive patriarchs—Dickens expressed his vision of a world which repressed, thwarted, and distorted human energies.

Early novels like *Martin Chuzzlewit* do not offer subtle explorations of the interplay between conscious and unconscious forces, romance and mimetic motifs, within a single personality trapped in this system. There is no character in them comparable to Pip, Esther Summerson, Arthur Clennam, or Amy Dorrit. In fact, the mimetic dimension of these novels exists primarily as a disguise or, for many in Dickens' contemporary audience, a subliminal expression of romance patterns. This undercutting of mimetic expectations does not weaken the early novels but gives them, instead, a unique power to expose the systemic, unconscious nature of the multiple abuses and disorders within the Victorian culture.

# The Novel as Fairy Tale:
## Dickens' *Dombey and Son*

### by Harry Stone

If one reads Dickens' novels chronologically, one is astonished, upon beginning *Dombey and Son* (1847–48), to find that Dickens has achieved a totally new mastery. The first half of *Dombey* is almost perfect in conception and execution; each scene connects with the next, each throws light on what has come before and what is yet to come. Dickens calls up intricate themes and images, develops them, sustains them, and finally merges them with one another. He introduces experimental techniques—the child's point of view, the microcosmic world of servants and tradesmen as chorus—and does so with great assurance. But most important he masters a new structural method which fuses autobiography, psychology, symbolism, and fairy-tale fancy.

This startling mastery, hardly hinted at in his six earlier novels, was advanced by a variety of circumstances. The two-year hiatus in novel writing which occurred between the completion of *Martin Chuzzlewit* (1843–44) and the beginning of *Dombey*—for Dickens an unprecedented pause—gave him his first real chance for leisurely observation and stock-taking since he had begun to write. He found that both he and his age were in a period of transition. What he now saw was the new iron era with its *sui generis* miseries, dislocations, and diminishments, a state of disorder paralleled by disturbing changes going on within himself. He was beginning to grow disenchanted with the fruits of success, and he had already begun to anatomize his mounting restlessness and unhappiness. He was also gaining a new objectivity and cosmopolitanism. He lived on the continent for almost half the four years between the completion of *Chuzzlewit* and

"The Novel as Fairy Tale: Dickens' *Dombey and Son*" by Harry Stone. From *English Studies*, 47 (1966), 1–27. Copyright© 1966 by Swets & Zeitlinger B. V. Reprinted by permission of the author and publishers.

the completion of *Dombey*. The vantage point of Italy and Switzerland enabled him to view the new English society—the commercial-industrial society about which he would now write—with a critical detachment.

But above all, the years between *Chuzzlewit* and the completion of *Dombey* provided him with unique opportunities for literary experimentation. In the Christmas books he wrote during that interval (*A Christmas Carol* [1843], *The Chimes* [1845], *The Cricket on the Hearth* [1846], *The Battle of Life* [1847], and *The Haunted Man* [1848]—the last conceived and partly written in the interval, but not finished until *Dombey* was completed) he had five opportunities to experiment with structure, symbol, and subject matter, to manipulate in exceptionally fluid and foreshortened form old elements which had troubled him, and new elements he had not yet used or mastered. The Christmas books, as I have demonstrated elsewhere, profoundly altered his artistic methods. And when he came to write his first post-Christmas-book novel, he adapted the techniques that had served him so well in the Christmas books. That he did so is not surprising. The first chapters of *Dombey* were written in Switzerland in the midst of planning and writing *The Battle of Life* and formulating *The Haunted Man*. As he worked on *Dombey*, therefore, his mind was preoccupied with devices and patterns, primarily cohesive in nature, which were helping him integrate the Christmas books. His problem in *Dombey* was almost identical. For in *Dombey*, as in the Christmas books, he self-consciously set out to blend autobiography, social criticism, story-telling, and fairy tales; as he put it, he was taking fairy tales and "giving them a higher form."

Dickens was using the term fairy tales in an idiosyncratic way; he was giving a convenient label to his special fusion of fairy story, fantasy, myth, magic, and folklore. He had created this blend out of materials familiar to him from childhood, out of the Gothic novel, the ghost story, the melodrama, the pantomime, the "Ancient Mariner" type of ballad, the Bunyanesque allegory, and the moral tract, as well as the fairy tale. But for Dickens all these elements were aspects of his suprarational view of life; he found such elements congenial because they touched his imagination, an imagination formed and sensitized by the logic and fancy of fairy tales. Following Dickens' authority, therefore, the term fairy tale may be used (and it will be so used in this essay) to designate this crucial confluence in his writings. To see how fundamentally the fairy tale shapes *Dombey and Son*, one must keep in mind its central plot, and then isolate its deftly integrated social, autobiographical, psychological, and fairy-tale strands; and one must also remember that Dickens, buttressed by his Christmas-book experiments, set out to do something he had never attempted before in a novel: to write a realistic story on the most up-to-date subject matter, a story which would be a detailed social and psychological analysis of the Victorian businessman, and yet, at the same time, be a magical fable of contemporary life.

*Dombey and Son* centers about the relationship of Mr. Dombey and his unloved daughter, Florence. Mr. Dombey is a cold, proud, self-centered business baron. He is not a bad man, but wealth and authority have made him arrogant, and his single passion is to see the great shipping and trading firm of Dombey and Son perpetuated once more by a male heir. Mr. Dombey is certain that money can buy everything—everything, that is, but perhaps a son—and when six years after Florence's birth his wife dies in giving birth to a son, Mr. Dombey's thoughts cluster obsessively about his infant heir. The book opens with the birth of Paul and the death of Mrs. Dombey, and the huge novel which follows is designed to explore Mr. Dombey's parental sin and to humble him and shatter his money ethic. Mr. Dombey's sin is his rejection of the freely offered love of his daughter; he must come to realize that what Florence yearns to give him is a gift more valuable than anything money can buy. He must also learn that love can never be bought; that to be loved, one must love, and one must allow oneself to be loved. This theme, fresh in Dickens' day, has become hackneyed through much imitation (one recalls nineteenth-century examples such as George Eliot's *Silas Marner* or twentieth-century examples such as D. H. Lawrence's "The Rocking-Horse Winner"), but Dickens' exploration of the theme, even after a century of recapitulations, is moving and illuminating.

Mr. Dombey's harrowing is thorough. At first he merely neglects timid Florence, but gradually he grows envious of her, then jealous of the love she inspires in others, and finally baffled and guilty, he hates her as the symbol of his own failure to inspire love. Dickens sets forth the father-daughter relationship at great length and with great subtlety. Mr. Dombey emerges from the book, in spite of a number of scenes which are unbearably painful, not as a villain, but as a helpless victim of his personality and the new times, as a lonely, bewildered, money-centered man, to be pitied rather than hated.

The humbling of Mr. Dombey is pointed up by a series of key episodes. The first inkling Mr. Dombey has that his money ethic may be wanting occurs when tiny Paul asks him (as Paul in "The Rocking-Horse Winner" asks his mother) what money is and what it can do. Mr. Dombey (again like the mother in "The Rocking-Horse Winner") is nonplussed by the question—he himself had always thought of money and its value as beyond examination—and he answers Paul in terms of his faith. "Money, Paul," he says, "can do anything." "Why," then asks Paul, "didn't money save my mamma?" The question is not sentimental, and it echoes through the remainder of the book. For Paul, with his strange fairy-tale prescience, intuitively perceives what his father must learn through disappointment and suffering; and when the little boy unwittingly emphasizes that money cannot buy life, he is foreshadowing his own death a few years later. That death is the first crushing lesson in Mr. Dombey's painful education, but it brings him closer to Florence. Paul had lavished all his love on his sister, and Paul's death intensifies Mr. Dombey's jealousy of that love and his resentment that his unwanted daughter lives while his son and the plans he had centered upon him perish.

But Mr. Dombey having failed to buy life seeks to buy love and thereby a new son. He buys Edith, a beautiful, accomplished woman who knows she is being bought, despises the marriage contract she enters into, yet accepts it as a fair bargain freely and openly arrived at. Edith is Mr. Dombey's female counterpart; she is proud, but she is not deluded by her pride as is Mr. Dombey, and it irritates him that she makes no pretence that their marriage is anything other than a commercial arrangement. Dickens lavishes much attention on this business courtship and marriage; he shows Mr. Dombey inquiring about the widowed Edith's fertility, testing her ability as an artist and a musician, and displaying his power to command her to perform and obey. The marriage soon degenerates into a humiliating contest of wills, and Mr. Dombey watches in growing frustration as Edith, like Paul, gives Florence the love she withholds from him. Mr. Dombey, in his pride, still cannot comprehend why this is so, and Florence's shy but still-offered love is now rejected as the cause of his misery. Florence, as he had dreaded many years before, has at last become hateful to him. He now looks upon her as a nemesis, a reminder of the insufficiency of his money and his mastery. Florence, in turn, feels guilty because her father rejects her. She has been a stranger to him since childhood, has long since become timid and inarticulate in his presence, yearns to discover the magic formula which will make him love her, and upbraids herself for not having won his love. Edith's position in the household at last becomes unbearable, and she agrees to run off with Carker, Mr. Dombey's trusted business manager. When the scandal of Edith's flight descends bolt-like upon Mr. Dombey, Florence rushes to him, her timidity overcome by love and pity, but he strikes her; and alienated at last, she flees from the house.

Mr. Dombey's proud world of money and power is now fast crumbling. Money has not saved his son, restrained his manager, bound his wife, or secured his daughter. When the neglected firm of Dombey and Son fails also, the world wags on with clucking tongue, the showy vanities of Mr. Dombey's wealth are auctioned off as an ironic reminder of what money can and cannot do, and his bought servants march out of his house in self-righteous indignation. Mr. Dombey can no longer delude himself; stripped of every defense, he must see himself as he really is. What he does see horrifies him, and tortured by the perversity of personality and values which have brought ruin to himself and those closest to him, he decides to kill himself. He is saved by the return of Florence, and after a long illness (symbolic of the death of the old Dombey and the birth of a new chastened Dombey) he is shown briefly in the humbled twilight of his life.

But *Dombey* is much more than a domestic novel. The full title of the book is *Dealings with the Firm of Dombey and Son, Wholesale, Retail and for Exportation*. The title, even when interpreted ironically as intended, emphasizes the centrality of the social or business aspects of the story. These aspects are not limited to tracing the bankruptcy of Mr. Dombey's money ethic, important as this feature is. Dickens wished to underscore the deleterious tendencies in the new industrial order and by depicting those tendencies in their multiplicity—in relation to machines, methods, persons—show their danger and their destructiveness. The real villain of *Dombey and Son* is the soullessness of the new business world; the most condensed emblem of that world is the manager Carker—clever, compulsive, ruthless, amoral—a representative of the new anonymous power breed.

The business theme, as we shall see, is wedded in Christmas-book fashion to the fairy-tale and autobiographical aspects of the story. And like these other aspects, the business theme is developed by contrast. Sol Gills' nautical instrument shop is a perfect counterpart to the great Dombey firm, for Sol's business, like Dombey's, takes its living from the sea. But while Dombey's firm prospers, Sol sits forlornly amid his instruments, watching the tide of commerce sweep by his door. Sol's business is beyond repair (he is saved at the end by investments which, in fairy-tale fashion, suddenly pour gold into his pocket), but his shop is a place of healing refuge where the simple, the good, and the uncorrupted can congregate and take strength from one another. To it come Captain Cuttle, Toots, and Susan Nipper, and finally Florence and Walter.

Dombey's empire is flourishing, but Dickens, again using parallel construction to underline and integrate his themes, makes Dombey's business, in contrast to Gills', a source of infection. Walter (in his role as originally planned), Carker's brother, Rob the Grinder, and other characters illustrate this blighting influence. Two segments of the business theme—the Toodles (a group of minor characters), and the railroad—will demonstrate how carefully Dickens was now elaborating his Christmas-book method, and how skillfully he was using it to integrate social, symbolic, and fanciful themes.

Rob the Grinder, for instance, is a Toodle gone wrong, a Toodle touched by the Dombeian business infection. But there are many other Toodles, and they also elucidate *Dombey*'s business fable. The Toodles are the new proletariat, clothed in the garb of their calling (Mr. Toodle is covered by the dirt and cinders of his railroad occupation even as Rob is branded by his Grinder uniform), taking their sustenance from the new world of business, but also contributing to that world and essential to it. Mr. Dombey in his pride refuses to recognize the latter fact; he only acknowledges the Toodles' dependency and servitude. It is one of the defects of the new business world (and an element in Mr. Dombey's harrowing) that this relationship—in effect the relationship between capital and labor—has not been humanely established.

How Mr. Dombey regards this relationship is apparent in the domestic as well as the industrial focus of the story. At the beginning of the book, Mr. Dombey hires Rob's mother, Polly Toodle, to nurse motherless Paul. Paul, symbolically, must take his sustenance from lower-class Polly, his very life depends upon her bounty and good will; the milk which turns into his blood and sinews emphasizes the commonalty of rich and poor, their symbiotic relationship. But for Mr. Dombey, placing Paul at Polly's breast is a degrading necessity, and in order to blur this necessity, he seeks to make the arrangement a mere matter of business. He emphasizes to Polly that her milk is only a commodity; he warns her against forming any attachments to

Paul; and he even buys her name—replacing the plebian "Toodle" with the businesslike "Richards."

But Mr. Dombey cannot entirely free his mind from the thought that Polly's Toodlish milk is contaminating his young son, and he has wild fears that this mixing process will go even farther, that Polly may substitute her own infant for his son. And a modern redaction of a fairy-tale changeling scene, a scene which emphasizes Mr. Dombey's money-centered obtuseness, does in fact occur. Paul is taken by Polly from his great rich nursery in Portland Place, Bryanstone Square, to Staggs' Gardens, the cindery slum where the Toodles live. The slum—and here Dickens begins to work intricate counterpoint on the Toodles, the railroads, and their many larger ramifications in the story—the slum is a wasteland, a landscape made hell-like by the new railroad which is being built in its environs.

The railroad landscape is doubly appropriate; it is an emblem of the new industrial order (and, as we shall see, of death) and the source of Mr. Toodle's livelihood. Paul, then, in being brought to the nether depths of the industrial world, is brought to the original source of his sustenance, an equivalence which is enforced whether one looks at that journey in terms of Polly's breast or of the new industrialism which undergirds his father's wealth. When Polly arrives home and sees her infant son in her sister's arms, she rushes forward and instantly exchanges him with Paul. She clutches her son to her breast, and the exchange Dombey fears occurs for the paradoxical reason that the lure of Dombeian wealth and advantage is not sufficient to make Polly forgo her motherhood. The exchange also emphasizes the essential equality of the infants, and by implication, despite the distance and outward distinction between Portland Place and Staggs' Gardens, and despite the fact that Polly is later dismissed for this lapse, the equality of all Dombeys and Toodles.

In the remainder of the book the Toodles reinforce the lessons of their earlier appearances. Dickens continues to show that an unfeeling ruling class sows the seeds of its own destruction. Whelplike Rob eventually becomes Carker's tool and helps Carker run off with Edith. Rob's Dombey-engendered delinquency thus plays a part in Dombey's own ruin. Dombey's ruin comes at the end of the book, and when it comes we acknowledge its justice. For Dombey rebuffs every attempt to reach his humanity. On the industrial level of the story there are several such attempts. These attempts parallel Florence's strivings on the domestic level; they show that the businesslike aridity which withers Dombey's personal life, also withers all his other relationships, and ultimately (since Dombey is representative of the new ruling class) endangers the whole structure of Victorian society. This message is made very clear by scenes which further interweave Dombey, the Toodles, and the railroad, with Dickens' theme.

After Paul's death, when Dombey is waiting at the railroad station for the train which will take him and Major Bagstock to Birmingham, he is approached by Mr. Toodle, the stoker of the train. Dombey fails to recognize him, then treats him with frosty haughtiness, and finally assumes that Toodle has approached him for money. Dombey can understand such an approach, but he cannot understand Toodle's real motivation. When Dombey discovers Toodle has come to commiserate with him, and wears mourning crepe, not for the death of one of his own children (Toodle assures Dombey they are flourishing in their usual apple-cheeked manner), but for Paul, Mr. Dombey is humiliated. Mr. Toodle's act of brotherhood, which again asserts the interdependence of Dombeys and Toodles and reawakens memories of Paul's nursing at Polly Toodle's breast, is intolerable to Mr. Dombey. He believes his money and position make him superior to Mr. Toodle; sonless Dombey never stops to think that Mr. Toodle possesses something which neither his money nor his position can buy. As a matter of fact, Mr. Dombey's train journey will emphasize this Dombeian obtuseness, for it will result in his meeting Edith, which in turn will lead to his disastrous attempt to buy her, and through her a son.

The symbolism here becomes extraordinarily rich. For after his colloquy with Mr. Toodle, Mr. Dombey is hurried toward his ruin on a train stoked by Mr. Toodle. Dombey's dependence on the Toodles and the new industrialism is absolute; ultimately, in generic terms, it is Toodle labor and machine power which insure Dombey's position and money. The train is an ambiguous industrial servant, rushing Dombey toward his desire, but since his industrial ethic is distorted, his desire is self-wounding, and the train hastens him toward his destruction: toward Edith and a money marriage, toward friction, scandal, and bankruptcy. For Toodle the railroad and the new industrialism mean salvation: the railroad gives him a livelihood and leads to advancement (he becomes an engineer, sends his children to school, learns to read, and so on).

As we have seen, this dual thesis, that an industrial society is symbiotic and that an individual reaps what he sows, has already been elaborated in the nursing and changeling episodes of the novel, but it is simultaneously elaborated by the railroad imagery—imagery which enters the novel and undergirds the business theme in three major integrating episodes. First we see the railroads being built and watch them change the face of the land. Here is the new Dombeian business world constructing its vital arteries and nerves:

> Everywhere were bridges that led nowhere; thoroughfares that were wholly impassable; Babel towers of chimneys, wanting half their height; temporary wooden houses and enclosures, in the most unlikely situations; carcases of ragged tenements, and fragments of unfinished walls and arches, and piles of scaffolding, and wildernesses of bricks, and giant forms of cranes, and tripods straddling above nothing. There were a hundred thousand shapes and substances of incompleteness.

This description of dislocation becomes more expressionistic as it goes on, until Dickens turns it into an image of hell: "Hot springs and fiery eruptions . . . lent their contributions of confusion to the scene. Boiling water hissed and heaved within dilapidated walls; whence, also, the glare and roar of flames came issuing forth; and mounds of ashes blocked up rights of way, and wholly changed the law and custom of the neighbourhood."

But if the railroad building is hell, the railroad built is death. In the next great railroad episode, the one in which Mr. Dombey converses with Mr. Toodle and then travels to Edith, Dickens makes this death identification explicit. The train forces "itself upon its iron way—its own—defiant of all paths and roads, piercing through the heart of every obstacle, and dragging living creatures of all classes, ages, and degrees behind it . . . a type of the triumphant monster, Death." The latter phrase, in Christmas-book fashion, is repeated with slight variations four times in the course of a two-page impressionistic description of a rapid rail journey, and becomes (along with imagery of the flowing seabound river—an even more persistent death image in *Dombey*) the ominous motif of Mr. Dombey's headlong journey. Yet it is Dombey and what he stands for, not the railroad itself, which is the villain. Dickens emphasizes that "as Mr. Dombey looks out of his carriage window, it is never in his thoughts that the monster who has brought him there has let the light of day in on these things [blight and misery]: not made or caused them."

The symbolism is heightened and completed in the last great railroad episode of the book. This episode climaxes the magnificent flight chapter in which Carker, pursued by Dombey, flees through France to England, where he waits for the train which will take him to safety. The phantasmagoric flight has been punctuated—again in Christmas-book fashion—by the reiterated leitmotif of "bells and wheels, and horses' feet, and no rest,"and now Carker, dazed and sick with weariness, shudders each time the ground trembles and a great train, dropping glowing coals and exhaling a deathlike breath, goes shrieking by. Confused by lack of sleep, bewildered by unearthly railroad noises, Carker suddenly sees Dombey emerge through the station door. He staggers back, loses his footing, and topples in front of a train. The wheels which rolled endlessly through his dreamlike flight now coalesce into the great avenging wheel of the locomotive "that spun him round and round and struck him limb from limb, and licked his stream of life up with its fiery heat." The death is appropriate. For Carker the manager, the new industrial man par excellence, is destroyed by the iron idol, that "type of the triumphant monster, Death," he had so inhumanly served. Dombey, for his part, goes from this scene of judgment to face his own imminent ruin, while Toodle and his apple-cheeked brood roll blithely forward.

Though the Toodles and railroads are subordinate elements in Dickens' larger design, they subserve major ends. For Dickens' design now dominates the detail as well as the grand sweep of the novel, and even minor or specialized elements (in this case primarily social or industrial elements) blend with—are actually a part of—his central conception. The blending is much richer than is suggested here, for it is compounded of the imagery of plants, plumages, clocks, jewels, rivers, and staircases, as well as railroads; it embraces characters such as Dombey, Edith, Paul, Florence, Mrs. Skewton and Major Bagstock as well as the lowly Toodles; and it works through leitmotifs more persistent and all-embracing than the wheel leitmotif of the flight chapter. All these interrelated and endlessly refracting aspects of plot, theme, image, and symbol give *Dombey and Son* an organic unity no previous Dickens novel had had. What he had done here was to elaborate and combine Christmas-book patterns and Christmas-book techniques with the basic organizing idea of the micro-macrocosmic novel, the novel which consciously depicts a whole society through a unified and manageable fragment thereof. In *Dombey* the fragment is the new business world, "Wholesale, Retail, and for Exportation"; in later works it is the legal world (*Bleak House*), or the prison world—the phrase taken in its metaphorical and psychological as well as literal meaning—(*Little Dorrit*). *Bleak House* has been cited by Edmund Wilson and others as the commencement of this micro-macrocosmic organization in Dickens, but in *Dombey*, six years before *Bleak House*, Dickens had introduced the fundamental form and attendant techniques of this powerful type of novel. The first appearance of this important innovation has been overlooked because the structure of *Dombey* falls below that of *Bleak House* and *Little Dorrit* and obscures Dickens' intent. The second half of *Dombey*, like the ending of the Christmas books, is inferior to the earlier portions; indeed the latter portions at times belie what Dickens set out to do. The micro-macrocosmic form and the Christmas-book method are present in *Dombey* nevertheless, and the reasons for *Dombey*'s initial superiority and subsequent falling off—very different from the reasons for the falling off of the Christmas books—throw light on how Dickens adapted the Christmas-book method to his new type of novel and the difficulties he encountered when pursuing that method at length for the first time.

Paradoxically, the fact that Dickens planned *Dombey* with greater care than any previous novel contributes to its falling off. In his earlier works improvisation was a central part of his method and led to some of his happiest effects. In intricately constructed *Dombey*, improvisation carried with it the danger that carefully planned groundwork would be left incomplete, or worse, would be completed by incongruous extensions. This is what actually occurred. Dickens, for instance, had originally intended that Edith commit adultery with Carker and then be killed, but at the last minute, at the urging of his close friend, John Forster, he decided to turn the episode into "an inverted *Maid's Tragedy*," have Edith run away from Dombey, meet Carker by prearrangement in a Dijon hotel suite, humble him by refusing to become his mistress, humiliate Dombey by letting the world think she had eloped with Carker and spent a night with him, and then flee into a lifetime of seclusion. The change weakened the novel, not merely because Dickens placed middle-class moral sensibilities above everyday probabilities, but because the Edith-Carker-Dombey denouement overthrew what he had carefully built into the novel earlier and what, as a consequence, the aesthetic structure of the story now required.

Carker, for example, is often projected through cat and snake imagery, Edith through bird and plumage imagery, and Dombey through gold imagery—imagery which forms and guides our expectations. Such imagery gives ominous meaning to Dombey's breakfast at Carker's residence (throughout the meal Carker's brightly plumed parrot—a symbol of Edith—plays in its symbolic cage and swings precariously on its great golden wedding-ring hoop), and such imagery gives terrible significance to the frantic scene with Carker in which Edith tears the decorative plumage from her wrist and rains it on the ground. These and similar imagistic foreshadowings are perverted by Edith's melodramatic escape. The escape is false not only to a web of imagery (for the bird imagery is reinforced by the imagery of Edith's magically sympathetic jewels, and by Carker's sinister catlike and snakelike stalking), but to the central thesis of the story. For the humbling of Dombey and all that Dickens attaches thereto demands that no mere appearance of disgrace be substituted for the irrevocable act; and Carker, for his part, should not be thwarted by a wilful woman (he should degrade her as he degrades everything he touches), but should be quelled solely by his idol, by the implacable wheels of industry. Furthermore, Dickens had designed Edith's money marriage and her relationship to her mother, Mrs. Skewton, to parallel the prostitution of Alice and her relationship to her mother, Good Mrs. Brown. His whole purpose was to demonstrate that the sale of one's body and one's accomplishments is prostitution no matter how exalted the contractors or how sanctified by marriage vows the contract. To imprison, transport, debauch, and kill Alice, and then cause Edith to escape her preordained adultery and death, is to overturn that demonstration.

The same damaging reversal also occurs with Walter. As Dickens' letters and avowals to Forster show, Walter was to have ended a wastrel, another sacrifice to Dombey methods and Dombey business. His degeneration was to have been accentuated by the *Cinderella* and *Dick Whittington* dreams of Sol Gills, Captain Cuttle, and himself—dreams to the effect that he was favored by Mr. Dombey, would rise to the top of the firm, marry Florence, and be rich and happy. The success imagery which surrounds Walter and Florence in the opening portions of the book was to have been ironic, it was to have served at the climax of the book to underline the blighting effect of the new business ethic—an underlining turned upside down by the revised ending.

These weakening changes were compounded by Dickens' decision in the midst of *Dombey* to abandon the business theme, a decision forced upon him by his mode of writing and publishing. Unable to go back and modify the monthly parts already published, unable to extend the monthly parts yet to be written, he found himself, now that the ending was looming before him, impossibly cramped. The detailed psychological analysis of the Dombey-Florence-Carker relationship—a type of analysis he had never attempted before—was taking an immense amount of room. Popular comic characters such as Captain Cuttle, Susan Nipper, Mrs. MacStinger, and Toots had to be paraded periodically and given scenes in which to display their talents. And the overriding requirements of the culminating plot and its abundance of melodramatic climaxes (Edith's spurning of Carker, Carker's flight and death, Walter's homecoming, Alice's death, Florence's return to her father, and Florence's last interview with Edith) could neither be eliminated nor postponed. As a result the world of business and all that revolved about it had to be severely attenuated in the second half. The complex initial unity of the domestic and commercial strands is perpetuated only by the reader's memory of Dickens' careful introductory weaving, and by a few major plot culminations planned from the first—the crash of the Dombey business, the symbolic railroad death of Carker, and the proliferation and staying power of the advancing Toodles.

But *Dombey*, though it fails to live up to the promise of its opening numbers, is a great achievement nevertheless. That achievement is made all the most auspicious by the departures it marks for Dickens—by its new emphasis on realism, psychology, and contemporary life, and by the successful transfer from Christmas book to novel of such mechanisms as leitmotif, symbolism, significant imagery, and fairy-tale episode and structure. It may seem strange that fairy-tale elements should wax strong when Dickens is emphasizing a new realism, but this is so, and *Dombey*, as we shall now see in greater detail, owes much of its special effectiveness to the fairy tale.

The central design of *Dombey*, for example, works changes on the *Cinderella* theme, and this familiar theme and the fears and fulfillments it embodies gives *Dombey* a part of its emotional appeal. The opening paragraph of *Cinderella* recalls the central situation of Dickens' business novel: "Once there was a gentleman who married, for his second wife, the proudest and most haughty woman that was every seen. . . . He had . . . by another wife, a young daughter, but of unparalleled goodness and sweetness of temper, which she took from her mother, who was the best creature in the world."

*Dombey*, of course, contains much more. For instance, Dickens also reworks the *Cinderella* theme—more subtly and psychologically than with Florence and Walter—through Florence and her father. Florence is the dispossessed, the cinder girl, the princess in disguise, the treasure whom Dombey must learn to recognize and appreciate. Dombey combines the roles of the wicked stepmother, the proud

vain stepsisters, and the searching prince: he neglects and humiliates
his princess daughter, leaves her home when he goes off to the balls
and fetes of the world, and persecutes her for his own failings.
Dickens gives this *Cinderella* (and poor-little-rich-girl) theme a mythlike power and fascination, but he also maintains the story's realism,
and infuses his fairy tale with autobiographical passion.

That passion stems from the waif theme; it grows out of the fact
that Dickens was able to project into Mr. Dombey's rejection of
Florence, his own sense of parental abandonment. Florence, like
Dickens (and like Oliver, Little Nell, Pip, and many other Dickens
characters) is an orphan. But Florence is the most pitiful kind of
orphan—and here Dickens' sense of his own abandonment makes
the Florence-Dickens identification most intense—she is an orphan
whose father is still alive. The scene in which Dickens gives this
notion explicit form is accompanied by great waves of emotion and
by an unusual richness of complementary imagery (imagery notably
of falling flowers and flowing water) and is followed by an interpolated exemplum, a reverse father-daughter story which accentuates Dickens' horror at the rejection he is depicting. The term
orphan is no critical subtlety, for Dickens himself applies the metaphor to Florence: "The flowers were scattered on the ground like
dust; the empty hands were spread upon the face; and orphaned
Florence, shrinking down upon the ground, wept long and bitterly."
The sense of being orphaned, of being a lonely waif in a great
unfeeling city, runs through all of *Dombey*, though usually by implication or dramatic demonstration rather than direct statement. Its first
strong enunciation occurs when Florence, as a child, is lost in the
city of London, a scene which recalls Dickens' similar childhood
experience, but which also mirrors his more general childhood
response to London. This crucial scene sets the pattern for what is to
follow, for the orphan label or the lost-child symbolism reappears at
climactic moments throughout the story. The predictability with
which Dickens sounds this chord at such moments testifies to its
profound meaning for him. When Dombey strikes Florence, Dickens
writes, "She saw she had no father upon earth, and ran out,
orphaned, from his house." And when she is running through the
streets, he has her think: "Where to go? . . . She thought of the only
other time she had been lost in the wide wilderness of London—
though not as lost as now—and went that way." Loss and abandonment become intertwined with rejection, and significantly (in view of
Dickens' own experiences), when Florence feels Walter also rejects

her, she summons up her childhood days, again remembers the trauma of her symbolic city experience, and recalls "when she was a lost child in the staring streets."

In such recurrent nightmare scenes fairy tale and autobiography coalesce. And by the same token (for it is the essence of Dickens' Christmas-book method to fuse fact and fairy-tale fancy into a more profound form of truth) the *Cinderella* structure of the Florence-Walter episodes carries with it suggestive autobiographical overtones. The Florence-Walter love relationship is treated through much of the book as a brother-sister relationship. It thus parallels the other central love relationship of the novel, the brother-sister relationship of Paul and Florence. Dickens counterpoises the love which exists between Paul and Florence to the love which is lacking between Florence and her father. The sisterly-brotherly love becomes for Florence (and for Paul) a substitute for the outgoing parental love Dombey is incapable of giving.

These relationships are similar to Dickens' early closeness to his sister Fanny and his turning to her for love in the face of what he took to be parental neglect and rejection. The importance of the brother-sister relationship is accentuated when Dickens insists upon making the Florence-Walter conjunction (despite its sexual and *Cinderella* aspects) a brother-sister situation. In a most curious way, the sibling quality of that relationship is emphasized at the same time that the possibility of sexual love and marriage is also underscored. In this respect, Dickens is perpetuating through Walter and Florence, little Paul's equally curious yearning. " 'I mean', said Paul, 'to put my money all together in one bank, never try to get any more, go away into the country with my darling Florence, have a beautiful garden, fields, and woods, and live there with her all my life!' " And when Paul dies, and the Captain Cuttle–Sol Gills circle views Walter's marriage to Florence and his accession to the head of Dombey and Son as certain, Dickens goes out of his way to make Walter a surrogate of Paul, and to give the brother-sister relationship of Walter and Florence an almost legal status. The day before Walter voyages into shipwreck on the *Son and Heir*, Florence visits him and says, "If you'll be a brother to me, Walter, now that he [Paul] is gone and I have none on earth I'll be your sister all my life, and think of you like one wherever we may be!" Walter accepts the offer, the clock strikes, Florence gets into a waiting coach, says "You are my brother, dear!" and the coach drives off. But Walter is to be Florence's husband, not her brother, and years later when he returns and realizes that he loves her sexually, the pledge of brotherhood becomes a torment to him, forces him to avoid her, and is dissolved only when Florence confesses her unsisterly love for him.

This strange brother-sister-husband-wife conjunction which Dickens idealizes in *Dombey* is similar to the one he strove to achieve in his own life. His sister Fanny, his parent substitute in childhood, who became the object of his love and then, so Dickens thought, betrayed him (even as his mother had earlier), was later, along with his mother and his first love, the equally unsteadfast Maria Beadnell, made his image of womanhood, an image which shaped his attitude toward love and his wife. What Dickens sought was a wife who would be a companion, a sexual partner, a bearer of children, but at the same time (and unlike his unforgiven mother or the inconstant Maria) be steadfast and innocent, untouched and untouchable, the matured and idealized image of his childhood sister. The very terms of his desire made it unattainable; for to find the paragon wife was to destroy the sister, and to preserve the immature sister, was to have no wife at all. Hence Dickens' curious domestic compromise, his anomalous household which from shortly after his marriage contained not only his wife, but his wife's sixteen-year-old sister, Mary Hogarth. And when adored Mary died in his arms at the age of seventeen (still budlike and perfect, still, in the words he wrote for her tombstone, "young, beautiful, and good," and thus forever so) he was able to convince himself that he had rediscovered, though again in fleeting form, the all-loving sister he had apotheosized in childhood. Now more than ever, therefore, he sought to give actual form to his dream of a sister-wife fusion. Five years later, he brought fifteen-year-old Georgina, another Hogarth sister, into his household. And there Georgina remained, unmarried and sisterly, sisterly even after her sister, Dickens' wife, moved out of his home, sisterly until his death, clinging to that portion of her brother-in-law which had need of a worshiping sister surrogate such as she. Yet what Dickens really wanted was not two women in his house, a wife and an aging sister substitute, but one woman who would be both wife and ever-young ever-adoring sister. His makeshift attempts to give his dream reality by means of resident sisters-in-law, infatuations with teenage girls (such as Christiana Weller), and finally, in his forties, by a liaison with an eighteen-year-old actress—these attempts and the will-o'-the-wisp dream which prompted them had much to do with his growing restlessness, his increasingly unsatisfactory marriage, and his latter-day unhappiness.

His need and the dream which embodied it also led to a host of female characters into whom he projected (and through whom he partly vicariously realized) the confused sister-wife ideal of his emotional yearning. In the early works the projection is usually an idealized blending of Fanny Dickens and Mary Hogarth, a combination of the perfect but vanished childhood sister companion and the doomed sister substitute: a figure who is most notably represented by Little Nell. Or more commonly, such female characters are sister-wife figures who are depicted both as perfect sisters and perfect wives. (One usually gets the feeling that the sister role is the important one, that happy wifehood is a vague status which comes late in the novel as a reward for loyal sisterhood.) In the typical case, the dutiful, loving sister, having proved her boundless devotion, is allowed to marry an impeccable but bloodless spouse: Rose Fleming, the foster-sister of Oliver (and his aunt, as it turns out), marries Harry Maylie (whose foster-sister—to compound the pattern—is the very same Rose); Kate Nickleby, the sister of Nicholas, marries Frank Cheeryble; Ruth Pinch, the sister of Tom, marries John Westlock. In each case the marriage occurs at the end of the book, and it is the sister relationship, not the lover relationship, which is important. Sometimes, as with Ruth Pinch, the sister perpetuates the brother-sister relationship after marriage by bringing the brother into (or next to) her new household; and in some cases, the sister never marries, but as with Harriet Carker, sacrifices her chance for marriage and happiness (nobly and fittingly as Dickens makes clear) in loyalty to her brother.

In later works the brother-sister relationship is more complex and usually reflects Dickens' feelings with greater insight. In *A Tale of Two Cities*, through Sydney Carton and Charles Darnay (two projections of Dickens, as Dickens himself recognized) he was again able to depict a love which combined sexual and brother-sister qualities. The pale married love of Lucie and Charles represents Dickens' ideal husband-wife relationship; the emotional Lucie-Sydney conjunction represents (as Chapter XIII of Book II makes clear) a forbidden sexual love which is repressed and finally sublimated into a precarious brotherly love. At the end of the book this brotherly love is purged of its remaining sexual taint when Sydney forgoes the possibility of marrying a widowed Lucie and saves Lucie's lawful sexual partner by sacrificing himself.

In *David Copperfield* the bifurcation of *A Tale of Two Cities* is reversed. David has two loves, one Dora, a provocative but immature lover and an unsatisfactory wife, the other, Agnes, a sister figure whom he finally recognizes, after Dora's death, as his proper spouse. In *Copperfield* Dickens came close to consciously understanding his dilemma and the impossibility of resolving it; for though David at last marries Agnes, he does so in a curiously asexual way, realizing that her love, no matter how deep, lacks something which his first love possessed. As Dickens later partly confessed, Agnes is a recrudescence of the sisterly Fanny-Mary-Georgina figure, while Dora is compounded of Maria and his wife, Catherine, that is, of his early sexual love and disillusionment.

Pip and Estella in *Great Expectations*, to cite only one more instance of this repeated pattern, also have an odd brother-sister-lover relationship. The brother-sister aspects of their relationship, built up by years of childhood association, make Pip a confidant, a person singled out for favorable treatment, a charmed being who is supposedly safe from a destructive sexual love for Estella. Yet his presumed immunity proves to be his curse, for his favored position causes him to love Estella all the more. He loves her as sister, as wife, and as ideal (as Estella, the star); he loves her though he knows he cannot, and for his well-being should not, attain her. But knowledge, reason, conscience are powerless to restrain him; he pursues her, and thus he pursues his own misery.

Dickens was probably only vaguely aware of the exact relationship between the loves he was depicting fictionally and his own emotional situation; yet his great urge to give creative objectivity to what he was feeling assured that the shaping pressures of the life would be projected into his fiction. His self-analysis therefore was partly unconscious and partly calculated. It was emotional and dramatic, not systematic. But is was not naive, and it was not static. *Copperfield* and *Great Expectations* examine the brother-sister-wife conjunction with a depth and sophistication that is beyond *Dombey* and the earlier novels.

Yet fittingly, as Dickens' first psychological novel, *Dombey* is also the first novel to deal with this node of his life with anything more than the idealized and impossible brother, sister, and wife figures of his early works. And *Dombey*'s fairy-tale structure helped give aesthetic form to the psychological complexities of the Florence-Walter, Florence-Paul, Florence-Dombey relationships—all of which body forth central aspects of his emotional life.

Mary Hogarth's death in Dickens' arms is a case in point. That death is projected into *Dombey* more than once, but with modifications important both autobiographically (in terms of the death's larger meaning to him) and aesthetically (in terms of his new care in constructing his novels). When Paul lies dying he recalls that his mother held Florence in her arms as she was dying, and therefore must have loved Florence much better than her father, "for even he, her brother, who had such dear love for her, could have no greater wish than that." Accordingly Dickens has Paul in his last moments (in the Dickens-Mary Hogarth manner), clasp Florence to his breast: "Sister and brother wound their arms around each other, and the golden light came streaming in, and fell upon them, locked together." Again the parent is excluded from this final gesture of love (a fact which makes Mr. Dombey jealous and helps turn him against his daughter), and the love of the sister is made to compensate for the inadequate love of the parent. That Dickens connected the brother-sister love of Paul and Florence with his love for Mary Hogarth, and Mary's death with Paul's, is made even clearer a few pages earlier. In the earlier scene, Paul, already in his prescient final illness, watches Florence, and thinks how "young, and good, and beautiful" she is—the words Dickens placed on Mary Hogarth's tombstone.

Although these parallels are not always true to the outward events of Dickens' experiences, they are true to the emotions of his experiences, and the parallels are subordinated to the larger demands of the novel—a new feature in Dickens' writing. The emotion-charged autobiographical relationships he projects into *Dombey* are modified, sometimes to accord with his wish-fulfilling desires, but more often to blend with his fictional purposes (though the two are not mutually exclusive). Similarly, the fairy-tale structures which carry his thesis, and the specific fairy-tale borrowings themselves, are also subordinated to the artistic whole. If Walter, owing to Dickens' change in plans, fulfills the *Cinderella* myth, Mr. Dombey in his *Cinderella* role can only enjoy his tardily recognized princess in diminished form—a switch from the old method which would have turned the converted Mr. Dombey into a fairy godmother and caused him to shower golden blessings on the elect.

Dickens' use of the fairy tale has changed. The fairy tale has become a more important force in his writings, but it has also become a more humanized, flexible, integrated force. This shift may be seen not only in *Dombey*'s complex double-tiered *Cinderella* framework, but in other areas. A portion of the plot is worked out through quasi-supernatural means, through the prophecy, special knowledge, portentous interference, and ultimately the astonishing blood relationship of Good Mrs. Brown, a realistic hag who is also a witch out of folklore and fairy literature. And the plot is unified by devices which for Dickens are allied to fairy tales, devices such as repeated phrases, leitmotifs, allegorical symbolism, and so on.

The Dombey mansion, for example, owes its mythlike potency to fairy-tale origins. The supernatural atmosphere of the mansion broods over the entire novel, but the scenes which wed the house most directly to the story's fairy-tale nimbus begin with the opening words of Chapter XXIII: "Florence lived alone in the great dreary house, and day succeeded day and still she lived alone; and the blank walls looked down upon her with a vacant stare, as if they had a Gorgon-like mind to stare her youth and beauty into stone." This introduction, with its repetition and its supernatural and fable elements (later, the whole sentence becomes a refrain repeated throughout the chapter) reminds one of Dickens' Christmas-book technique, a similarity strengthened when Dickens goes on in the next sentences to introduce a host of fairy-tale allusions. "No magic dwelling-place in magic story, shut up in the heart of a thick wood, was ever more solitary and deserted to the fancy, than was her father's mansion in its grim reality." Although there were not "two dragon sentries keeping ward before the gate of this abode, as in magic legend are usually found on duty over the wronged innocence imprisoned," there was a "monstrous fantasy of rusty iron"; and though there were "no talismanic characters engraven on the portal," neighborhood boys had chalked the neglected railings and pavements with ghosts. The decaying mansion is bewitched: "The spell upon it was more wasting than the spell that used to set enchanted houses sleeping once upon a time, but left their waking freshness unimpaired." The allusion is to *Sleeping Beauty*; but the spell on Dombey's mansion is far different from that on Sleeping Beauty's enchanted castle. In the Dombey mansion, curtains droop, mirrors grow dim, boards creak and shake, keys rust, fungus proliferates, and spiders, moths, black beetles, and rats multiply in frightening multitudes. Dickens makes the decaying house and its spell-like isolation mark the passage of time, underscore Dombey's neglect of Cinderella-Sleeping-Beauty Florence, and dramatize her magical transformation into lovely womanhood. The interlude (like the interlude in Virginia Woolf's *To the Lighthouse* which describes a similar scene and achieves an identical effect) goes on for several pages without slackening in tautness or evocativeness. The house is now boldly termed "an enchanted abode," and in this supernatural mansion, Florence "bloomed . . . like the king's fair daughter in the story." The interlude continues, associating the staircase, flower, and lost-child imagery with the fairy-tale atmosphere, and after further allusions to the "circle" which enabled Florence to live on while "nothing harmed her," and references to "an enchanted vision," and "a haunted house," and after an intricate juxtaposition of the mansion with Florence's solitary life and frustrated will to love, Dickens concludes by repeating the Gorgon refrain for a third time.

This synthesis of prosaic detail, suprarealistic atmosphere, and fairy-tale point of view is not confined to interpolated interludes. Mrs. Pipchin, for example, the dour and redoubtable teacher of little Paul, and his later overseer and nurse, combines meticulous realism with the most artful supernaturalism. Mrs. Pipchin is the old fairy-tale ogre-witch, but so thoroughly transformed that she bears little relationship to the one-dimensional witches and godmothers of Dickens' early writings. For Mrs. Pipchin's diablerie is more than Gothic trimming, it is a reflection of Paul's view of her. Mrs. Pipchin was modeled on two real persons, a Mrs. Roylance, a hard and unresponsive lady who took Dickens in to board during a portion of his blacking-warehouse days, and another woman, probably the keeper of a dame school he attended briefly several years earlier; but his childhood sufferings (especially those of his blacking-warehouse days) caused him to transform his flesh-and-blood models into a flesh-and-blood witch. Mrs. Pipchin is a young child's image of evil—it is noteworthy that Dickens in his self-pity makes Paul younger than he himself was—and her representation accentuates the child's view of the world that Dickens is depicting in this portion of the book.

Mrs. Pipchin is a "marvellous ill-favored, ill-conditioned old lady" with a "stooping figure," "mottled face, "hook nose," and "hard grey eye." Her witchlike appearance is accentuated by her "black bombazeen" clothing of a "lustreless, deep, dead, sombre shade," and by the fact that her presence is always a "quencher." Dickens then goes on to describe the hostilely animistic contents of the "Castle of this ogress and child-queller." Paul's first conversation with Mrs. Pipchin adds still other touches to the frightening fairy-tale atmosphere:

> 'Well, sir', said Mrs. Pipchin to Paul, 'how do you think you shall like me?'

'I don't think I shall like you at all', replied Paul. 'I want to go away. This isn't my house.'

'No. It's mine', retorted Mrs. Pipchin.

'It's a very nasty one', said Paul.

'There's a worse place in it than this though', said Mrs. Pipchin, 'where we shut up our bad boys.'

This "worse place," an empty basement at the back devoted to correctional purposes, Dickens calls the "Castle Dungeon." Paul's predicament, in his childish view, is catastrophic. He is trapped in a horrible fairy-tale castle presided over by a merciless witch. Words such as "ogress," "castle," "black," and "dungeon" reverberate through the remainder of the passage, and harmonize with Mrs. Pipchin's "black teapot," "coiled" black cat, and "hard grey eye."

Paul, who was not lacking in supernatural qualities himself, is fascinated by this horrific old lady, even as Dickens was fascinated by his own lady mentors and nursemaids and their terrifying folklore stories. Soon a strange fairy-tale rapport develops between Paul and Mrs. Pipchin. The two would sit before the fire and Paul would stare at his keeper "until he sometimes quite confounded . . . [her], ogress as she was." The atmosphere of the scene, despite its foundation of realism, becomes charged with an ever-increasing supernaturalism. "The good old lady," writes Dickens, "might have been—not to record it disrespectfully—a witch, and Paul and the cat her two familiars, as they all sat by the fire together. It would have been quite in keeping with the appearance of the party if they had all sprung up the chimney in a high wind one night, and never been heard of any more."

"This," continues Dickens in the next sentence, "never came to pass," and with that remark (though the supernatural atmosphere continues to hover over the chapter) the emphasis shifts from the fairy-tale level to the realistic. The passage is a good example of Dickens' method of combining the realistic and the fantastic, and the passage illustrates what he gained thereby; a suggestive atmosphere, an evocative point of view, a flexible suprarealism, and a unity of vision.

Dickens puts this synthesis to work throughout the novel. Another, even more important, case in point is the Walter-Florence-Good-Mrs. Brown conjunction, a conjunction which appears mystifyingly vexing and unorganic until viewed from its fairy-tale conception. So viewed, the conjunction emerges as one of the chief symbolic nodes of the story, a node at which the *Cinderella*, lost child,

business world, witch, and enchantment themes meet and inter-
mingle. Florence had accompanied Polly Toodle and Susan Nipper
on Paul's fateful visit to Staggs' Gardens, but in a moment of confusion
on the way home, had become separated from them. An old woman
hobbles up to Florence, grasps her by the wrist, and promises to
bring her back to her friends. The old woman has "red rims round
her eyes, . . . her mouth that mumbled and chattered of itself," and a
"shrivelled yellow face and throat" that went through "all sorts of
contortions." When the old woman seeks to soothe Florence and
lead her away, Florence asks, "What's your name?" "Mrs. Brown,"
answers the old woman, "Good Mrs. Brown."

Good Mrs. Brown leads Florence through dirty lanes and muddy
roads to a "shabby" "closely shut up" house. She unlocks the door,
and pushes the child into a room with black walls, black ceiling, and
no furniture. On the floor there is "a great heap of rags of different
colours, . . . a heap of bones, and a heap of sifted dust or cinders."
"Sit upon the rags," says Good Mrs. Brown. And then Good Mrs.
Brown, taking her own seat on the bones, warns, "Don't vex me. If
you don't . . . I won't hurt you. But if you do, I'll kill you. I could
have you killed at any time even if you was in your own bed at
home."

So little Cinderella sits near her heap of identifying cinders and
confronts her own Mrs. Pipchin, a witch and child-queller infinitely
more terrifying than Paul's. But the episode and its symbolic implications have only begun. Good Mrs. Brown (who all through the
episode, and elsewhere in the novel, in addition to being a witch, is
also a realistic Victorian rag and bone scavenger) now commands
Florence to take off her clothes. The command and its consequences
are deeply emblematic, for in *Sartor Resartus* fashion, Florence's
garments, like Rob the Grinder's, Mr. Toodle's, Mr. Toots', and
those of other characters in *Dombey*, proclaim and conceal identity.
Florence trembles and obeys. Off come her costly frock, bonnet,
petticoats, and shoes; on (taken from the heap of rags) go two wretched
substitutes for shoes, an old worn girl's cloak, and the "crushed
remains of a bonnet that had probably been picked up from some
ditch or dunghill." Florence is now clothed in an outfit which
correctly represents her outcast state. Then, suddenly, in a frightening scene, she almost undergoes a more crippling transformation. In
putting on her filthy substitute bonnet, she had entangled it in her
"luxuriantly" beautiful hair, and Good Mrs. Brown, watching like a
great black spider, falls into a strange fit of excitement. Trembling

with desire, the old woman "whips[s] out a large pair of scissors," ruffles Florence's very saleable curls "with a furious pleasure," and prepares to cut them off. But then, remembering her distant daughter's long hair, she pauses, finally stops, and at last gives way to a "wild tossing up of her lean arms" and a passionate parental grief that "thrilled to the heart" of the unloved Florence. The old woman tells Florence to hide her curls under the bonnet and "let no trace of them escape."

Mrs. Brown's passionate daughter, Alice, tossing her wild hair, will later appear in the story, a transmutation of the innocent Florence, and a foil to upper-class Edith (just as Good Mrs. Brown is a foil to Edith's mother Mrs. Skewton); and Alice and her mother will also serve as one more study of a blighting parent-child relationship. But the talismanic hair episode, with its frightening despoliation implications, and its many fairy-tale and legendary analogues, is more than a clue to a character who must appear much later. It is part of the terrifying fairy-tale evil which hovers about the immature Florence, and it is part of the enchanted atmosphere of the entire story. For the whole episode is a way of objectifying in a magical and exceptionally evocative manner—and also, from a child's point of view, in a brilliantly appropriate manner—the mortal peril which encompasses innocent Florence. And it follows that Florence's brief sojourn in the hell-like charnel house (a house which is identical, emotionally, to her bleak palace home) epitomizes the hellishness of her daily life. The symbolic significance of the episode is carried forward when Good Mrs. Brown returns with Florence to the London streets.

The two leave the black room of cinders, rags, and bones, but only after Mrs. Brown has insisted that Florence not go home but find her way "to her father's office in the City." Mrs. Brown accompanies this injunction with terrifying threats, and enjoins Florence to wait at the street corner "until the clock [strikes] three." Florence waits in fear and bewilderment. She looks back to see "the head of Good Mrs. Brown peeping out of a low wooden passage . . . likewise the fist of Good Mrs. Brown shaking towards her," but at last the witch disappears, London's many clocks toll the magic number three, and Florence ventures into the London thoroughfare, seeking her father's offices. Of the offices she knows fittingly and ironically only "that they belonged to Dombey and Son."

Lost and in rags, Florence goes through the commercial heart of the city asking the way to Dombey and Son. Symbolically, Florence has begun the great pilgrimage of her life—she is seeking the way to her father's heart, the way into the cold commercial citadel which is her father's life. At last, she comes to a dock where Dombey's name is known. Walter, Dombey's office boy, is nearby, and when she hears that he is from Dombey and Son, she runs eagerly up to him, leaving one of the slipshod shoes upon the ground. "I am lost," she cries, bursting into tears. At the same time her bonnet falls off, her hair comes "tumbling down about her face," and Walter, moved to "speechless admiration" by this magical sign, falls into a worshipful daze of love. But he is not too dazed to champion Florence and guide her through the city labyrinth. His first act is to pick up the shoe "and put it on the little foot as the Prince in the story might have fitted Cinderella's slipper on." This done, they walk arm-in-arm through the London streets, Walter neat and prosperous and Florence dirty and neglected, in a reversal of their social roles but in accordance with their spiritual status—and also in ironic reversal of the planned regeneration of Walter and the apotheosis of Florence.

Walter brings her to Uncle Sol's nautical instrument shop (the refuge she will again come to when she flees her father's house and once more hurries dispossessed through London streets), and he calls out to his uncle, "Here's Mr. Dombey's daughter lost in the streets, and robbed of her clothes by an old witch." After dinner, Florence falls asleep and Walter goes off to tell Mr. Dombey what he has found. Sol remains by Florence's side, "building a great many airy castles of the most fantastic architecture; and looking, in the dim shade, and in the close vicinity of all the instruments, like a magician . . . who held the child in an enchanted sleep."

Walter returns with Susan, Florence's maid, and with fresh clothing. Florence once more takes off her garments, again dons her usual clothes, and reassumes her former appearance. Walter and Florence exchange a kiss, Florence gets into the waiting coach, and the coach carries her off to her father's palace. "The entrance of the lost child," comments Dickens, made "a slight sensation, but not much," for Mr. Dombey "had never found her."

This remarkable episode, so striking in its fairy-tale analogues, so momentous in its symbolism and foreshadowing, encompasses in foreshortened form much of what Dickens was trying to do in *Dombey*. The groundwork is here laid for the intricate interaction of many of Dombey's central characters: for the interaction of Florence, Walter, Mr. Dombey, Uncle Sol, Good Mrs. Brown, and Carker Junior; and for the interaction of characters who have not yet appeared or who have not yet been entangled in the enchanted web—Edith, Mrs. Skewton, Alice, Harriet Carker, and Carker himself. But Dickens has also succeeded in casting a penumbra of magic, myth, and fairy lore over this scene. The events and characters take on an overwhelming significance; and for Dickens they had such a significance, for they embodied crucial engrams of his experience— the waif or lost child (especially in city streets), the inadequate parent, the witchlike child-queller, the fairy-tale refuge, and the magical transformation. The real and the supernatural mingle and strengthen one another, and the union helps produce Dickens' special vision of life.

That vision enhances reality. For Dickens' re-creation of his everyday world, even when he records it with hypnotic exactitude, possesses a fairy-tale essence which is projected and works upon the reader even when the reader has no clear notion of what he is responding to. Like *Gulliver's Travels*, *Moby-Dick*, and similar works of literature, *Dombey* and the later Dickens novels can be read pleasurably on the most superficial levels. Readers accustomed to thinking of Dickens as a popular author, and remembering their youthful introduction to him, do not often look in him for the hidden meanings, ambiguities, and wordplays they have been taught to search for in Joyce. Joyce demands such attention. Portions of *A Portrait of the Artist as a Young Man*, much of *Ulysses*, and all of *Finnegans Wake* are unintelligible without precise exegesis. But *Dombey* is more like *Dubliners*, for *Dombey* can be read meaningfully, and to all appearances, satisfactorily, on a casual perusal. This universal availability is a virtue and a trap; it enables the work to speak unencumbered to a huge differentiated audience, but it also leads to misinterpretation. For if a reader responds to elements of a work of art without knowing they are there or why he is responding, he may respond erratically and incompletely. If the symbolism, the fairy-tale core, the recurring themes of *Dombey* are missed, the book's meaning is attenuated, and the novel's impact is lessened. One can see this very quickly if one follows Good Mrs. Brown through the rest of *Dombey*. For the fairy-tale filaments which knot momentarily in the opening Good Mrs. Brown scene, float in thousands of threadlike spinnings through the rest of the book, knotting again here and there, until they form an intricate web which binds together one whole movement of the novel. Good Mrs. Brown retains her witchlike nature throughout the novel; indeed her role is scarcely intelligible unless one constantly views her as a double image: as an evocation of a miserable London scavenger, and as a full-fledged necromancer.

The scene in which Good Mrs. Brown's magical associations are projected with the greatest force occurs halfway through the book. The episode takes place in Leamington. Dombey is courting Edith, testing her accomplishments, and displaying her to Carker whom he has called down from London. Carker, like most of the important characters in *Dombey*, has his share of fairy-tale qualities. He is the folklore devil who often appears disguised as an animal—in *Dombey* he is described most frequently as a cat, but notably also as a wolf and a snake. Carker, the sinister stalking cat or hypnotizing snake, affects Florence, Edith, Rob the Grinder, Diogenes the dog, and others, in supernatural ways. Florence shudders whenever he comes near, and almost faints when he fixes his serpent's eyes upon her; Diogenes growls and barks ferociously when he appears; and Rob is so terrorized and hypnotized by him that he follows him trance-like through the London streets, his eyes never wavering from Carker. Carker often imposes his silent will upon others and speaks to them without articulating. In his passionate interviews with Edith, his malignancy, magnified by the surrounding supernatural symbolism, creates truly terrifying effects. In one interview, he looks at her, and Dickens writes, "He saw the soft down tremble once again, and he saw her lay the plumage of the beautiful bird against her bosom for a moment; and he unfolded one more ring of the coil into which he had gathered himself." The horror condensed into these words is difficult to convey, for the terror of the scene accumulates from associations which have been building around Carker from the first. This aura of terror always clings to Carker. It is with him in the Leamington scene, and it adds its special appropriateness to the meaning and effect of that scene.

The scene occurs before breakfast in the countryside. Carker has strolled beyond the town, and on his return he goes by way of a "deep shade of leafy trees." Once in this grove, he begins a strange serpentine ritual: "Mr. Carker threaded the great boles of the trees, and went passing in and out, before this one and behind that, weaving a chain of footsteps on the dewy ground." As he softly glides round the truck of one large tree "on which the obdurate bark was knotted and overlapped like the hide of a rhinoceros or some kindred monster of the ancient days before the Flood," he sees a figure sitting on a nearby bench "about which, in another moment, he would have wound the chain he was making." The figure is that of a beautiful, elegantly dressed lady who is struggling with herself. The lovely lady in distress is Edith, whom Carker has not yet met. But even as he looks at her from behind his antediluvian tree, a "very ugly old woman scrambled up from the ground—out of it, it almost appeared—and stood in the way." The old woman—who is Good Mrs. Brown, although never so identified in this scene—disturbs Edith with her demands for silver and her threats to call out her fortune. Edith, frightened, rushes toward the hidden Carker, who snakelike is "slinking against his tree," and who seizes this moment to cross her path and assume her defense. But Good Mrs. Brown is not put down. "Give me something," she tells Carker, "or I'll call it after *you*!" Carker throws her a piece of silver, and Good Mrs. Brown, in Shakespearian image, "munching," Dickens writes, "like that sailor's wife of yore who had chestnuts in her lap, and scowling like the witch who asked for some in vain," picks up the coin, crouches "on the veinous root of an old tree," and utters the following gnomic spell: "One child dead, and one child living; one wife dead, and one wife coming. Go and meet her!" Carker, in spite of himself, is startled by the prescience of the old hag's utterance, and turns to look at her. Munching and mumbling, she "pointed with her finger in the direction he was going, and laughed." Carker pauses, but then hurries on. As he leaves the wood, however, he looks over his shoulder "at the root of the old tree." "He could yet see the finger pointing before him, and thought he heard the woman screaming, 'Go and meet her!' "

The scene is penetrated with suggestion and foreshadowing. The enchanted grove, the chain of fate, the forbidden antediluvian, Biblical tree, the serpent in the garden, the piece of silver, the gnomic prophecy, the finger pointing the way to adultery and destruction—all these signs heighten the events which are to come, underline their inevitability, and give the episode a cosmic significance.

That significance and the fairy-tale contributions to it are forged bit by bit. For example, much of the irony and tension of a scene which occurs several pages later are lost if the implications of the episode in the magic woods are missed. The new scene takes place after breakfast on the day of the meeting in the enchanted grove. The Dombey party is exploring the neighborhood of Warwick Castle, and Dombey is again testing and displaying Edith, now by requesting her to sketch for him. She asks him negligently what he would like her to sketch, and Dombey chooses a nearby view. The view is portentous:

"There happened to be in the foreground, at some little distance, a grove of trees, not unlike that in which Mr. Carker had made his chain of footsteps in the morning, and with a seat under one tree, greatly resembling, in the general character of its situation, the point where his chain had broken." Carker suggests that it is "an interesting—almost a curious—point of view." His statement, meaningful only to Edith, is the beginning of the skillful psychological process whereby he forces upon her a peculiarly personal and secret relationship. "Will you like that?" Edith asks Mr. Dombey. "I shall be charmed," is Dombey's unwitting reply. "Therefore," continues Dickens, "the carriage was driven to the spot where Mr. Dombey was to be charmed"; and a few moments later Carker, watching Edith sketch, commends her "extraordinary skill—especially in trees."

Such ironies and directives, underlined and extended by *Dombey*'s fairy-tale structure, save scene after scene from having only melo-dramatic or coincidental significance, for episodes which would be impossibly contrived in a purely realistic novel become acceptable and meaningful in so expressionistic a work as *Dombey*. Good Mrs. Brown's integrating supernatural-realistic role continues through the remainder of the book: through the Dombey wedding, the return of Alice, and the threatening of Rob. As the book progresses we begin to understand Good Mrs. Brown's unforgivable sin and its relationship to Dickens' fundamental purpose. Her sin is avarice, a willingness to sacrifice everything—she has already so sacrificed her daughter—for money. A money ethic has turned her into a veritable witch; yet her sin is identical with Mrs. Skewton's and Mr. Dombey's sin (and one might add, with Dickens' conception of his parents' sin—especially his mother's—in the blacking-warehouse days). Good Mrs. Brown is therefore another permutation of *Dombey*'s central fable; she is a character who forces the reader to see that placing money before human values is witchlike and disastrous. That these characters are part of the central fable and exhibit the same sin is made explicit through a confrontation scene, with strong supernatural overtones, involving Good Mrs. Brown, Alice, Mrs. Skewton, and Edith, and by the revelation at the end of the book, in fairy-tale fashion, that Alice is Good Mrs. Brown's illegitimate daughter by Edith's father's brother, so that Edith and Alice—whose physical as well as emotional and moral resemblances have been pointed up throughout the novel—are first cousins. Finally, parallelism, poetic justice, and fairy-tale coincidence are additionally served by Good Mrs. Brown's thauma-turgic part in the destruction of Edith, Carker, and Mr. Dombey.

This intricate interdependence and compensation, like that developed in the industrial and domestic levels of the story, points Dickens' theme of the essential unity of society. The coincidences serve Dickens' moral purpose, but they are more than mere happenstance and moral juggling, for the atmosphere of myth and fairy tale he blends with them gives them a poetic appropriateness which helps universalize the novel.

As the novel progresses, Dickens develops other fairy-tale characters and themes. The original *Cinderella* conjunction of Florence and Walter (associated from its outset with Good Mrs. Brown's fairy-tale abduction of Florence) is elaborated by many subsequent *Cinderella* touches. Walter preserves Florence's slipshod shoes and enshrines them in his room. This act, and Dickens' later references to it, keep our memory of the *Cinderella* meeting alive and prepare us for what is to come. But Walter's action also reflects his personality, and his romantic gesture links the realistic and fairy-tale levels of the story. Dickens tells us that Walter has a "strong infusion" of the "spice of romance and love of the marvellous" in his nature, and attributes to this trait Walter's "uncommon and delightful interest" in the adventures of Florence with Good Mrs. Brown. Walter, then, is attracted to Florence by a fairy-tale episode, but he exemplifies in his own relationship to her another fairy tale. He not only preserves the *Cinderella* shoes, he dreams fairy-tale dreams. He will go to sea, come back an admiral with epaulettes of "insupportable brightness," and bear Florence off to the "blue shores of somewhere or other triumphantly." And when Walter does go to sea, sent there for very unromantic reasons by Mr. Dombey, he takes with him Florence's slipshod shoes.

But the *Cinderella* atmosphere does not evaporate with Walter's nautical exile. Just before he leaves for his ship, Florence comes to Sol Gills' shop in a coach. This visitation casts a fairy-tale aura over Walter's departure and holds his future in suspense. In depicting the atmosphere of the scene, Dickens speaks specifically of a "fairy influence," and that influence, which clings to Walter and shapes our lasting impression of him (for he now disappears from the book for hundreds of pages), hovers about Florence in all her subsequent relations with the Sol Gills-Captain Cuttle world.

Much later, for example, when Florence seeks sanctuary in Sol Gills' shops (now in charge of Captain Cuttle, owing to Sol's wandering search for the missing Walter), Dickens uses *Sleeping Beauty* and *Beauty and the Beast* imagery to maintain the reader's sense of the

marvellous and to intensify Florence's aura of fairy-tale enchantment. Florence has fled her father's house, hurried once more
through the frightening streets, and come at last to the nautical
instrument shop. She is led through the shop to a high upstairs room
and there falls asleep on a couch. The beautiful girl, slumbering on a
couch, isolated from the bustling world, is a Sleeping Beauty who has
come to an enchanted sanctuary and who waits for the wakening kiss
of her absent prince. She even has her magical warders. Her dog,
Diogenes, miraculously follows her and becomes a protective dragon
who keeps guard by her side (Sleeping Beauty also had a dog who
slumbered by her side); and good Captain Cuttle, sensing her fairy
lineage, goes softly into her room and gazes upon the sleeping girl
"with a perfect awe of her youth and beauty."

When the action is resumed (for Dickens used the above scene to
conclude a monthly part), the fairy-tale atmosphere is maintained,
but now primarily in *Beauty and the Beast* imagery. Dickens contrasts
Florence's "youth and beauty" (echoing the *Sleeping Beauty* words of
the month before) with Captain Cuttle's "knobby face," "great broad
weather-beaten person," and "gruff voice." The situation, Dickens
remarks, was "an odd sort of romance, perfectly unimaginative, yet
perfectly unreal." And a few lines farther on he tells the reader that "a
wandering princess and a good monster in a story-book might have
sat by the fireside, and talked as Captain Cuttle and poor Florence
thought—and not have looked very much unlike them." This conjunction of the real, the grotesque, and the fanciful, bound together
and made viable by a fairy-tale essence, shapes the remaining adventures of Florence in her castle sanctuary. High up in that sanctuary,
in her magical chambers, Florence lives on, safe at last from the
cruelties of the commercial streets. It is while in her new home, an
enchanted castle under a different and more benign spell than that
which grips her father's house, that Florence finally receives and
returns the love of the resurrected Walter. The imagery surrounding
their castle trysts and the rapturous emotion Dickens lavishes on
their romance meetings maintain the fable atmosphere: "Florence
never left her high rooms but to steal downstairs to wait for him
when it was his time to come, or, sheltered by his proud encircling
arm, to bear him company to the door again and sometimes peep
into the street."

The wedding which finally unites Florence and Walter rounds out
one major fairy-tale motif. The wedding is symbolic and magical: it
exorcises the childhood trauma of the London streets (Florence had

only dared "peep" into the streets, even though in the castle sanctuary and encircled by Walter's protective arm), and it unites Cinderella with her Prince Charming. "It is very early, Walter," says Florence on her marriage morning, "and the streets are almost empty yet. Let us walk." Walter asks if walking to church will not tire her, but Florence answers, "Oh no! I was very tired the first time that we ever walked together, but I shall not be so to-day." And so "Florence and Walter, on their bridal morning, walk through the streets together." "Not even in that childish walk of long ago," Dickens reminds the reader, "were they so far removed from all the world about them as to-day. The childish feet of long ago, did not tread such enchanted ground as theirs do now." And with this cyclical ritual, in which the symbolic and unsatisfactory walk to Dombey and Son is replaced by the equally symbolic but satisfactory walk to church, one great tension of the novel is resolved.

Dickens weaves this complex *Cinderella* imagery and action, like his other fairy-tale elements—his witches, child-quellers, enchanted abodes, spells, sacred groves, and magic circles—into functional patterns. Taken together, experienced concurrently as they actually appear, buttressed by the other fairy-tale episodes of the book, aided by hundreds of additional fairy-tale touches ranging from isolated words to recurrent symbolic motifs, and blended with the other major strands of the story—with the industrial, psychological, and autobiographical strands—these fairy-tale elements become a central foundation of *Dombey*'s method and meaning.

That fact is momentous. In *Dombey*, for the first time in a Dickens novel, fairy-tale juggling—the arbitrary interposition of supernatural agencies—becomes far less significant than subtle and pervasive fairy-tale enhancement. Dickens had learned the lessons of the Christmas books well. He had found a congenial means of organizing and enriching his writings, and he had successfully adapted that method to the novel. All his subsequent works would be fairy tales raised to "a higher form." He would fuse the magic, the suggestiveness, and the patterned order of fairy tales into the heart of his writings, endowing his mature masterpieces with the power and harmony of myth.

# A Psychoanalytic Rereading of *David Copperfield*

*by Gordon D. Hirsch*

If conventional, non-psychologically oriented "moralistic" critics of *David Copperfield* have tended to overstate the case for David's growth, learning, and personal development toward a mature, adult state in which "the undisciplined heart" will no longer hold sway, traditional psychoanalytic critics have perhaps also erred in focussing too narrowly on David's Oedipus complex—on the way in which Mr. Murdstone, the sexualized parent, cuts David off from the exclusive love of his mother and sets in motion David's book-long search for an image of the mother he can possess, a search that finds expression in both his marriage choices, Dora Spenlow and Agnes Wickfield.[1] Undeniably, both of these traditional interpretations contain portions of the truth. There *is* an Oedipal drama depicted in this novel, a drama which sends David off on a quest for an idealized image of his mother, while other characters, most notably Steerforth and Uriah Heep, have projected onto them all the aggressive and sexual impulses that are split off from David. Surely, too, it is Dickens'

"A Psychoanalytic Rereading of David Copperfield" by Gordon D. Hirsch. From *The Victorian Newsletter*, Number 58 (Fall, 1980), 1–5. Reprinted by permission of the author and publishers.

[1]Many critics have written on David's emotional and intellectual growth in *David Copperfield*, but the classic study is Gwendolyn B. Needham's "The Undisciplined Heart of *David Copperfield*," *NCF*, 9 (1954), 81–107. Among the others taking this approach are George Ford in his introduction to the Riverside edition of *David Copperfield* (Boston: Houghton Mifflin, 1958), pp. v–xv; Sylvère Monod in *Dickens the Novelist* (Norman: Univ. of Oklahoma Press, 1968), pp. 275–369; and Jerome H. Buckley in *Season of Youth: The Bildungsroman from Dickens to Golding* (Cambridge: Harvard Univ. Press, 1974), pp. 28–43.

The major psychoanalytic studies of the novel are these: Jack Lindsay, *Charles Dickens: A Biographical and Critical Study* (London: Andres Dakers, 1950), pp. 288–292; Leonard Manheim, "The Personal History of David Copperfield," *AI, 9* (1952), 21–43; Manheim, "Floras and Doras: The Women in Dickens' Novels," *TSLL*, 7 (1965), 181–200; Mark Spilka, *Dickens and Kafka* (Bloomington: Indiana Univ. Press, 1963); and E. Pearlman, "David Copperfield Dreams of Drowning," *AI*, 28 (1971), 391–403.

conscious intention to depict David learning about the value of mature love in contrast to youthful infatuation—however many doubts we readers may finally have about the attractiveness of discipline (when we contemplate the Murdstones) or about the unattractiveness of immaturity (as it is manifested in, say, the Micawbers). I would suggest, however, that both the exclusive focus on David's Oedipal neuroses and the easy optimism of the didactic, intentionalist critics on the subject of David's growth to maturity are finally inadequate to describe the complexity and psychological verisimilitude of this book. Recent psychoanalytic theories may enable one to chart a course between the Scylla of moralism and the Charybdis of Oedipal reductivism.

A major thrust in the psychoanalytic theory of the past thirty years has been the recognition of the importance of "the self" or identity— the sense in the individual of continuity, coherence, and integrity. The self as a psychic structure, analysts have found, begins to be formed in the first months of life, starting with the infant's initial attempts to differentiate his own body from otherness, to discover his separateness from the mother.[2] When the mother withdraws her breast from the suckling infant, or later when she leaves the room and the child finds himself temporarily alone, she precipitates a crisis which produces fear and anxiety in the child, while at the same time she initiates a process of development by which the child comes to recognize his separateness, a process that ends in what some analysts call "individuation." Typically, such temporary separations and losses are experienced not only as crises but also as opportunities for making a game of the experience, for mastering one's feelings of grief and rage, for discovering one's inner resources and strength. The self as a principle of psychological integrity has its origin in these early events, then, but this process of identity-formation continues beyond infancy, into childhood, and even through adult life. At times it is progressive, while at other times there may be a reversion to earlier modes of relating to the world. But a life history may be seen as a process with enough consistency that an individual's behavior at any given point can be related in some way, however complexly, to a continuum of behavior that extends back to his early experiences of self-object differentiation.[3]

---

[2] Or mothering persons of whichever sex. Issues of separation and individuation are developmentally crucial whether or not the mothering person is actually the child's mother.

[3] The psychoanalysts whose ideas are reflected in this discussion are Erik H. Erikson, George S. Klein, Heinz Kohut, and Margaret S. Mahler. Their most relevant works

In light of the emphasis placed by recent psychoanalytic theorists on the experiences of separation and loss, and on their importance to the developmental process, the number of times these two words actually appear in *David Copperfield* is quite striking. The word "loss," for instance, figures prominently in two chapter titles (Chapter 30 is "A Loss" and Chapter 31 is "A Greater Loss," referring respectively to the death of Barkis and the elopement of Little Emily with Steerforth). Steerforth's mother touches on the book's recurring motif of "separation" between parent and child when she compares her grief to Mr. Peggotty's: "What compensation can you make to *me* for opening such a pit between me and my son? What is your separation to ours?[4] David himself expresses Dickens' intuitive recognition of the importance of these psychological themes when he generalizes about the "separations that had marked my life" (830). These two words, "separation" and "loss," in fact appear prominently throughout the novel.

When one stops to consider, though, one should hardly be surprised that these words do figure conspicuously in the book, because the plot is actually based upon recurring experiences of separation and loss. The opening phase of the novel sounds this keynote by recording David's loss of his exclusive intimacy with his mother. As David leaves his old home with Peggotty to stay with her family in Yarmouth, during which absence from home his mother will marry Murdstone, this motif of separation and loss is heard clearly: "It touches me nearly now, although I tell it lightly, to recollect how eager I was to leave my happy home; to think how little I suspected what I did leave for ever" (26). David also muses here about "whether, if Peggotty were employed to lose me like the boy in the fairy tale, I should be able to track my way home again" (27)—a

---

for my argument are: Erikson, *Childhood and Society*, 2nd ed. rev. (New York: W. W. Norton, 1963); Klein, *Psychoanalytic Theory* (New York: International Universities Press, 1976); Kohut, *The Analysis of the Self* (New York: International Universities Press, 1971); Kohut, *The Restoration of the Self* (New York: International Universities Press, 1977): Mahler, *On Human Symbiosis and the Vicissitudes of Individuation* (New York: International Universities Press, 1970); and Mahler *et al., The Psychological Birth of the Human Infant: Symbiosis and Individuation* (New York: Basic Books, 1975). Mahler's studies of the process of separation and individuation particularly inform this paragraph, though I have been eclectic here as elsewhere. Freudians of the old school may take some comfort, however, from the fact that a recognition of the importance of the child's mastery of his separation anxiety is clearly already present in Freud's analysis of the *fort-da* game in *Beyond the Pleasure Principle* (1920).
[4]Charles Dickens, *David Copperfield* (Oxford: Oxford Univ. Press, 1974), p. 469. Subsequent references to this edition appear parenthetically in the text.

reference, I presume, to a tale of the Hansel and Gretel type. Indeed, while the separation of David from his mother by Murdstone clearly enacts an Oedipal drama—note the unmistakable symbolism: "My old dear bedroom was changed, and I was to lie a long way off" (43)—it can also be argued that the father in the Oedipal stage should really be seen as "the principle of separation" who merely reactivates the child's earlier sense of loss at the conclusion of the symbiotic phase of his relationship with his mother, a phase in which the infant behaves as though he and his mother were essentially fused, a single system with a common boundary. In a sense the Oedipus complex is a reenactment of these earlier crises in the process of individuation, and in *David Copperfield* many things point to the earlier, pre-Oedipal phases of human development as offering the best way for understanding the psychological issues in the novel. It is significant, for example, that an important aspect of David's response to the loss of his mother, first through her marriage to Murdstone and later as a result of her death, is to remember her "only as the young mother of my earliest impressions" (133) and to recall "the days when my mother and I and Peggotty were all in all to one another, and there was no one to come between us" (108). At the time of his mother's death, David expresses this same wish for reunion with the mother of his infancy in a rather more grisly fantasy: "The mother who lay in the grave was the mother of my infancy: the little creature in her arms [David's dead half-brother], was myself, as I had once been, hushed for ever on her bosom" (133).

And it is not just David's loss of his mother that defines the predominant psychological pattern of this novel, but a whole series of experiences involving separation, loss of love, loss of love object, and blows to David's sense of himself and to his self-esteem (which I shall refer to as "narcissistic blows"). Thus David suffers from his neglect by the Murdstones after his mother's death; from being put to work at a menial occupation; from his loss of Little Emily, first to Ham and then to Steerforth; from his loss of Steerforth as a friend and idealized self-object; from the blow to his sense of self accorded by Aunt Betsey's apparent financial setbacks, which force David to set out once again on a new course in life; from the death of his wife Dora; and from the blows to his self-esteem inflicted throughout his life by such figures from the hostile or indifferent world at large as the young man with the donkey-cart who steals his trunk, the tramps and old-clothes dealers who threaten him on the road to Dover, and finally the numerous waiters, public house operators, coach drivers, and inn keepers who always manage to eat his food, assign him to inferior quarters, or cheat and swindle him in one way or another. Nor should one forget David's dealings with such characters as his landlady, Mrs. Cupp, and Steerforth's servant, Littimer, who are always infantilizing David, even as he aspires to manhood and independence. In short, the world of this novel is one in which there is little room to be found even for a modicum of self-esteem, let alone for the acting out of an occasional fantasy of grandiosity or omnipotence.

Nor is this persistent threat of loss or narcissistic blow by any means confined to David in the novel. Mr. Wickfield loses control over his affairs as a result of Uriah Heep's frauds; Aunt Betsey apparently loses the investment from which she lives; Peggotty loses her husband, Barkis, when he "goes out with the tide"; Ham and Mr. Peggotty lose Little Emily to Steerforth; later Mr. Peggotty will lose Ham in a drowning; Steerforth deserts Little Emily after they have lived together abroad for a time; Martha Endell loses her place in the community of Yarmouth and flees to London, where she becomes suicidal; Miss Mills, Dora's friend, is "unhappy in a misplaced affection; and ready to retire from the world as a result of this blow"; and so on.

If these "losses" of love, or loved ones, or narcissistic blows generally are a recurrent cause of psychological crisis in the novel, the book also depicts problems derived from the failure of love objects sufficiently to individuate, to separate from one another, to perceive themselves to be separate entities. The classic example of this failure is the relationship between Mr. Wickfield and his daughter Agnes. Wickfield's problem, as Dickens tells us, is that he has made Agnes his "one motive in life" to the exclusion of all else; we are also told, interestingly, that the reason for this "fusion" with his daughter is his attempt to counteract his grief, the sense of loss he felt upon the death of his wife, Agnes' mother. Steerforth and his mother also represent an instance of unsuccessful individuation, and so too, probably, do Uriah and his mother, Dora and Mr. Spenlow. Though Dickens tends to show these problems arising in parent-child relations, he also seems to recognize that they can persist into adult relationships as well. Dora Spenlow's basic problem is, after all, that she has no self-esteem, no independence, no maturity. To reason with her is, from her perspective, as David discovers, to scold her. She insists on being treated in her marriage as a baby, as a "child wife."

Losses, separations, and narcissistic blows are, then, practically universal and inevitable in the world of *David Copperfield*. But to avoid them by failing to individuate, by failing to form a secure and independent identity apart from one's parent or spouse, is clearly an inadequate and even a dangerous response. The central question of this novel becomes, then, how these various blows may be surmounted and overcome, or, to adopt Shakespeare's familiar words, the *uses* of adversity. One of the best, if also one of the strangest, examples of this sort of "working through" is Mrs. Gummidge, who is the widow of a former sea-faring partner of Mr. Peggotty. Throughout the first part of the novel she lives with that gentle man, always brooding about her being "a lorn creature" and always "thinking of the old 'un," her late husband lost at sea. However when a still greater blow strikes the Peggotty household, Little Emily's affair with Steerforth, Mrs. Gummidge undergoes a radical transformation— becoming "devoted, . . . forgetful of herself, and . . . regardful of the sorrow about her" (458). For the first time, she becomes "loving and patient" (740), "the willingest, . . . the honestest-helping woman" (870).

Mrs. Gummidge's eventual ability to overcome her sense of loss and despair, her ability to turn a blow to some use—to learn from it and be changed for the better by it—seems to exemplify, if in a somewhat sentimental fashion, what Dickens shows happening to David Copperfield as well. David transcends his losses in at least four ways—as a child who defines himself by running away, as a mourner who can overcome his grief and even be strengthened by it, as a young man who can accept the "risks" of active courtship, and as a writer able to use his unhappy experiences for the material from which to weave his public, literary fictions.

When David takes his first extended decisive action in the novel— running away from the Murdstone and Grimby wine warehouse to his Aunt Betsey—he justifies himself to his aunt in this way: "I have been slighted, and taught nothing, and thrown upon myself, and put to work not fit for me. It made me run away to you" (191). The pronoun "it" here lacks a clearly stated antecedent, and the syntactical gap thus created between the two sentences invites commentary and elaboration. "It" certainly refers to "this kind of treatment by the Murdstones," to supply the implicit antecedent, but the ungrammatical "it" also suggests that what is really important here is how David feels about that treatment. In other words, the first sentence suggests, upon rereading, that David is being offered a self-image by the Murdstones which he finds simply impossible, and the second sentence expresses David's determination not to accept this definition of himself which has been supplied by his new guardians. David is using his misfortune, using his anger at this attack upon his self-image, and in the best sense he is exploiting his narcissism and indulging his grandiosity to "form [the] great resolution" of running away to "make another beginning," as two chapter headings from this part of the novel put it. By repudiating an unacceptable self-image, in short, he is in fact defining himself. Feeling rejected and lost, he runs away in order that he may discover who he is.

Second, David learns how to mourn. There are hints that he will learn the uses of grief even when his mother dies early in the novel. There is an affecting passage describing David's behavior at school when he is told of his mother's death: he reports that he feels "an orphan in the wide world," but he also recalls that the importance which this distinction gave him among his schoolfellows "was a kind of satisfaction to me" (124). This may sound a bit selfish, but it is also touching and rings oddly true; surely one of the consolations in mourning is the attention, concern, and sympathy of others. A more significant process of mourning, though, is recounted in David's response to the death of Dora. David is greatly shaken at first, but he gradually works through his grief as he follows the customary Romantic prescriptions of travel and communion with Nature in the Swiss Alps. Agnes Wickfield's letter to David abroad makes very clear the uses of such grief and affliction, which the novel dramatizes:

> [Agnes] knew (she said) how such a nature as mine would turn affliction to good. She knew how trial and emotion would exalt and strengthen it. . . . She knew that in me, sorrow could not be weakness, but must be strength. As the endurance of my childish days had done its part to make me what I was, so greater calamities would nerve me on, to be yet better than I was. (815)

Third, the love for Agnes Wickfield which David is at last able to recognize and to express upon his return to England after three years' absence should not be underestimated, whatever uneasiness a reader might feel about Agnes' identification with a pre-separation maternal image—a difficulty to which I will return later. Still, it is significant that David can at least broach his love to Agnes, even at the risk of upsetting their long-standing platonic "brother/sister" relationship. In other words, David's decision actively to court Agnes after a period of depression and loneliness should be regarded as important and must not be dismissed as merely a resort to a wishful

Oedipal fantasy. David's movement from isolation to interaction once again is presented by the novel in a context where the risks of failure are underscored.

Finally, since I have just been speaking about *Liebe*, love, I should address that other area of human behavior in which Freud thought a good measure of mental health might be taken, *Arbeit*—in this case David's discovery of his life's work as a novelist. It is worth noting that David's first reference to the world of fiction appears early in the novel when he describes his "being daily more and more shut out and alienated from his mother" (55), in compensation for which he turns to reading his father's library. As David puts it himself: "It is curious to me how I could ever have consoled myself under my small troubles (which were great troubles to me), by impersonating my favorite characters in [books]—as I did" (56). Participation in the world of fiction, in other words, begins for David as an attempt to compensate for his feelings of separation and loss. As everyone knows, David gradually discovers his vocation as a novelist, and the repeated tributes in the novel to his growing fame suggest much about the importance of this sort of reinforcement not only for David but also for Dickens. One significant passage, too, describes the way that David, during his period abroad of mourning for Dora, writes a work of fiction "with a purpose growing, not remotely, out of my experience" (816). Once again, the uses of the past, even past griefs, are terribly important: they may provide the impetus for writing and even the material out of which one constructs one's fiction.

Clearly this attitude toward past losses, separations, and narcissistic blows is relevant to Dickens' own perspective on his experience and its relation to his fiction, particularly its relation to *David Copperfield*. This is, after all, Dickens' "autobiographical novel," and it represents his only full, published account in fiction of his feelings associated with being rejected by his parents and sent to work at Warren's Blacking. Even the terrifying early parts of this novel, however, in which David is pretty much a child-victim, are distanced by the temporal shifts which characterize the narrative—particularly the sense that these events are being recalled by an adult novelist who is no longer very threatened by them. And the presentation of these once terrific experiences in the context of the narrator's tone of humor or pathos or wise detachment marks the extent of their transformation into something that is in fact usable by the older David Copperfield, who sets them down in words. In short, the style of the novel itself consistently underscores David's magical transformation of his past.

Yet Dickens also makes it clear that this is not an easy or unequivocal victory. Mr. Dick, whose name of course suggests Dickens', is another author, like David, but he is so fixated on the traumas of the past that he is unable to keep them out of his writing, where they take "the figure" of King Charles's head—a metaphor that again points to *Charles* Dickens' own obsessions. Mr. Dick, then, is unable to transform or disguise the traumas in his life successfully; he has failed to master them. Psychological crises may be worked through, as in the examples from David's life discussed above, but Dickens is painfully aware that they may alternatively result in some rather debilitating compulsions or other neuroses, as is the case with Mr. Dick. Another indication, perhaps, of just how seriously Dickens intends this less happy outcome to be taken is suggested by the presence of the "poor lunatic gentleman" who "was always sitting at [David's] little window" in his childhood home (320); Dickens seems to be suggesting that there, but for the grace of God, goes David. Indeed, many of those classic Victorian passages in *David Copperfield* which describe David's commitment to "earnestness" and hard work also glance at such things as his "many talents neglected, many opportunities wasted, many erratic and perverted feelings constantly at war within his breast, and defeating him" (606). In other words, the commitment to work is made in the face of, and in part as a response to, a nearly overwhelming sense of personal neurosis, as seems to be the case also with Thomas Carlyle, from whose anti-selfconsciousness theories of labor this part of Dickens' ideology is derived. David's novel-writing, then, is a largely successful attempt to work through, master, and indeed make use of his past experiences and traumas, but even this achievement is viewed as not so far removed from other, more compulsive, less healthy responses to similar traumata— witness Mr. Dick.

Perhaps this will explain why one must not read this novel as a simple sort of *Bildungsroman*—at least if one associates the term *Bildung* with a notion of the complete and harmonious development of the personality—because the reader is aware that what David achieves at the end is a rather fragile, tenuous, and probably reversible kind of mastery. Still, this potential reversibility of outcome is, after all, part of Dickens' mimetic excellence, part of his fidelity to life. For example, however welcome and "progressive" David's rather late active courtship of Agnes may be, it is also clear that she represents a regressive and wishful answer to his longings; there can be no question but that his dear "sister" embodies an image of the all-good "pre-separation" mother who is unfailingly devoted to David. This maternal identification has of course been frequently remarked upon by critics and comes through in many different ways, but since I have been focussing here on issues of separation and fusion, I would note particularly one description of David and Agnes walking in the fields together after their marriage, "never to be divided more" (863).[5] Agnes is merely a less absurd version of Mrs. Micawber, who will "never desert" her husband and who will constantly have one child or another nursing at "Nature's founts"; she is an image of the nurturing, faithful, supportive, pre-separation mother. She is David's "good angel" in more senses than one; in a way, David is also marrying an image of his best self. So David's marriage contains within itself elements that are both narcissistic and mature, both regressive and progressive—as is so often the case with marriages in real life as well.

Another way of measuring the limits of David's maturation is to note that he is able to turn only certain portions of his life around from passivity to activity. He does run away from Murdstone drudgery, work through his grief for Dora, actively court Agnes, and learn to write from his personal experience. But he stands rather idly by while that pair of unlikely heroes, Wilkins Micawber and Tommy Traddles, undertake the exposure of Uriah Heep. It is significant in this regard that Uriah expresses his conviction that David has organized this "conspiracy" to unmask him (747), whereas in fact David has had little or nothing to do with it. Similarly, it is oddly enough Mr. Dick, not David, who is left to reconcile Dr. Strong and his wife. And David keeps some distance away from Little Emily after her return from the continent; even when Emily suffers from Rosa Dartle's tongue-lashing, David remains passive and concealed, refusing to intervene.

The novel *David Copperfield* is, then, a *Bildungsroman* in which the protagonist's personal development is conspicuously mixed, partial, and incomplete. The book is more faithful to psychological reality and to life itself, perhaps, than to any simple thesis about personal

[5]This wish for an end to all separations at the close is a powerful image in Dickens' novels generally. Compare the last words in the revised ending of *Great Expectations:* "I saw no shadow of another parting from her."

growth and development. It shows instead the way that losses and narcissistic blows may produce different results; the crises they precipitate may on the one hand end in grief, passivity, madness, wishful fantasy, or regression; or they may on the other hand result in a kind of growth, activity, working through, and transcendence. But these different outcomes are related, linked, and always reversible. The close of the novel does not portray a David who is fully mature and free from all neurosis, fantasy, and conflict, but rather a David-author who has grown and changed in some areas of his life, while he has reached an impasse in others. In this way the novel resembles those other favorite mid-nineteenth century literary forms, the dramatic monologue and the Victorian quest poem, as much as it does the *Bildungsroman*. Like the trumpet blast of Browning's Childe Roland as he comes at last to his dark tower, the note that David sounds as he emerges at the end of his journey through what he calls the forest of difficulty seems less an announcement of his completion and fulfillment than a self-progressive statement. Its message is: "I am the sum of my experiences. You have read about them and now know how to understand who I am." Such a conclusion implies that David's psychological development, like that of the author of this book in 1850, is yet in process and unfolding.

# Esther Summerson Rehabilitated

*by Alex Zwerdling*

## I

The critics have not been kind to Esther Summerson. From the first, her prominence in *Bleak House* has been treated as one of Dickens' disastrous mistakes. George Henry Lewes was not the last critic to consider her a "monstrous failure."[1] The portrait of Esther is said to be unrealistic and unconvincing, since a girl with so little experience of the world could hardly be expected to understand the complex institutions and devious characters she is asked to describe. It is regularly assumed that Dickens tires of the "mask" of Esther and uses her as a mouthpiece at will, a practice that would certainly create a hopelessly inconsistent character. Esther is also frequently accused of coyness, particularly in her insistence on disclaiming the compliments heaped upon her while faithfully recording them. In the sarcastic words of the original review in the *Spectator*: "It is impossible to doubt the simplicity of her nature, because she never omits to assert it with emphasis."[2]

These attitudes seem to me based on a serious misunderstanding of Esther Summerson and of Dickens' purpose in making her so prominent in *Bleak House*. She is, I think, one of the triumphs of his art, a subtle psychological portrait clear in its outlines and convincing in its details. But in order to understand what Dickens was doing, we must rid ourselves of certain critical clichés: that he was not interested in point of view, that his characters are static and shallow, and that his psychological penetration was not remarkable. In calling

"Esther Summerson Rehabilitated" by Alex Zwerdling. From *PMLA*, 88 (1973), 429–39. Copyright © by the Modern Language Association of America. Reprinted by permission of the author and publishers.

[1]"Dickens in Relation to Criticism," rpt. in *The Dickens Critics*, ed. George H. Ford and Lauriat Lane (Ithaca, N.Y.: Cornell Univ. Press 1961), p. 65.

[2]Rpt. in *Dickens*: Bleak House: *A Casebook*, ed. A.E. Dyson (London: Macmillan, 1969), p. 57.

these attitudes critical clichés, I am not ignoring a number of studies which have treated Dickens' interest in psychology more positively, but suggesting that this new perspective has still not become dominant.[3]

An accurate assessment of Dickens' portrait of Esther must, I think, begin with his interest in first-person narratives. In *David Copperfield*, *Bleak House*, and *Great Expectations* he used this technical device to record in depth a long process of psychological development. Dickens' (and the reader's) attitude toward these narrators is seldom straightforward. Our perspective must be detached and critical, since we are intended to see more than the narrator sees. In all three novels, Dickens further makes use of a double perspective even in the narrator by shifting back and forth from his childish to his adult vision. This temporal double perspective is much more consistently used in *David Copperfield* and *Great Expectations* than in *Bleak House*, however, because in that novel Dickens is interested in portraying someone who remains trapped between childhood and real maturity. Such a narrator is not a transparent medium for the author's impressions. We are asked to look very much *at* Esther rather than *through* her, to observe her actions, her fantasies, even her verbal mannerisms with great attention. For Dickens' attitude toward her is essentially clinical, and the major aim of her portion of the narrative is to study in detail the short- and long-range effect of a certain kind of adult violence on the mind of a child.

"The crime against the child," as Dorothy Van Ghent has suggested, is one of Dickens' major themes.[4] Between *Oliver Twist* and *Bleak House*, his vision of childhood suffering became much more psychological. Oliver's deprivation is primarily physical, external. By the time Dickens came to write *Dombey and Son*, he had become more interested in the child deprived of love than of food and shelter, and this shift is clearly reflected both in *David Copperfield* and in *Bleak House*. Esther's first memories of her aunt (the "godmother" who brought her up) obliquely record both the withholding of love and the overwhelming sense of failure it imprints on the child:

[3]Useful studies of Esther Summerson along psychological lines include James H. Broderick and John E. Grant, "The Identity of Esther Summerson," *MP*, 55 (1958), 252–58; William Axton, "The Trouble with Esther," *MLQ*, 26 (1965), 545–57, and his "Esther's Nicknames: A Study of Relevance," *The Dickensian*, 62 (1966), 158–63; and F. R. and Q. D. Leavis, *Dickens the Novelist* (London: Chatto & Windus, 1970), pp. 155–60.

[4]"The Dickens World: A View from Todgers's," *Sewanee Review*, 58 (1950), 431.

I was brought up, from my earliest remembrance—like some of the princesses in the fairy stories, only I was not charming—by my godmother. . . . She was handsome; and if she had ever smiled, would have been (I used to think) like an angel—but she never smiled. . . . I felt so different from her, even making every allowance for the differences between a child and a woman; I felt so poor, so trifling, and so far off; that I never could be unrestrained with her—no, could never even love her as I wished. It made me very sorry to consider how good she was, and how unworthy of her I was; and I used ardently to hope that I might have a better heart; and I talked it over very often with the dear old doll; but I never loved my godmother as I ought to have loved her, and as I felt I must have loved her if I had been a better girl.[5]

There is very little independent judgment in this passage, hardly any sense of a code that would justify the child and condemn the godmother, although of course Dickens relies on the reader to supply such a perspective on Esther's words. Rather, Esther seems to have accepted the values by which she is found "poor" and "trifling." All the guilt and shame are taken upon herself. Such self-denigration becomes Esther's essential life-style. Deprived of the sense of her own merit from earliest infancy, she is never sure that she is worthy of love and respect. The innumerable compliments of her wisdom, shrewdness, affectionate nature, and beauty she compulsively records and compulsively dismisses as absurd. She has an insatiable hunger for them, yet they are never the right food, for the damage to her sense of self-esteem has been permanent. This complex behavior is what critics of the novel have usually called her "coyness."

It is appropriate, rather, to use the word trauma, to see Esther's childhood as a wound that never fully heals. The traumatic experience in the narrow sense of the term is the scene in which her illegitimacy is revealed, when on her birthday she asks her godmother about her parentage. The stern reply etches itself on her mind in precise detail and is never forgotten:

Your mother, Esther, is your disgrace, and you were hers. The time will come—and soon enough—when you will understand this better, and will feel it too, as no one save a woman can. . . . Submission, self-denial, diligent work, are the preparations for a life begun with such a shadow on it. You are different from other children, Esther, because

---

[5]Charles Dickens, *Bleak House* (London: Oxford Univ. Press, 1966), pp. 15–16, Ch. iii (*The Oxford Illustrated Dickens*). Subsequent citations are to this edition.

you were not born, like them, in common sinfulness and wrath. You are set apart. (pp.17–18, Ch. iii)

I hope to show that Esther's reaction to this speech can be understood along the lines of Erik Erikson's description of trauma: "an experience characterized by impressions so sudden, or so powerful, or strange that they cannot be assimilated at the time and, therefore, persist from stage to stage as a foreign body seeking outlet or absorption and imposing on all development a certain irritation causing stereotypy and repetitiveness."[6] Years later, on two subsequent occasions, Esther accurately recalls portions of this speech (Chs. xvii, xxxvi). Her godmother's words (and the coldness of her heart behind them) become the most powerful determinant of her adult personality and life choices. This has often been recognized; what has not so generally been understood is that Dickens creates, in Esther's narrative, a detailed life pattern that records both the long-range effects of this childhood trauma and the stages of an attempt to triumph over it.

Esther is wounded by her godmother's speech but she is not crushed. She has a supremely practical turn of mind, and her first impulse is to formulate a strategy for survival. "Submission, self-denial, diligent work" is what her godmother proposes. Esther's own plan is a subtle but significant variant: "I would try, as hard as ever I could, to repair the fault I had been born with (of which I confessedly felt guilty and yet innocent), and would strive as I grew up to be industrious, contented, and kind-hearted, and to do some good to some one, and win some love to myself if I could" (p. 18, Ch. iii). An instinct for self-preservation is at work in this formula. Although she has been told to feel only guilt, she also feels a paradoxical innocence. And the grim words "submission, self-denial, diligent work" are transformed into more social and less self-destructive terms: contentment, kindheartedness, industry. Above all, Esther sees even these devices as means to an end: to "win some love to myself if I could." It is as if the child instinctively understands this basic psychological necessity and determines to direct all its energies toward obtaining it.

Esther envisages love as a reward for strenuous effort, however, not as something that may come naturally; and she does not specify what *kind* of love she is talking about. It would, of course, be absurd

[6]*Gandhi's Truth: On the Origins of Militant Nonviolence* (New York: Norton, 1969), p. 98.

to expect a child to distinguish among the various kinds of love, parental, romantic, conjugal, filial, and so on. But in fact the ambiguity of the phrase illuminates Esther's most important adult conflicts. As we gradually begin to understand, she has great doubts about her right to love and marry, and she accepts with misgiving the role of an affectionate spectator of other people's attachments. There is a buried but potent feeling that the "sin" of being illegitimate makes her unfit for romantic love.

Others conspire to make Esther see herself in this light. It is curious, for example, that she is never for a moment considered a possible match for Richard, that she is instantly cast in the role of duenna in his romance with Ada. Richards meets the two girls at the same time. They are approximately the same age, both attractive, and both attracted to him. Yet from the first Jarndyce takes Esther into his confidence concerning his hopes for the union of the other two. Esther's reaction to this arrangement is complex, though she does her best to make it simple: "My fancy, made a little wild by the wind perhaps, would not consent to be all unselfish, either, though I would have persuaded it to be so if I could. It wandered back to my godmother's house, and came along the intervening track, raising up shadowy speculations which had sometimes trembled there in the dark, as to what knowledge Mr. Jarndyce had of my earliest history . . ." (p. 80, Ch. vi). Such ungrateful and dangerous speculations must be suppressed; indeed, they can hardly be recorded without guilt, even in the deliberately obscure and general terms Esther uses. She instantly calls her errant "fancy" back to duty: "It was not for me to muse over bygones, but to act with a cheerful spirit and a grateful heart. So I said to myself, 'Esther, Esther, Esther!, Duty, my dear!' " (p. 80, Ch. vi).

In this impatient command, Esther temporarily resigns her own hopes of romance and begins to live vicariously in the love of Richard and Ada. She cannot treat the idea of having a lover as a serious possibility or as her right. She begins to think of herself as (and allows people to treat her as) "a methodical, old-maidish sort of foolish little person" (p. 92, Ch. viii). She offers no objection to being called a whole string of pet names—"Old Woman, and Little Old Woman, and Cobweb, and Mrs. Shipton, and Mother Hubbard,and Dame Durden, and so many names of that sort, that my own name soon became quite lost among them" (p. 98,Ch. viii). These names have a double function: they substitute the image of an old, maternal, drudging woman for the image of a young girl; and they suggest that the only fit mate for such a person is an aging, paternal man like Mr. Jarndyce.

Her buried romantic impulse is almost entirely invested in her vicarious participation in the Ada-Richard courtship. She is the Nurse in the lovers' acting out of *Romeo and Juliet*, and her fantasies are obviously filled with displaced romance: "They brought a chair on either side of me, and put me between them, and really seemed to have fallen in love with me, instead of one another" (p. 178, Ch. xiii). When the marriage finally takes place, there is very little romance left. Richard is nearly penniless and driven half-wild by the Chancery suit; Ada marries him in secret against her guardian's wishes. When Esther realizes that their marriage will exclude her, as all marriages must, she is driven wild with grief: "I walked up and down in a dim corner, sobbing and crying" (p. 698, Ch. li). On the same evening, she steals back to their house and stands by their door, listening for "the murmur of their young voices" (p. 699, Ch. li). After the court-ship the duenna must turn voyeur.

The strangest aspect of Esther's relationship to the lovers is her attitude toward Ada. Her intense attachment is irrational and mys-terious and no commonsense explanation of it will serve. In part, Esther's adoration of Ada is a displaced form of romantic love, inhibited from expressing itself normally by her fear that she is forbidden to marry. But she has also from the first treated Ada as an idealized second self, as the girl she might have become if she had not been born "different from other children" and "set apart." Her fantasy-identification with Ada makes it possible for Esther to bear a great deal of humiliation and deprivation. It is as though she lived in the belief that no evil could affect her alter ego, no matter what happened to herself. When she realizes she is ill, she commands her maid to bar the door to Ada: "Charley, if you let her in but once, only to look upon me for one moment as I lie here, I shall die" (p. 442, Ch. xxxi). Not "she will die," but "I shall die." Her need to protect Ada is an oblique form of self-preservation. When, after her dis-figurement, she calls Ada "my beauty," as she frequently does, the phrase is charged with meaning.

We are dealing here with one set of consequences arising from Esther's childhood wound, her surrender of the normal expectation of love and marriage and the attempt to feed her need for romance vicariously. These are not the only long-range consequences of her unsponsored childhood: there is also the inhibition of her natural intelligence. She has been made to feel inferior to others in every way. What then is she to make of the fact that her natural intelligence and her power of observation are unusually acute? She consistently tries to deny her abilities, as in her first words to the reader: "I have a great deal of difficulty in beginning to write my portion of these pages, for I know I am not clever. I always knew that. . . . I had always rather a noticing way—not a quick way, O no!—a silent way of noticing what passed before me, and thinking I should like to understand it better. I have not by any means a quick understanding. When I love a person very tenderly indeed, it seems to brighten. But even that may be my vanity" (p. 15, Ch. iii). The reflex quality of the disclaimers in this passage ("not a quick way, O no!" "But even that may be my vanity") suggests how efficiently she has been bullied into denying any sense of her own worth. Vanity and pride are her great fears; she has never been taught a comparable fear of underestimating herself.

Esther does indeed have "rather a noticing way," a sharp analytic intelligence and a keen sense of the disparity between peoples' words and their actions. Yet her observant satirical eye is regularly reproved by her conformist conscience. Here she is, for example, on Mrs. Badger:

> She was surrounded in the drawing-room by various objects, indicative of her painting a little, playing the piano a little, playing the guitar a little, playing the harp a little, singing a little, working a little, reading a little, writing poetry a little, and botanising a little. . . . If I add, to the little list of her accomplishments, that she rouged a little, I do not mean that there was any harm in it. (p. 173, Ch. xiii)

If Dickens were describing Mrs. Badger in his own voice, only the last phrase would be out of place. It would have to be made obviously (rather than ambiguously) ironic or else eliminated altogether. But for Esther to draw in her claws and play the kitten in this way is essential to her image of herself. Her critical sense is often disguised as mere reportorial accuracy. When its satiric content becomes too dangerous, it is suddenly replaced by a fraudulent generosity of spirit. It is no wonder that critics are confused about Esther's intelligence and tempted by the theory that she becomes, at moments, merely Dickens' mouthpiece. But the difference between Dickens and Esther as narrators lies not in their perspectiveness but in their self-confidence *about* their perceptiveness. The savage sarcasm of the other narrator of *Bleak House* is simply a psychological impossibility for Esther.

It should be clear from these illustrations that Dickens' interest in Esther is fundamentally clinical: to observe and describe a certain kind of psychic debility. The psychological subject matter of Dickens' later novels demanded a new narrative technique, in which the character could present himself directly, rather than being described and interpreted by an omniscient narrator. Esther Summerson is Dickens' most ambitious attempt to allow a character who does not fully understand herself to tell her own story. There are obvious dangers in such a technique. The reader may not be able to see beyond the narrator's vision, although he needs to do so if he is to comprehend the book. Furthermore, a neurotic character will be obsessive, and the narrative will inevitably keep recording his obsessions, often at the price of variety. Certainly *Bleak House* does not escape these dangers. Yet the portrait would be less subtle, detailed, and vivid if it were not done in the first person. Esther's story must be told from the inside; and if we are to feel that the damage to her psyche has in some sense been permanent, it cannot be told by a fully mature woman looking back on the troubles of her youth.

There are important thematic, situational, and psychological parallels between Esther's case and those of other people in the novel. In allowing her to tell her own story, Dickens gives selflessness a voice and tries to provide words for some of society's usually inarticulate victims. She is the unconscious representative of the many characters in *Bleak House* who have not known parental love—Jo, the Jellybys, the Pardiggles, Guster, Prince Turveydrop, Richard, Ada. The breakdown of the parent-child relationship is one of the major themes of the novel. Parents behave like children; children must take over parental roles. The Lord High Chancellor "appeared so poor a substitute for the love and pride of parents" (p. 31, Ch. iii). And the universe, as Mr. Jarndyce points out sadly, "makes rather an indifferent parent" (p. 72, Ch. vi). Yet all the other victims of this parentless world are seen from the outside. We are conscious of their numbers and of their superficial trials, but we know little of the internal cost of this absence of nurture. The function of Esther's narrative, then, is to show us the deeper and more lasting effects of such neglect.

Esther is also the representative of another inarticulate character in *Bleak House*—Lady Dedlock, whose *inner* history Dickens could not write for a Victorian audience. The two women seem totally different yet are in a similar position. Each is alienated from her true self and unable to acknowledge her deepest feelings. Each is incomplete:

Lady Dedlock searches for a child; Esther for a mother. Lady Dedlock has given up her lover and married an affectionate and protecting man a generation older than herself, whom she respects but does not love—the very doom that Esther narrowly escapes. The mother's haughtiness and isolation are as much aspects of a frustrating role as the daughter's cheerfulness and immersion in the community. The two women specialize in opposing parts of themselves rather than allowing their complex natures full play.

The final reason that Esther must tell her own story is connected with Dickens' attitude toward the qualities she embodies. Whether that attitude is at all ironic has always been one of the major problems in interpreting the book. First-person narratives frequently produce such disagreements, and for understandable reasons, since it is impossible for the author to comment directly on the character he has created. Yet this deliberate surrender of the power of judgment can be useful to a writer whose response to a particular way of life is fundamentally divided. Its poetic equivalent—the dramatic monologue—has frequently been used in the same way. Both make it possible for a writer whose feelings about a character are simultaneously sympathetic and hostile to write about him without self-contradiction. Esther Summerson's narrative may finally be a way for Dickens to study the psychological roots of selflessness, a trait about which his feelings were profoundly ambiguous, without committing himself to either praise or blame.

## II

I have suggested that Esther is not a static character, and that Dickens is interested in tracing various patterns of behavior in her from infancy to adulthood. In becoming the ward of Mr. Jarndyce, Esther is given a chance to relive her childhood with a radically different parental figure, generous, loving, and open. Consequently, she acquires two entirely different images of herself, the rejected and the sponsored child, and these two identities engage in a long civil war for control of her psyche. It is the task of her early adult years to absorb the new image and permit it to affect every aspect of her life, her sense of her own abilities and rights, her assessment of other people, and her life plans. Dickens has a remarkable feeling for the difficulty of this task and understands how potent the curse of childhood deprivation can be, no matter what may happen in later life.

The first signs of a new self-appraisal are seen in Esther's judgment of other people, which becomes steadily more self-confident, independent, and unapologetic. She begins by taking characters such as Mrs. Jellyby or Harold Skimpole at face value and inhibiting her critical uneasiness about them. Her guardian tells her that Skimpole is childish goodness incarnate, and her initial reaction confirms this vision: "He was so full of feeling, too, and had such a delicate sentiment for what was beautiful or tender . . ." (p. 71, Ch. vi). Yet her own acute observation eventually leads her to a very different and more accurate assessment and even allows her to understand why her guardian is taken in by Skimpole's "innocence." She is soon convinced that Skimpole's "display of guileless candour" was not as "artless as it seemed" (p. 522, Ch. xxxvii). The same self-confidence and clear-sightedness are evident in her ability to judge other deceptive or deluded characters in the book accurately—Mrs. Jellyby, Mr. Turveydrop, Richard.

The blossoming of Esther's working intelligence is a continuous and uninterrupted process in the book. The same can hardly be said for her realization that she has a right to love and marry a man to whom she is attracted. Her romantic nature is much more completely crushed than her intelligence, in this case with the complicity of her guardian and her closest friends. It is surprising that her need for a lover has survived at all, in no matter how buried a form; but that it is very much alive despite all discouragement is evident for the first time when Mr. Guppy proposes. Esther's reaction to the offer of marriage from this absurd and vulgar man is totally unexpected yet, I think, completely convincing. She is anything but grateful, and her decisive rejection of him introduces a tone which we have never heard before in her words, and will seldom hear again: "Get up from that ridiculous position immediately, sir, or you will oblige me to break my implied promise and ring the bell!" (p. 124, Ch. ix).

The haughty dismissiveness and sheer command of these words sound more like Lady Dedlock than Esther Summerson. Esther here finds herself face-to-face with the kind of man who might be willing to take a piece of damaged goods, and her spirit rebels violently against the insult to her own pride. Her response suggests an extremely healthy sense of her own innocence and worth, a facet of her nature that is so regularly repressed that it can only declare its

existence in such unexpected explosions. Esther's later reaction to
the scene illustrates better than anything else in the novel how clearly
Dickens connects adult with childhood experience:

> But, when I went up-stairs to my own room, I surprised myself by
> beginning to laugh about it, and then surprised myself still more by
> beginning to cry about it. In short, I was in a flutter for a little while;
> and felt as if an old chord had been more coarsely touched than it ever
> had been since the days of the dear old doll, long buried in the
> garden. (p. 126, Ch. ix)

The doll had been the sole companion of her childhood, the
faithful listener to whom she could tell her troubles without fear of
rejection or reproach. When her godmother dies, she buries the doll
in the garden as if in penance. The ceremony reveals her guilt about
any form of self-indulgence, even such a sorry substitute for maternal
acceptance. Its return in her fantasy at this moment shows how
Dickens uses childhood associations to explain adult behavior. For
the doll is a symbol of her "selfishness," her need for someone who
loves her absolutely. Faced with the prospect of the parody-lover Mr.
Guppy, the doll springs inevitably into her fantasy. It will not stay
buried, just as her adult truce with the past cannot altogether pre-
vent the occasional "coarse" reassertion of the primary feelings of
childhood.

Yet the pride and self-assertion evident in the scene with Guppy
desert her completely when she encounters a man to whom she is
fully attracted, Allan Woodcourt. It is at first impossible for her even
to acknowledge her interest. Her references to Woodcourt are
incredibly tortured and coy; yet she is being neither "insincere" nor
girlishly silly. She is so terrified of losing him that she can hardly bear
to mention his existence. Her first reference to Woodcourt is absurdly stilted and confused, especially for such a lucid and methodical narrator:

> I have omitted to mention in its place, that there was some one else at
> the family dinner party. It was not a lady. It was a gentleman. It was a
> gentleman of a dark complexion—a young surgeon. He was rather
> reserved, but I thought him very sensible and agreeable. At least, Ada
> asked me if I did not, and I said yes. (p. 181, Ch. xiii)

This might be the "before" exhibit in a grammar book exercise on
how to construct complex sentences. Esther regularly becomes a
grammatical cripple whenever she mentions Woodcourt: "I believe—

at least I know—that he was not rich." "I think—I mean he told us—that he had been in practice three or four years. . . ." "And so we gave him our hands, one after another—at least, they did—and I did" (pp. 238, 239, Ch. xvii).

Her grammatical disarray is an expression of her anxiety. Deeply convinced that her illegitimacy makes her unfit to marry a man of worth, yet desperately hoping that the conviction is false, she turns Woodcourt into a test case. To acknowledge her feeling for him is to invite disappointment; hence the evasiveness and insincerity of practically everything she says about him until he actually proposes. Since Woodcourt loves Esther, and since there are no real obstacles to their marriage, one might have expected their romance to proceed uninterrupted and Esther's self-confidence to grow as steadily as did her trust in her own intelligence. But the plot presents two crucial yet seemingly arbitrary setbacks: her illness and consequent disfigurement, and her guardian's proposal of marriage.

The effect of both these events is regressive. The loss of her beauty convinces her that any thought of marriage is now out of the question. The ambiguous phrase in her childhood vow, to "win some love to myself if I could," must now be interpreted to mean only the communal affection of those around her, not the romantic love for which she longs. After seeing her new face in the mirror, she tries desperately to convince herself to be satisfied with what she has. This attempt clearly takes her back to an earlier stage, to her childhood vow:

> The childish prayer of that old birthday, when I had aspired to be industrious, contented, and true-hearted, and to do good to some one, and win some love to myself if I could, came back into my mind with a reproachful sense of all the happiness I had since enjoyed, and all the affectionate hearts that had been turned towards me. . . . I repeated the old childish prayer in its old childish words, and found that its old peace had not departed from it.[7] (p. 495, Ch. xxxv)

But to rededicate oneself to an ideal formulated in childhood, particularly if it has already become a reality, is to make further progress impossible. Esther is in fact ready to go beyond the vow at the moment of her illness; but her disfigurement makes it impossible for her to proceed. She seems trapped in the present and resigned to surrendering the future.

[7]It is significant that in the earlier scene she had vowed to be "kind-hearted," not "true-hearted," although she does not seem to be aware of the shift.

The treatment of Esther's illness is difficult to explain on the literal level: she loses and then regains her sight without explanation; her disfigured face is magically restored to its former beauty; Dickens even conspicuously avoids giving the illness a name. Yet as a symbol of Esther's psychological state at a particular moment in her development, it makes a good deal of sense. It comes when the circumstances of her birth—the fact that she is Lady Dedlock's child—are exposed. At about this point in the novel, her mother recognizes and reveals herself to the child she had long thought dead, and Mr. Tulkinghorn acquires the crucial piece of evidence that will make the facts public. The symbolic connection of these events with Esther's disfigurement seems clear. Her illegitimate birth is no longer a secret. She is made ugly in the eyes of the world. Her scarred face is the outward and visible sign of an inward and spiritual sin. Her two sharpest anxieties, about her birth and her disfigurement, come together in Chapter xxxvi, in which Lady Dedlock reveals herself and Ada sees her for the first time since her illness. Esther's violent reaction to her mother's revelation, which brings her to the nadir of her own self-confidence, feeds directly into her fear that Ada will not recognize her new face.

Her despair is suicidal. She is "possessed by a belief that it was right, and had been intended, that I should die in my birth; and that it was wrong, and not intended, that I should be then alive." And she reflects on "the new and terrible meaning of the old words, now moaning in my ears like a surge upon the shore, 'Your mother, Esther, was your disgrace, and you are hers. The time will come—and soon enough—when you will understand this better, and will feel it too, as no one save a woman can' " (p. 514, Ch. xxxvi). It is as though the childhood curse had until this moment slept in her ear, for Esther has consistently evaded a fuller knowledge of the circumstances of her birth. But at this point in her life, when she stands at the threshold of maturity, the bare facts must be brought into the open and faced.

She recovers from the terrible despair into which her mother's revelation has thrown her, however, and the passage in which she declares her own innocence has often been quoted to suggest that her sense of confidence is fully restored. This seems to me a misinterpretation, though not an obvious one. Esther says: "I knew I was as innocent of my birth as a queen of hers; and that before my Heavenly Father I should not be punished for birth, nor a queen rewarded for it" (p. 516, Ch. xxxvi). Although this has the ring of confidence, it should be noticed that Esther is planning to be vindicated in death, not in life. God will recognize her innocence and heaven will bring the rewards she has been denied on earth. But this reliance on a heavenly reward barely masks her despair about the possibility of earthly fulfillment. She has indeed already resigned herself to giving up Woodcourt *until* heaven where, she says, "I might aspire to meet him, *unselfishly, innocently, better far than he had thought me when I found some favour in his eyes, at the journey's end*" (p. 502, Ch. xxxv; italics added).

In such passages Esther tries to construct a possible life out of the elements of duty, selflessness, and the hope of a heavenly reward. She struggles to convince herself that they will do; but they will not. There is a strong intuitive awareness that these elements can only be oppressive if they are not combined with self-realization. These buried misgivings are brilliantly suggested during Esther's illness, as her fantasy takes over from her conscious mind. In her feverish reverie, she identifies her present household tasks with all the former duties of her life. The stream of reminiscence inevitably leads back to her godmother's house and oppresses her with the sense that every stage of her life, including the supposedly happy present, has merely presented her with a new set of "cares and difficulties." At this point she begins to hallucinate:

> I am almost afraid to hint at that time in my disorder—it seemed one long night, but I believe there were both nights and days in it—when I laboured up colossal staircases, ever striving to reach the top, and ever turned, as I have seen a worm in a garden path, by some obstruction, and labouring again. . . . I would find myself complaining 'O more of these never-ending stairs, Charley,—more and more—piled up to the sky, I think!' and labouring on again.
>
> Dare I hint at that worse time when, strung together somewhere in great black space, there was a flaming necklace, or ring, or starry circle of some kind, of which *I* was one of the beads! And when my only prayer was to be taken off from the rest, and when it was such inexplicable agony and misery to be a part of the dreadful thing? (pp. 488–89, Ch. xxxv)

In these dreams, Esther can no longer force herself to be content. The frustration of a life made up solely of duties is sharply expressed. Her obligations "mount up" like the endless staircases of her dream; there is no surmounting them in this life. The image of the starry circle probably expresses her intense though unacknowledged need to break out of the chain of commitments to the community, "to be taken off from the rest" and be a separate self. The whole passage is a powerful example of Dickens' use of fantasy, association, and dream to reveal elements in the psychological makeup of his characters that are systematically repressed in action and in speech.

Esther's illness (and the shame of her illegitimacy which is so closely related to it) has made her greatly more dependent on Mr. Jarndyce. As her obligations to her guardian increase, her sense of gratitude begins to mix with a kind of bleak helplessness. His protection envelops her; thanking him becomes a full-time duty, even a burden. Just before she reads Mr. Jarndyce's proposal of marriage, Esther exclaims, "I thanked him with my whole heart. What could I ever do but thank him!" (p. 608, Ch. xliv). The question seems rhetorical but its answer is critical for her development. To spend her life in thanking Jarndyce is to surrender to the obstacle in her path.

Her guardian's proposal, coming at this point, is like Esther's illness, no arbitrary twist of the plot but a symbol of a particular moment in her development. The marriage would freeze her at the stage of filial dependence; she would be forever safe and adored. It is precisely because her relationship to Jarndyce has been a substitute for so much—a mother's love, a father's guidance, the sense of being accepted despite her birth—that it threatens to become her final human tie. But such sponsorship is a stage, hopefully leading to the child's sense of his own independent power and right of choice. If it lasts forever there has been a crucial failure in the educational process.

This, it seems to me, is the meaning of the proposal. The setback of her illness and the full revelation of her illegitimacy make Esther retreat to the safe world in which she knows she is loved. Yet when she realizes that the door may shut upon her there forever, she is profoundly disturbed. Her first reaction to Jarndyce's offer of marriage is far from joyous. She thinks of the proposal

> as the close of the benignant history I had been pursuing, and I felt that I had but one thing to do. To devote my life to his happiness was to thank him poorly, and what had I wished for the other night but some new means of thanking him?
>
> Still I cried very much . . . as if something for which there was no name or distinct idea were indefinitely lost to me. I was very happy, very thankful, very hopeful; but I cried very much. (p. 611, Ch. xliv)

Esther sees her marriage to Jarndyce as an end, not a beginning, and she is convinced that she has no choice. ("I felt I had but one thing to do.") Although she does not understand exactly what she is giving up in accepting him, it becomes clear enough a few paragraphs later. Even after her illness she had kept some flowers that Woodcourt had given her, although she doubted then whether she had a right to keep them. Now they must be destroyed. She puts them for a moment to the lips of the sleeping Ada, recalls Ada's love for Richard, and then burns them. The ceremony is the first act of a novitiate.

Esther's deeply unsettled feelings about her engagement are also evident in her unwillingness to make it public. She delays as long as possible in telling anyone about it and then regularly insists on using the euphemism that she will become the mistress of Bleak House. The feeling that she is marrying the house rather than its owner is entirely appropriate. At the same time, Ether's busy cheerfulness begins to show signs of hysteria: "I resolved to be doubly diligent and gay. So I went about the house, humming all the tunes I knew; and I sat working and working in a desperate manner, and I talked and talked, morning, noon, and night" (p. 686, Ch. 1). Violent industry is Esther's characteristic response to misery she cannot acknowledge.

Yet even immersion in work will not allow her to ignore her fundamental need to be loved passionately rather than paternally. Her romantic longing has fastened on Woodcourt, and at this moment in her history he must therefore reappear. It is worth noting how many apparently arbitrary plot elements in Dickens are determined by his need for symbolic manifestations of internal states. When Esther sees Woodcourt again, she at first instinctively avoids his glance because she is "unwilling that he should see my altered looks." She has a strong impulse simply to run away, but she forces herself not to do so: "No, my dear, no. No, no, no!"(p. 623, Ch. xlv). Her resistance is the first indication since her illness that her willpower can be used to confront her self-doubt rather than suppress it. Only very gradually does Woodcourt's love convince her that she is not hopelessly tainted, "disfigured," after all. When she is ready to entertain this radical idea, she is finally ready for his offer of marriage.

The proposal intensifies rather than resolves Esther's problems, however, because it confronts her with a need to choose when she is not yet psychologically ready to do so. She is still bound to her guardian. Her first response to the knowledge that she can be loved passionately, that there are in fact no obstacles to normal life for her, is not joy but violent regret: "O, too late to know it now, too late, too late. That was the first ungrateful thought I had. Too late" (p. 833, Ch. lxi). Her natural impulse is rebellious. She feels that her engagement, her dependence on Jarndyce, fetters her, but the bond is too powerful for her to break.

She is terrified not of hurting Jarndyce but of pleasing herself. Nothing in her childhood or young adulthood has prepared her to think she has a right to do so. After her first uncontrollably bitter reaction, Esther can only allow herself to use Woodcourt's proposal as a way of fulfilling her childhood vow: "He had called me the beloved of his life, and had said I would be evermore as dear to him as I was then; and *I felt as if my heart would not hold the triumph of having heard those words*. My first wild thought had died away. It was not too late to hear them, for *it was not too late to be animated by them to be good, true, grateful, and contented*" (p. 835, Ch. lxi; italics added). Her "selfish" impulse is immediately translated into duty, and she can only think of ways to make herself worthy of Woodcourt's faith. It is impossible for her to assume that she already *is* worthy; all her plans are for self-improvement.

The effect of such contradictory impulses can only be paralysis. The need to depend on her guardian and the need to break away from him seem equally strong. Yet a few pages later, the conflict has been mysteriously resolved and Esther is married to Woodcourt. This conclusion to Esther's history seems to me sheer fantasy. Everything in her narrative has stressed the potent nature of her conflicts and the feebleness of her own will in dealing with them. Indeed, she must not even allow herself to acknowledge them. Such a situation demands a tragic ending—or a deus ex machina. Dickens chooses the latter. Esther's decision is made for her by Jarndyce, who surrenders her to Woodcourt even without consulting her. The whole scene is dominated by magical and fantastic elements whose function is to dissolve the contradictions inherent in the situation. Where conflict was, there harmony shall be.

All the plans for Esther's future life deny the presence of conflict or the necessity of exclusive choice. The house where she and Woodcourt will live was purchased and furnished by her guardian. It too is to be called Bleak House, so that Esther will be its mistress after all. It is decorated inside and out like her old home and will even have a replica of the Growlery, where her guardian plans to spend much of his time. Esther had hoped to be vindicated by God, and it is notable

that Jarndyce becomes indistinguishable from a benevolent Providence in the book's concluding section. He denies the part of himself
which had once wanted her as a wife: "I am your guardian and your
father now" (p. 857, Ch. lxiv). Esther sees him in a new way: "As I sat
looking fixedly at him, and the sun's rays descended, softly shining
through the leaves, upon his bare head, I felt as if the brightness on
him must be like the brightness of the Angels" (p. 857, Ch. lxiv).
Such religious references relate to the Ada-Richard plot, which
comes to a tragic conclusion simultaneously, and in which it is made
clear that *only* eternity can resolve the conflicts of earthly life: "A
smile irradiated his face, as she bent to kiss him. He slowly laid his
face down upon her bosom, drew his arms closer round her neck,
and with one parting sob began the world. Not this world, O not this!
The world that sets this right" (pp. 870–71, Ch. lxv).

The treatment of Esther's internal conflicts has been so detailed,
painstaking, and psychologically plausible that the sudden miraculous resolution, in which fantasy elements are presented within a
realistic framework, seems totally unconvincing. Yet several critics
have treated the change in Esther as a triumphant self-assertion. J.
Hillis Miller, for example, writes of "her liberation into an authentic
life when she chooses to accept the self she finds herself to be."[8] I can
see no such existential choice. Esther cannot properly be said to
choose at all, and much of her old self manages to survive her change
of situation. This is illustrated obliquely and symbolically in Ada's
return to Jarndyce after Richard's death. Esther has treated Ada as a
second self throughout the novel, but they are really alternative
aspects of a single nature. Esther's marriage to Woodcourt is possible
only after Ada loses her husband and returns to her loving guardian.
The two girls change places. Only one of them can venture into the
world of love and marriage at a time; the alter ego must stay at home.
The psychological complexity of the book is often revealed in such
symbolic ways just when the literal events seem least plausible and
convincing. In the interstices of Dickens' magical solution, he cannot
help planting these grains of truth.

Dickens characteristically resorts to fantasy whenever his sharp
eye for human suffering has uncovered more than he can bear to
contemplate. His detailed realistic observation stops short at the
borders of despair. The resolution of the Esther plot is only one case

---

[8]*Charles Dickens: The World of His Novels* (Cambridge, Mass.: Harvard Univ. Press,
1958), p. 223.

in point. There are two other significant instances of a resort to fantasy
in the book, the first of which also involves Esther. I have tried to
show how psychologically plausible Dickens' portrait is, but there is
one crucial fact this analysis has ignored: that a child brought up in a
totally loveless home, as Esther was, is almost surely doomed to grow
up unable to love anyone. Yet Esther is an open, affectionate,
thoroughly responsive person. Here Dickens' realism comes into
conflict with his desire to present his victims as purely victimized.
The portrait of the bitter Miss Wade in *Little Dorrit* suggests that he
knew how unlovable a person who had never been loved could be;
but Miss Wade is a minor character, not the heroine of the novel, and
we are not asked to waste very much sympathy on her. Esther, on the
other hand, is an example of Dickens' myth of the innocent child,
whose goodness must be absolute. Her harsh upbringing can leave
her incomplete and vulnerable, but not selfish or corrupt. Dickens'
vision of society depends on the idea of victimization, on the absolute separation of the oppressors from the oppressed. That the
oppressed can go on to become oppressors in their turn is an
example of the sort of pessimistic conclusion his fantasy exists to
deny.

The same element of fantasy enters into his resolution of the
sociopolitical plot of *Bleak House*. Here Dickens comes much closer to
acknowledging the darkness of his own vision, which has led Jo, Lady
Dedlock, Tulkinghorn, Gridley, and Richard to their deaths. The
institution of Chancery goes on. The government remains in the
same incompetent hands. The Church and the charitable organiza-
tions are as corrupt as ever. All this can hardly be called a retreat
from pessimism into fantasy. Yet the book ends not in London but in
Eden, where a small group of good and permanently innocent
people transform the new Bleak House into a community of love
existing outside the blighted world described in the rest of the novel.
As Dickens' satire becomes more savage, his need to invent an escape
from the world he satirizes becomes more desperate and increasingly forces him to resort to fantasy.

It is possible that the myths he characteristically uses—the innocent child, the pure victim, the community of the saved, the good
rich man, etc.—gave him the courage to describe his society with
much greater fidelity and candor. The promise of an ultimate escape
in fantasy from the black world of the novel may well have unlocked
his ability to describe its misery—both social and psychological—in

such extraordinary and vivid detail. If this is so, then the savage indictment of social institutions in *Bleak House*, as well as the detailed psychological realism of the portrait of Esther, are both dependent on the element of fantasy at the borders of each.

# "The Prison of This Lower World"

## by Gerald Coniff

Man's condition of imprisonment is not, for Dickens, limited to nineteenth-century England. As J. Hillis Miller comments, "All the world's a prison," for the lord of the Circomlocution Office as well as the Marshalsea debtor, and the term of bondage is lifelong. Dickens' work reflects, of course, the great trauma of his childhood, his father's incarceration in a debtor's prison. That trauma is represented throughout the fiction, from the *Pickwick Papers*, with its imprisonment sequence, to the last completed novel, *Our Mutual Friend*, with its evocation of the terrifying Poor House, and even the uncompleted *Edwin Drood*, with its dismal crypt and opium den, the last chapters of which according to Forster's *Life* were to have been written as from the prison cell of the murderer. Pickwick hints how captivity and freedom are to constitute a ubiquitous polarity in the Dickensian narrative. The startling and apparently irrational court action against Mr. Pickwick, his being jailed, and his refusal to accept the hard factual side of a world he has hitherto examined in the light of a freely inquiring mind, these plot developments pose a problem more serious than Pickwickian. None of the novels or tales ignores this problem. Imprisonment is often a fact or immediate threat; yet, more broadly, it is a metaphor of the human condition.

The metaphor is not, finally, Christian. For Dickens the Christian feeling *is* pervasive if sometimes expressed in a perfunctory way. When Florence Dombey flees her home, she is said to have "no father upon earth." But if she does have a Heavenly Father instead, that vaguely suggested figure can be meant only as a force to transform real child and father into an earthly family where divine love is freely given, unbound and unbinding. Often, the family is in Dickens as much a form of constraint as other institutions, the poor

"The Prison of This Lower World" by Gerald Coniff. This essay appears for the first time in this volume.

house, the house of detention, the school house, ；
which should be a house of God.

The prison in Dickens amounts to more than ；
what Carlyle saw as an atheistic, soul-enslaving ag
the conventional religious belief that mankind's flesɪ⌐
home must be accepted as a vale of tears. It amounts to a vision ㄴɪ ⌐
human laspe from true humanity in a world where society makes
prisons for its people and individuals imprison themselves.

In *Oliver Twist* there are the workhouse and the den of thieves; in
*Nicholas Nickleby* there is Dotheboys Hall; in *Martin Chuzzlewit* there is
slavery, enacted by law and economic laws; in novel after novel there
are chains, cells, jails, prison ships, dungeons. From *Pickwick* to *Edwin
Drood* the prison and its shadows define, darken, and limit the world
of Dickens' novels. They function not only as elements of plot and
setting but also as recurrent tropes.

These figures of speech themselves emerge from the common
language and the grim settings. Often, like the slang they echo, these
are ironic phrases: a singing bird in the nightmare scenes of *Barnaby
Rudge*, with its bigotry and hideous violence, becomes the jail bird,
and that image of the bird as prisoner in crowded cities or dank cells
is to recur in later novels. Sometimes the irony is lighter. Mr.
Micawber is actually more at home in jail, more free of care, than out
of it. But even the comic-relief effect of character and language in
*David Copperfield* underlines the fact that home is a prison for the
improvident or unfortunate; the images of caged creatures, of jail-
house shadows, fetters and bonds, recur here and from here on in
the fiction.

Yet it is not until the later novels, especially *Little Dorrit*, *A Tale of
Two Cities*, and *Great Expectations*, that Dickens brings himself to deal
directly with prisons, prisoners, and self-imprisoning as controlling
idea and cohesive agent. He exposes his hidden wound (in Edmund
Wilson's image) to open air as he explores how an imprisoning lower
world—a profound psychological state as well as a socially restrictive
order—can be exposed and transformed.

Each of these novels establishes its crucial symbol in plot and in
images of suffocation and of shadows, in the metaphor of the bird in
the cage; in comparisons direct or indirect, stated or unstated, of
locales, situations, and persons with actual prisons or the elements of
prison cells and prison life; in the many things that are bound,
fettered, bolted, locked, buttoned-up, or crushed; in the suggestion

this lower world is itself a prison whose form is a labyrinth or ze; and at last in the very lives of the characters, in their ability or nability to escape from mental fetters that are largely of their own creation.

## II

The "villainous prison"of Marseilles in *Little Dorrit* literally casts its shadow on the city: "A prison taint was on everything there . . . [the prison itself] like a well, like a vault, like a tomb." As the prison is morbid and polluted, so is the whole place, its harbor foul, its smell noxious, its air suffocating. Enclosure and staleness are repeated in descriptions of one locale after another in the novel, from Mrs. Clennam's house to Tite Barnacle's (and he himself is closed "tight" as well as smothering in white cravat) to the Marshalsea and the palaces of Venice—to London, where the scene reminds Arthur Clennam of his childhood Sundays, when he was marched to chapel "like a military deserter" by a guard of teachers, feeling "morally handcuffed to another boy" and terrified when told of his going to "Perdition." As Arthur looks around, he feels surrounded by prisons of one sort or another. Seeing the slums, he wonders if those who once lived there "were ever conscious of them, how they must pity themselves for their old places of imprisonment."

When Arthur goes to his mother's house, she greets him in her room, reclining on a "black bier-like sofa . . . propped up behind with one great angular black bolster like a block at a state execution." Again, the metaphors of tomb and prison house—or death house—are combined. But now the sin-obsessed Mrs. Clennam is the para-lyzed prisoner, her room an airless cell, suggesting the dark prison house that Miss Havisham makes for herself. With the confrontation scene between Mrs. Clennam and Rigaud in Book II, Dickens reverts to the imagery of bierlike sofa and block, indicating that the room is exactly the way it has always been, with one exception: the window is open. In that scene, the truth of the family secret finally comes out, and as the open window allows fresh air into the long closed room the secret is unlocked. For now Mrs. Clennam's past is exposed and she is herself "judged" as Arthur's true father and mother were judged and condemned by her. Now the room becomes a final earthly prison for Rigaud, suffocated in dust as the ruined house collapses. She and he have formed their own prison and sentenced themselves.

Houses in *Little Dorrit*, commonly filled with stale, dead air, express their inhabitants. Frederick Dorrit's apartment is "close," with "an unwholesome smell." Tite Barnacle's home is a bottle, in which he is squeezed and stopped up. The expensive houses of people who care only for surface, for a good address, are supposedly stylish "little coops" and "hutches" that confine them. The Casby's house is "somber, silent, air-tight," fitting the Patriarch who, like Tite Barnacle, does not want change and is concerned with maintaining *his* "surface" or image. The faded scents of rose leaves and lavender in the house are "like wintry breath that had a faint remembrance in it of the bygone spring"—just as the atmosphere of the Marseilles prison is that of "six months ago . . . six years ago." Bitter, repressed Miss Wade lives in a "close back house" in London and a place equally grim in Calais. Fanny, like Miss Wade seeking revenge and like the Barnacles concerned with status, marries Sparkler to live in her own prisonlike house. "It's like lying in a well," she cries, echoing the well-vault-tomb images of the Marseilles prison, once more.

The suffocating closeness is most evident in the actual prison, the Marshalsea, near the end of *Little Dorrit*. But even this prison house can be as much a projection of character as a description of external fact. Some of Arthur's dread, laboring to breathe in the hated atmosphere, is shared by his mother who, in Little Dorrit's room, looks "down into this prison as it were out of her own different prison"—and her cell-like room has not really been so very different. She seems for a moment now on the verge of being released, but as she must reiterate her need to be an "instrument of severity against sin" she turns back, is pent up again and still, and she becomes "a statue."

In contrast, what appears to be a prison may not be so. Externals, walls of stone, do not make a place of confinement that is false or self-denying for the monks, although ironically the still psychologically imprisoned Dorrit—pretending to be a gentleman "not used to confinement"—assumes that they must. But Dorrit values surfaces, seeks only surfaces, and for him (in Holloway's phrase) "seeming imprisons reality." All of those in the novel who worship surfaces and seeming are self-imprisoned, and few escape those illusions that bind them—although perhaps Dorrit himself briefly does at the end, hallucinating about the Marshalsea but no longer a Carlylean "clothes-screen."

Prisoners of their own illusions are as various and many in the pages of *Little Dorrit* as caged birds. The English society of Venice prowl "in the old dreary prison-yard manner," Mr. Merdle has the habit of "clasping his wrists as if he were taking himself into custody," Daniel Doyce is stifled by the red tape of the Circumlocution Office until Clennam replaces him as inmate, the discontented inhabitants of Hampton Court, former government officials or their widows, speak of "going out" directly as Marshalsea prisoners talk of getting out—but never do. As for the birds, Mrs. Merdle is as "caged" as her parrot, Cavaletto and Rigaud and the quarantine group are called jail birds in Marseilles while the Marshalsea people are equally birdlike, Mrs. General the specialist in varnish is described as a phoenix (with sharp irony) as she takes new life in new social stations, and Little Dorrit is a "small bird, reared in captivity."

The Dorrit family is of course central to this work, and Little Dorrit herself its very center. She can be more than a prisoner, a caged bird. The crucial irony of the novel is that Amy, "Child of the Marshalsea," is able to escape the shadow of the wall, although her father and her family regard her as tainted by the prison precisely because she is honest, because she has not been imprisoned by illusions, lies, by surfaces. The child of imprisonment, she is the only adult in the family. This means that like Florence Dombey, like Sissy Jupe, and other children in some ways orphaned or abandoned (and perhaps like Dickens himself, whose novels are full of these children), she has to forgive and protect her father. It means, as well, that she can serve as an example to help others transcend imprisonment. John Chivery's love for her is all that makes the prison of his class, his prospects, bearable; his romanticism is funny, not fatal. Pancks' public revelation of Casby's hypocrisy frees him, as does his kindness and decency. Doyce escapes the tape of the Circumlocution Office and goes abroad to work, in countries where his talents are appreciated, while Flora can overcome *her* limitations.

III

Far aslant across the city, over its jumbled roofs, and through the open tracery of its church towers, struck the long, bright rays, bars of the prison of this lower world.

This virtually epigraphic passage with its ambiguous church towers, its curious juxtaposing of bright rays and prison shadow, and its problematical "lower world" suggests that there is more in the novel than the political and social message that Shaw and others have found there, more even than a fervent Carlylean attack on *laissez-faire* smugness. The murky depths of this world are those of the soul that needs imaginative liberation. Dickens perceives that liberating as a possible process for his characters—and for himself as the self-liberating teller of tales—in *Little Dorrit* and in other novels.

Something of the mixture, light and hope along with darkness which is the imprisoning shadow of the past, a sense that the present is at once the best and worst of times, gives *A Tale of Two Cities* the extraordinary chiaroscuro effect that makes it more than the obvious and sentimentalized melodrama it is sometimes taken to be. Within *this* lower world, the cities of which—both London and Paris—are prisons, willingly to accept imprisonment may be to achieve freedom. The irony is not subtle but it is powerful. Again, it need not be explicitly Christian: Sydney Carton is not the blameless Christ who is sacrificed, although he may be rather like the monks of Saint Bernard who judge themselves and will their own confinement, their own penance. Free people like the Manettes are imprisoned by a cruel society (cruel because of its being cruelly victimized), and they rightly resist. But the free have the right, as well, to judge and even to sacrifice their own lives. It is, once more, a matter of seeing oneself, one's own lower world, a matter of moral vision. Once more, to accept one's real imprisonment is to be free, to escape the prison.

In *Great Expectations*, there are degrees of freedom and imprisonment. Virtually at the beginning of the novel we encounter the prisoner who is to be a substitute father—like and at the same time very much unlike the novelist's father—and the source of Pip's expectations. Magwitch escapes the prison ship for a time, escapes again and lives when he returns to England in a tenuous state of freedom, haunted as Pip is now by the shadow of Newgate Prison. He is always a prisoner of his own mysterious past. So is Jaggers' housekeeper. So are his many clients. Even Pip the orphan, who hardly has a past, is trying to escape, forget, deny his limitations so as to be a gentleman—when in fact the London to whose society he aspires is itself more dark and dreary, more confining, with the law courts and the prison in its heart, than the old Gargery house with the hulks, the prison ships, nearby. But the most profoundly imprisoned character in the story until almost the end of her life, because hers is indeed a self-imprisonment, is Miss Havisham.

When Pip first goes to Satis House, that manor house that has become for both Estella and its owner a dark tomb and dungeon, the place is described first of all as though it were a jail house: it

> was of old brick, and dismal, and had a great many iron bars to it. Some of the windows had been walled up; of those that remained, all the lower were rustily barred. There was a courtyard in front, and that was barred.

Here are the lower windows of this lower world; the house is a symbol of the woman, who has immured herself from fresh air and from all free communication with humanity. When she explains to Pip the meaning of Satis House, and comments wryly on it ("Whoever had this house could want nothing else. They must have been easily satisfied in those days") she does not fully explore the implications of that curious name. For "Satis"-"satisfaction" can also mean "expiate-atonement." At the end, Miss Havisham longs only to atone, to be forgiven.

She recognizes, that is, that she has imprisoned, stunted, not only herself but also Estella, and she begs repeatedly that the girl be asked to sign the statement, "I forgive her." Pleading for this forgiveness is pleading for freedom from her prison, her past. It is as much a moral act as Magwitch's return to England, which can be the return to an actual prison.

A vision of the human situation that informs each of these novels and that has been anticipated in earlier novels by metaphors, hints, and passages, imprisonment acts in several ways. The dominant fact, which becomes a symbol, is the actual prison or house or building with prisoners' cells. But the ultimate thematic idea is that of our being imprisoned by illusions, social, economic, religious, and by our acceptance of illusion, of false appearance, an acceptance that constrains us psychologically, emotionally, and, most important, morally.

# Storytelling and the Figure of the Father
## in *Little Dorrit*

*by Dianne F. Sadoff*

"Look'ee here, Pip. I'm your second father."

The discovery is made [that Ralph Nickleby was Smike's father], Ralph is dead, the loves have come all right, . . . and I have now only to break up Dotheboys and the book together.[1]

Doubling and discovery inhere in a classical narrative's metaphors and in its structures. Doubling implies resemblance, analogy, identity, but also difference; the elements of a narrative—structure, character, plot—all make use of metaphor and its opposite (double), catachresis. The hinges in a story hang events together: and then this happened, and it was like—or unlike— that earlier thing that happened. Event sometimes carries the weight of forecast, of destiny, of prophecy: this will or might well happen. Scenes in stories, actions symbolic and narrative, would make no sense without metaphor and catachresis as figures of comparison. So we might say that doubling and metaphor as a structural device inhere especially in all long narratives, all "loose and baggy monsters." Dickens, Eliot, and Trollope, among others, bind the triple-decker together with metaphor to create a story of several classes, a tale with many centers. Reading the multiple-plotted novel, in fact, the reader engages in a metaphorical activity based on perception of resemblance and

"Storytelling and the Figure of the Father in *Little Dorrit*, by Dianne F. Sadoff. Reprinted by permission of the Modern Language Association of America and the author from *PMLA*, 95 (1980).

[1]The first quotation is from Charles Dickens, *Great Expectations* (London: Oxford Univ. Press, 1953), p. 303. The second is from Dickens, Letter to John Forster, 9 Sept. 1839, in *The Letters of Charles Dickens*, ed. Madeline House and Graham Storey, I (Oxford: Clarendon, 1965), 581. Hereafter cited as the Pilgrim Letters.

difference during reading time: Does one "central" plot make other stories subplots? Do all the plots together create one inevitable meaning, one transcendental signified? Do the several plots demonstrate discontinuities, ironics, and differences among themselves?[2] Dickens and his recent critics would have us, as readers, choose our middle alternative, which is to define stories as metaphorical, as creating similarity and resemblance—the matrix of analogy. Yet Dickens' narratives often demonstrate inevitable discontinuity. *Bleak House*, for example, attempts to persuade us of the ultimate and inevitable congruence between public and private versions of order, but ironically persuades us of the incongruence between public disorder, embodied in the omniscient narrator's tale of Chancery, and private order, embodied in Esther Summerson's tale of her life.[3] The reader interprets a life, then, and its larger context with the help of metaphor, the figure of doubling, resemblance, and failure to resemble.

The story of a life, even the life of a public institution like Chancery or the Circumlocution Office, is a tale of origins and ends, of purposes, motivations, consequences, outcomes, genealogies, fatherhood. The reader interprets a life with the tools of metonymy: *first* this happened, *then* that. When Silas Marner, the figure of discontinuity and wandering, appears in Raveloe with a pack on his back, the community fails to explain his presence because no one knows his father or mother, his home, or his origin. The novel ends when Silas himself becomes a "father" and his "daughter," Eppie, rejects her "real" father in favor of her foster and "present" father. As *Silas Marner* demonstrates, the structures of multiple-plotted narrative combine issues about the family with temporality; genealogy provides a chronology, a linear and causal sequence, within which a story resides.[4] Narrative acquires its authority by reference to familial

---

[2]I am indebted in this discussion of the relationship among plots in the multiple-plotted novel to J. Hillis Miller's talks in a National Endowment for the Humanities summer seminar held at Yale University in 1977.

[3]Peter K. Garrett, "Double Plots and Dialogical Form in Victorian Fiction," *Nineteenth-Century Fiction*, 32 (1977), 1–17, also makes this observation about *Bleak House* in his application of Mikhail Bakhtin's terminology to multiple-plotted Victorian novels.

[4]For a longer discussion of genealogy and narrative structure, see Patricia Drechsel Tobin, *Time and the Novel: The Genealogical Imperative* (Princeton: Princeton Univ. Press, 1978). Applyig Edward Said's structure-anthropological terminology to narrative structure, temporality, and genealogy. Tobin chronicles the breakdown

and other origins, by forewarnings of deaths and ends, however equivocal those origins and ends appear. In this sense, the multiple-plotted narrative, like all texts structured by the double—figurative and grammatical—nature of language, never achieves total congruity or closure of its several stories. According to George Eliot's narrator, for example, "Every limit is a beginning as well as an ending."[5] Narrative teleology, that is, narrative purpose, tendency, and end-point, shapes, and is shaped by, a life story, a father begetting and generating, a mother giving birth, a child marrying and begetting or dying or both.

Narrative origins and narrative endpoint, or knowledge, disen-tanglement, and undoubling—in short, the narrative urge—are figured, according to Roland Barthes, by the father:

> The pleasure of the text is not the pleasure of the corporeal striptease or of narrative suspense. . . . This is an Oedipal pleasure (to denude, to know, to learn the origin and the end) if it is true that every narrative (every unveiling of the truth) is a staging of the (absent, hidden, or hypostatized) father—which would explain the solidarity of narrative forms, of family structures, and of prohibitions of nudity, all collected in our culture in the myth of Noah's sons covering his nakedness.
>
> Death of the Father would deprive literature of many of its plea-sures. If there is no longer a Father, why tell stories? Doesn't every narrative lead back to Oedipus? Isn't storytelling always a way of searching for one's origin, speaking one's conflicts with the Law, entering into the dialectic of tenderness and hatred?[6]

Barthes's principal metaphor for narrative sequence, for the origina-tion and engendering of a story, is paternity, or the son's search for the father. The author seeks patriarchal authority, and narrative sequence embodies that search. Narrative discovery, as the Nickleby epigraph is meant to suggest, defines the father's relationship to his son, the closure of narrative as the death of (or accommodation with) the father, and, by analogy, the legitimacy of authorship as paternal. In fact, the *OED*, using references to Pope, Lamb, and Thackeray,

---

of such narrative assumptions in the modern and postmodern novel. She believes that aside from a few quirky exceptions, Victorian fiction fails to interrogate its own genealogical structures and ideologies; my essay fundamentally disagrees with Tobin's assumptions about Victorian narrative.

[5]Eliot, *Middlemarch*, ed. Gordon S. Haight (Boston: Houghton, 1956), p. 607.

[6]Barthes, *The Pleasure of the Text*, trans. Richard Miller (New York: Hill and Wang, 1975), pp. 10, 47. Barthes's paradigm, of course, valorizes masculine aesthetics; his perspective of the son-as-writer is the one from which I view Dickens here.

gives one definition of "author" as "one who begets," a "father," an "ancestor." Dickens himself used the metaphor of paternity to deny the legitimacy of writing spuriously attributed to him; of an ersatz continuation of *Pickwick* and a paper by Father Prout, Dickens announced that he "decidedly objects to fathering anybody else's articles" (Pilgrim Letters, I, 217, 433). We also know that Dickens spoke metaphorically of himself as parent to his characters, most notably in the preface to *David Copperfield*: "It will be easily believed that I am a fond parent to every child of my fancy, and that no one can ever love that family as dearly as I love them. But, like many fond parents, I have in my heart of hearts a favourite child. And his name is DAVID COPPERFIELD."[7] As that novel demonstrates, in becoming an author the unhappy son attains maturity and becomes his own father, fathers himself.

In *Little Dorrit*, Dickens likewise demonstrates, although in a different way, that the purpose of narrative, including the narrative about purpose or vocation, is to seek the figure of the father, to write the paternal metaphor, and to acquire paternal authority. This multiple-plotted novel tells two major stories—or a double story—one about Amy Dorrit, the other about Arthur Clennam, and attempts to bring the two narratives (and characters) together at the novel's close with a marriage that bridges antithesis and creates symbolic unity. Behind this narrative project stands the father, the figure of law and of Oedipal prohibition and desire. Both the story of a son and the story of a daughter involve confronting the father, one absent (dead), the other all too present. The father, a figure of resemblance and difference, of origin as aim and as end, links the two narratives and provides the novel's teleology. Dickens associates the figure of the father with purpose and authority: creating children, like creating the sons and daughters of *Little Dorrit*, should cure aimlessness, empower authority, adumbrate genealogical continuity, and shape narrative sequence. Yet Dickens discovers in telling the stories of Amy and Arthur that the narrative search for the father's authority makes the father, authority, and narrative knowledge of end and origin problematic. The curiously overdetermined ending of *Little Dorrit* represses the narrative's discoveries about paternity, about the father's failure to create "children" authoritatively and responsibly.

Dickens' story of a son, Arthur Clennam, narrates a public search

[7]*David Copperfield* (New York: Random, 1950), p. xv.

for purpose, for vocation. Yet when we first encounter Clennam, in the Marseilles quarantine, he confesses his utter lack of direction to Mr. Meagles: "I am such a waif and stray everywhere, that I am liable to be drifted where any current may set. . . . I have no will. That is to say . . . next to none that I can put in action now. . . . Always grinding in a mill I always hated; what is to be expected from *me* in middle life? Will, purpose, hope?"[8] In a chapter Dickens ironically titles "Nobody's Weakness," Clennam ponders "what he was to do henceforth in life; to what occupation he should devote himself, and in what direction he had best seek it" (p. 231). Clennam is the weak "nobody," but he is also blameless in the face of his embraced, even courted, failures. Thinking he goes to the Circumlocution Office to help the Dorrits, for example, Clennam goes in part as an "exercise in perseverance" (p. 154), for he expects that he will fail to beat the system as others before him have failed. In fact, as he knows, the "purpose" of this revolving office is to destroy his already damaged will, "to set bounds to the philanthropy, to cramp the charity, to fetter the public spirit, to contract the enterprise, to damp the independent self-reliance, of its people" (p. 455).

A vocation, in the form of the helpless Daniel Doyce, however, providentially finds Clennam at the Circumlocution Office. What is the business of the newly formed firm of Doyce and Clennam, and is this really Clennam's long-sought vocation? We hardly know. Despite our uncertainty about what Clennam makes or accomplishes at The Works, Clennam claims a "feeling of pleasure in his pursuit that was new to him." Yet we never see Clennam working or enjoying his work. Dickens makes his usual claims for the value of work but fails to show us that value in the action of the novel, just as he fails to do so at the end of Pip's great expectations. In fact, Dickens fills his metaphorical description of work at The Works with a violence and ambiguity: the benches, vices, tools, straps, and wheels, "in gear with the steam-engine, went tearing round as though they had a suicidal mission to grind the business to dust and tear the factory to pieces"; a trapdoor lets in a shaft of light that reminds Clennam of "the child's old picture-book, where similar rays were the witnesses of Abel's murder" (pp. 312–13). Clennam works with the money, however, not with the machines, and in the counting-house Dickens removes Clennam from the noise and the devilish figures covered with iron

---

[8]Dickens, *Little Dorrit*, ed. John Holloway (Baltimore: Penguin, 1976), p. 59. All page references in the text of the essay are to this edition.

and steel filings; he protects Clennam from the self-destructive violence and fratricide he figuratively associates with The Factory and so refuses Clennam's implicit identification with Cain, a murderous and exiled son and brother. Dickens' figurative language of violence aimed at the brother, or double, and ultimately at the self creates and mediates ironic, Oedipal tensions in Clennam's public vocation.

Clennam's troubles with vocation, as metaphor demonstrates, are intimately bound up with his sonhood. Early in the narrative, he declares will, purpose, and hope "extinguished before [he] could sound the words" (p. 59). Clennam apparently lost his sense of purpose as an infant, before he attained the power of speech; his language, his sense of himself as still a child incapable of speech, metaphorically blames his family for his continuing will-lessness and identifies him as a son. Indeed, the "mill he grinds in" is his father's business, which "exiles" the metaphorical Cain and crushes his sense of purpose. The father asserts his power of precedence over the son, metaphorically castrating him, making him infirm and aimless. Yet this powerful father resembles, as well as differs from, his son. Like the "slip-shod, purposeless, down-at-heel" Tip Dorrit (p. 116), Clennam has a constitutional, or genealogical, problem with idleness: Clennam's father, like Clennam himself, was "an undecided, irresolute chap" (p. 224). The paternal metaphor identifying the son with the father has worked too well: the son becomes a repetition of the father, and genealogy proves to be an ironic, paradoxical inheritance of paternal failure and lack of authority. Clennam carries a double burden of guilt with regard to the father: the ironic double reference to the Bible—Clennam as Cain and Clennam as Prodigal Son—implies that only when the father is dead can the unprodigal, exiled son return home to confront, surreptitiously, his sonhood.

Clennam's first vocation, once begun, gives way to a second: his attempt to help the Dorrit family get out of prison. Clennam, however, again deceives himself with regard to his purpose, with which he unconsciously attempts to alleviate his mysterious and motiveless feelings of guilt. Whenever Clennam thinks about vocation and occupation, he finds his ability to act blocked by the "misgiving that there was some one with an unsatisfied claim upon his justice" (p. 231). Because his mother is kind to Little Dorrit and to no one else, Clennam irrationally connects Little Dorrit's family with his own pervading sense of guilt and family hatred: "What if any act of [his mother's] and of his father's, should have even remotely brought the grey heads of those two [Dorrit] brothers so low" (p.

129). No logical reason can be given why Clennam makes such connections, primarily because the narrative motive is sexual: "purpose" gets mixed up with the family as origin, with potency and engendering, as Clennam unknowingly attempts to become father to Little Dorrit by "altering her whole manner of life, smoothing her rough road, and giving her a home . . . as his adopted daughter" (p. 231). The second vocation, then, becomes as metaphorically double as the first. In liberating a family apparently connected to his own, Clennam seeks to liberate his sense of his purpose and to transform himself from family-bound son to freedom-engendering father.

Clennam's second vocation succeeds better than he could have hoped, but ironically its success is also its failure. When the newly rich Dorrits leave the Marshalsea, Clennam once more finds himself vocationless; when he has apparently fulfilled his purpose of righting an old wrong, Clennam's feelings of guilt, idleness, passivity, and lack of purpose reassert themselves. Clennam's guilt now centers on his mother, and his vocation now consists of finding out the "secret" of her house in order to "shake off" his "paralysis." His "indomitable" mother, however, renders him "completely powerless" and makes his "energy, activity, money, credit, all his resources whatsoever . . . useless." His desire to track down his feelings of guilt, to name their origin, becomes inextricably linked to a mysterious "shame and exposure" that hangs over his mother and over "his father's memory" (pp. 742–43). Dickens' evasive rhetoric and his body metaphors reveal the sexual component of Clennam's vocation: his impotence—or his mother's castration of him—can be cured only by his exposing her shamefully and learning her secrets, of both body (house) and identity. Again, Clennam's vocation signifies an attempt to become, to replace, the father. Clennam feels guilty—but doesn't know it—primarily because of his father's adultery and his mother's resulting disinheritance of Amy Dorrit. His purpose is to track down his parentage, to discover the history of his bastardy through metaphorical sexual knowledge of his mother. This aggressive act of incest will metaphorically cure the aggressions and desires structured into the Oedipal family and will place Clennam in the position of replacing his own father.[9] Clennam's search for

---

[9]Albert D. Hutter, "Reconstructive Autobiography: The Experience at Warren's Blacking," *Dickens Studies Annual*, 6 (1977), 1–14, believes the reason the blacking warehouse factory scarred Dickens so deeply was just this childish fantasy of replacing the father and the seeming confirmation of the fantasied replacement

vocation appears as a metaphor for sexual and paternal knowledge, for incest and self-origination.

Yet knowledge and replacement of the father are central to a story of sonhood. The myth of Oedipus is a drama of discovery, a tragedy of a son who comes to know his parentage too late. The tale told by many tellers makes paternity a metaphor for narrative sequence and insists on the son's knowledge of origin as a consequence of story-telling. Dickens' tale of paternity in *Little Dorrit*, however, averts Oedipal tragedy and exile by eliding the son's knowledge. But Clennam's equivocal and metaphorical vocations find their op-posites in his two grotesque and knowing doubles, Rigaud and Miss Wade. The criminal Rigaud pervades the novel, yet he is paradoxi-cally absent from it and disguised throughout. Although we never see him actually perform a criminal act, his alleged crimes are legion; he kills his fiancée for money and social status; he kills Pet's dog "dead as the Doges" for no reason; he bribes and blackmails Mrs. Clennam. As Alexander Welsh points out, only Clennam connects Rigaud—also likened to Cain—to the mysterious crimes of the narrative.[10] Rigaud, the motiveless villain, is Clennam's dark double (just as Old Nandy is Dorrit's "poor old foil"),[11] and he acts out versions of Clennam's hidden and unconscious motives—incest and parricide—through sexual exploitation and murder.

Rigaud's criminality, like Clennam's figurative violence, originates in his confused lineage, the mysterious circumstances of his birth. Like Clennam, Rigaud is a metaphorical orphan, waif, and bastard through his indeterminate nationality: his father is Swiss, his mother is French by blood and English by birth, and he himself was born in Belgium. Rigaud, however, imagines himself deprived of aristo-cratic birthright. This fiction compensates for his orphanage and lack of origin: a gentleman knows his family history and his place in it; he knows his father and accepts his sonhood as a prelude, in a sequential genealogy, to his own fatherhood. Social acceptance hinges on this genealogy. To be a pariah is to have no nameable and verifiable father and thus no patriarchal line that defines inheritance

---

when his family lived in prison while Dickens worked and lived outside. In *Little Dorrit*, of course, Dickens recreates this "scene" from his experience by making himself female and submissive, turning violent emotions toward the self.

[10]Welsh, *The City of Dickens* (Oxford: Clarendon, 1971), pp. 134–35.

[11]Paul D. Herring, "Dickens's Monthly Number Plans for *Little Dorrit*," *Modern Philology*, 64 (1966), 38.

and identity. Rigaud's mysterious parentage, his metaphorical orphanage, deprives him of both money and substance, of personal and social authority.

Rigaud takes revenge against society by enacting disguised, violence against members of the upper and middle classes. Having no origin himself, he spitefully reveals hidden origin by selling the secrets of genealogy. He bribes Mrs. Clennam because he knows her secret, Clennam's parentage. Thinking himself a man whom "society has deeply wronged," Rigaud maintains that "society shall pay for it" (p. 174); "society sells itself and sells me," he says, "and I sell Society" (p. 818). Rigaud attempts to revenge his own unjust bastardy, disinheritance, and consequent social rejection by punishing those who know their fathers. Rigaud's motives parody Clennam's vocational researches, Dorrit's gentlemanly poses, and Merdle's capitalistic exploits—all of which demonstrate the doubleness of social authority and personal identity.

Like Rigaud, Miss Wade tries to revenge her lack of origin. Again like him, she has little function in the narrative. Yet she too experiences a strange kinship with Clennam, to whom she eventually exposes her indignant history. No narrative reason can be given for her act; it appears to be motiveless, but it reveals an important motivational relationship between Clennam and Miss Wade. Like Clennam, Miss Wade is an orphan and a bastard. Pancks says of her, "I know as much about her as she knows about herself. She is somebody's child—anybody's—nobody's. Put her in a room in London here with any six people old enough to be her parents, and her parents may be there for anything she knows" (p. 595). Miss Wade becomes a perfect paradox: she has an origin and yet has none; she is somebody yet nobody; she knows all yet knows nothing. She too takes revenge against society and the concept of sexual guilt. Tattycoram and her illegitimacy becomes Miss Wade's instrument of revenge against the Meagleses. Because she believes in the substantive, constitutive properties of birth and blood, however, Miss Wade also feels guilty about her origin. She speaks of herself as a dark double of Tattycoram: "She has no name, I have no name. Her wrong is my wrong" (p. 379). Name (birth, genealogy, blood) defines substance; to be nameless signifies sexual guilt.

The constitutive power of the name means that language is able to engender. Miss Wade knows this as no other character in *Little Dorrit* does. Aware of her nameless origin, she rebels against bourgeois society's false names: Tattycoram, Pet, Blandois. She rises against "swollen patronage and selfishness, calling themselves kindness, protection, benevolence, and other fine names" (p. 734). Miss Wade—Esther Summerson gone cynical and paranoid—represents the absolute urge to know and to name in the narrative: in a suicidal, murderous rage, she exposes all human intersubjectivity as debased authority and competition. She exposes her lack of origin through her writing, in the "history" she gives Clennam to read. As a "writer" in a narrative full of real victims and apparent rebels (like Pancks, whose castration of The Patriarch is purely symbolic), Miss Wade does what Dickens cannot bring his hero, Clennam, or himself, as author, to do: by writing a narrative about her origin, she exposes orphanage and bastardy as the central motivation that unites social patronage, exploitation, petit-bourgeois capitalism, and murder. Miss Wade's story covers over the primary gap, the plotted evasion of the narrative; namely, that the consequence of sexual intercourse is fathering. She accepts, even glorifies, the emptiness Clennam tries to fill, the father he seeks to replace. Miss Wade's *history* exploits the duplicity implicit in the act of exposure, in naming: does her history, like the written history of a nation, recount "real," literal events or does it, like *Tom Jones: The History of a Foundling*, for example, recount another fiction of origin? Miss Wade's narrative, which Dickens, not she, entitles "The History of a Self-Tormentor," acts out Clennam's self-hatred in the way that Merdle metaphorically acts out his business-related suicidal urges. His history reveals, behind its angry rhetoric of self-justification, that revenge is an appropriate if not efficacious motive, that writing out the hidden vocation of seeking one's origin is dangerous because it confirms what it attempts to deny: the father's inadequacy and his ultimate absence. As every son knows (and Dickens' exaggerated version of Miss Wade's lesbian seductions implies a masculine knowledge), the symbolic father is the dead father.

Who, then, is the father in *Little Dorrit*? Clennam's, Rigaud's, and Miss Wade's stories recount versions of the dead, absent, and missing father. Yet the narrative as a whole offers us as a present father only William Dorrit, a weak and unauthoritative father, both publicly and privately. Dorrit's authority as Father of the Marshalsea depends wholly on an ironic and debased precedence, his seniority as a prison inmate. His humbug gentlemanliness, his patronage and condescension as public Father cover up an "effeminate style" and "irresolute hands": he lacks will and helplessly depends on those who should be dependent on him. Little Dorrit knows that "a man so

broken as to be the Father of the Marshalsea, could be no father to
his own children" (p. 112). Dorrit finds a paradoxical freedom inside
the prison walls. The "old jail-bird," Dr. Haggage, tells an unnamed
debtor on the day the debtor's daughter is born inside the Marshalsea, "Elsewhere, people are restless, worried, hurried about, anxious
respecting one thing, anxious respecting another. Nothing of the
kind here, sir. We have done all that—we know the worst of it; we
have got to the bottom, we can't fall, and what have we found?
Peace" (p. 103). That debtor is Dorrit, already relieved by his quiet
refuge and destined, as the turnkey prophesies, to become Father of
the Marshalsea. As Father, Dorrit disowns paternity and purpose and
abdicates authentic authority; he appears to be as absent and as dead
a father as Clennam's.

Although Dickens scorns Dorrit's refusal to be responsible for his
actions, the secure stability of the "place of refuge" nonetheless
attracts Dickens and represents the drive in the novel toward
becoming "nobody." The pastoral interludes in the novel embody
this longing for rest, stasis, and death: the Meagleses' little home and
its river, which Clennam would like to float down; the Plornishes'
parodic "Happy Cottage"; the turnkey's and Amy's imaginary fields
outside the prison walls; Maggie's dreams of the hospital, with its
appropriately oral gratifications, especially "chicking"; Amy's tale of
the princess spinning in her cottage. Despite the differences among
these pastoral scenes and imagings, all appear metaphorically related
to the prison's freedom from conflict. Dorrit's acceptance of this
otherwise unacknowledged narrative desire earns him Dickens'
conscious scorn, which is affirmed by the reader's disrespect; yet
Dorrit's passivity also surreptitiously reveals Dickens' sympathy for
the father, forever incarcerated in his imagination.

Hidden within *Little Dorrit*'s assault on the Victorian paterfamilias,
then, are Dickens' deeply buried guilt, his complex contradictions,
and his fears about fathering. Much has been written about Dickens'
ambivalent relationship to his own father, John Dickens, portrayed
as the improvident yet good-humored Micawber and the tyrannical
usurper Murdstone in *David Copperfield*. Much has also been written
about Dickens' hopes for *his* sons when he became a father, the good
provider whose father became his dependent (financially and psychologically), a "son" among his own failing, unsuccessful sons.[12] In

---

[12]See, in addition to Hutter, "Reconstructive Autobiography," Leonard Manheim, "The Law as Father: An Aspect of the Dickens Pattern," *American Imago*, 12

*Little Dorrit* the autobiographical urge seems less clear than it is in *Copperfield*, but the representation of fathering appears no less con-fessional because more fictional.[13] Guilt over the lack of a nameable origin and anger over the absence of paternal support and discipline balance the belief that one doesn't deserve a fatherly mentor, a family, a lineage, a constitutive name. Outside and prior to the nar-rative is its originating yet untold act: the father's adultery—his faithless sexuality, his false engendering, his duplicitous authority. Being a father means creating bastardy, becoming deceptively tyran-nical, and necessarily failing to provide for offspring. The narrative displaces and then replaces the father, as the son attempts, and fails, to shortcut genealogy and become his own engenderer. The father, like the son, is indeed "nobody."

*Little Dorrit*, however, also tells the story of a daughter, Little Dorrit. Amy performs the functions Dickens himself performed while *his* family lived in prison; the youngest child, and a daughter at that, takes "the place of the eldest of the three," and "in all things but precedence" becomes the "head of the fallen family" and bears its "anxieties and shames" (pp. 111–12). Amy serves her father in a perfect union of love and duty. She does not think of herself or "trouble any one with her emotions" (p. 139); she sacrifices her life for others; she submits absolutely to her father's authority although he is clearly unworthy of her submission. Amy habitually sits silently

---

(1955), 17–23, and "The Personal History of David Copperfield," *American Imago*, 9 (1952), 21–43 (rpt. in *The Practice of Psychoanalytic Criticism*, ed. Leonard Tennenhouse [Detroit: Wayne State Univ. Press, 1976], pp. 75–94); Steven Marcus, "Who Is Fagin?" in *Dickens: From* Pickwick *to* Dombey (New York: Simon, 1968), pp. 358–78; Albert D. Hutter, "Crime and Fantasy in *Great Expectations*," in *Psychoanalysis and Literary Process*, ed. Frederick Crews (Cambridge, Mass.: Winthrop, 1970), pp. 25–65; Pearl Chesler Solomon, *Dickens and Melville in Their Time* (New York: Columbia University Press, 1975); Lawrence Jay Dessner, "*Great Expectations*: the ghost of a man's own father,'" *PMLA*, 91 (1976), 436–49; Branwen Bailey Pratt, "Dickens and Father: Notes on the Family Romance." *Hartford Studies in Literature*, 8 (1976), 4–22. Randolph Splitter, "Guilt and the Trappings of Melodrama in *Little Dorrit*," *Dickens Studies Annual*, 6 (1977), 119–33, mentions the father with regard to Clennam's guilt but blames primarily the mother for the hero's guilt and self-repression. Welsh, however, says, "In *Little Dorrit*," the supplanting of the father is . . . thorough" (p. 153); William Myers, "The Radicalism of *Little Dorrit*," in *Literature and Politics in the Nineteenth Century*, ed. John Lucas (London: Methuen, 1971), claims that "the middle-class *paterfamilias* penetrates the novel at every level" (p. 80).

[13]See Barry Westburg, *The Confessional Fictions of Charles Dickens* (Urbana: Nothern Illinois Univ. Press, 1977), for a definition of the difference between autobiography and confessional fiction.

by her father's side or falls piteously "at her father's feet" (p. 421) or "obey[s] without a murmur, ... little patient hands folded before her" (p. 517) in her characteristic pose of deference to, and respect for, authority.[14]

The figure for Amy's willful, almost grotesque submission, for her ability to nurture in deprivation, is breast feeding: "There was a classical daughter once—perhaps—who ministered to her father in his prison as her mother had ministered to her. Little Dorrit, though of the unheroic modern stock and mere English, did much more, in comforting her father's wasted heart upon her innocent breast, and turning to it a fountain of love and fidelity that never ran dry or waned through all his years of famine" (pp. 273–74). The almost shocking collapse of the metaphor into the literal betrays this passage's contradictions: despite Amy's metaphorical and daughterly "self-sacrifice" (Dickens' running title for this page), the motherly act of breast feeding upsets the generations, make the father dependent, and sexualizes the father-daughter relationship. Although Dickens attempts to distance these associations with the analogy to Euphrasia and her father, the King of Syracuse, the figure stands for the double horror of incest. If the story of a son relates the search for a father's authority, the story of a daughter tells of incestuous structures of desire.

Freud discusses incest as fantasy and desire, the sexual aspects of a nurturing relationship. These aspects represent the personal horror of incest, and its structures of desire appear widely in our literature. The cultural horror of incest, however, relates to genealogy, to the "swallowing up" by the family of other social institutions and commitments. Society collapses onto the family as the family becomes the voracious devourer of wider human connection.[15] *Little Dorrit's*

---

[14]J. Hillis Miller, *Charles Dickens: The World of His Novels* (Cambridge: Harvard Univ. Press, 1958), believes Little Dorrit's "voluntary refusal to will" makes her a "human incarnation of divine goodness" (p. 246). This providential view of Amy and of the novel in general, a view with which I strongly disagree, is also articulated by Avrom Fleishman, "Master and Servant in *Little Dorrit*," *Studies in English Literature*, 14 (1974), 575–86, and Jerome Beaty, "The 'Soothing Songs' of *Little Dorrit*," in *Nineteenth-Century Literary Perspectives: Essays in Honor of Lionel Stevenson*, ed. Clyde deL. Ryals (Durham, N.C.: Duke Univ. Press, 1974), pp. 219–36. In contrast, Janice M. Carlisle, "*Little Dorrit*: Necessary Fictions," *Studies in the Novel*, 7 (1975), 195–214, presents Amy as a figure of practical deception and fictionalizing.

[15]For an extended discussion of Freud's evasions of culture in his early theories of the Oedipus complex, see Paul Ricoeur, *Freud and Philosophy: An Essay on Interpretation*, trans. Denis Savage (New Haven: Yale Univ. Press, 1970), pp. 194–211.

version of incest represents this double bond of incest—familial desire and the temporal collapse of generation. The narrative collapses the family onto two figures: the daughter whom the father seduces becomes the mother who nurtures him, while the fatherly figure of the law becomes, through regression, the son. This dyad combines all the roles possible in an incest matrix: father, daughter, mother, and son. Self-sufficiency, nurturing, satisfaction of all need and desire, temporal regression, and narcissism make this matrix a figure for the Dickensian family; it is a representation of bliss, the assuaging secret that attempts to atone for patriarchal authority and guilt in the narrative.

We begin with familial desire. Amy Dorrit nurses her father, ministers to him, thinks of living always with him, and occasionally sleeps in the same bed with him. William Dorrit, however, upsets this father-daughter idyll when he thinks of replacing Amy with the prunes-and-prism Mrs. General. After this sexual betrayal of the daughter, the father-as-lover finds himself displaced by his brother, his double, Frederick Dorrit:

> As he stopped here, looking in unseen, he felt a pang. Surely not a jealousy? For why like jealousy? There was only his daughter and his brother there: he, with his chair drawn to the hearth, enjoying the warmth of the evening wood fire; she seated at a little table, busied with some embroidery work. Allowing for the great difference in the still-life of the picture, the figures were much the same as of old; his brother being sufficiently like himself to represent himself, for a moment, in the composition. So had he sat many a night, over a coal fire far away; so had she sat, devoted to him. Yet surely there was nothing to be jealous of in the old miserable poverty. Whence, then, the pang in his heart? (p. 699)

While the earlier incestuous scene was evaded by historical metaphor, this one is distanced by pictorial representation: the past made still life in the present. Yet the jealousy at replacement is clear, as is the familiar, comfortable, silent, habitual intimacy Dorrit voyeuristically views. This replacement drives Dorrit mad and kills him: although Dickens hints at Dorrit's impending breakdown and overtly blames the Marshalsea for his madness, William Dorrit dies because a different father-lover sits with Amy. William breaks in on the idyllic scene, calls Frederick (his double) mad, then goes mad himself; Frederick, inordinately guilty over his brother's death, dies the same night at his brother's bedside.

The father, then, becomes lover, and the uncle replaces him. In a final narrative replacement in this series of fathers and daughter, the lover becomes father. Throughout the novel, Clennam plays father to Little Dorrit, while she plays his child.[16] "Don't mind me," he tells her, "who, for the matter of years, might be your father or your uncle. Always think of me as quite an old man" (p. 434). Amy writes Clennam from Italy:

> What I have to pray and entreat of you is . . . that you will remember me only as the little shabby girl you protected with so much tenderness, from whose threadbare dress you have kept away the rain, and whose wet feet you have dried at your fire. That you will think of me . . . and of my true affection and devoted gratitude, always without change, as of your poor child, LITTLE DORRIT. (p. 524)

At the center of the novel, a crucial "recognition"—knowing-and-revelation—scene announces the identity of lover and father. Clennam tells Amy that her family will be free of prison and rich as well, through inheritance; "as he kissed her, she turned her head towards his shoulder, and raised her arm towards his neck; cried out, 'Father! Father! Father!' and swooned away" (p. 465). This remarkable naming of the lover "father" becomes accurate later when Clennam, having got into debt like William Dorrit, committed a "crime" to justify his pervasive sense of guilt, advertises himself as scapegoat and goes to prison—in a metaphoric sense, for all speculators. Clennam chooses to be incarcerated in the Marshalsea and winds up in the room the Father of the Marshalsea once inhabited; he dreams of Little Dorrit, and she suddenly appears, his "own poor child come back!" Amy performs for Clennam the loving tasks she once performed there for her father: she sits by his side, her "nimble fingers busy at their old work"; she "never move[s] from his side, except to wait upon him"; she sits by his bed at night "tending" him. In response, Clennam takes her "in his arms, as if she had been his daughter." Just as she nursed her father in that room, she "nurses and restores" Clennam: "Drawing an arm softly round his head, [she] laid his head upon her bosom, put a hand upon that hand, nursed him as lovingly, and GOD knows as innocently, as she had nursed her father in that room when she had been but a baby" (pp. 825–29).

The structural similarity of Clennam's and Dorrit's actions, the figural repetition of breast feeding, allows Clennam finally to replace

---

[16]Welsh, pp. 153–54 and 172–73, also discusses the relationship between father and lover in *Little Dorrit*, and my discussion of this issue is indebted to his.

the father, but in a scene different from the one he had envisioned. The father-daughter idyll creates a snug little space of peace and stasis, nurturing activities from both partners, intimate work and caring, unspoken affection and communication, both familial and sexual. Whether in the prison or at the hearth, this father-daughter idyll represents the same sweet death Clennam dreamed of by the Meagleses' river, the same peace Dorrit found in prison, the same deceptive snugness of the Plornishes' "Happy Cottage." Father-daughter incest represents a choice of willful submission, of temporal regression, of bourgeois isolation and privacy; it privileges values apparently scorned in the narrative search for originating paternity. Replacing the father, then, means bearing a burden of contradictory forces, love and death. Both lead, however, to the void that creates "nobody."

Metaphorical father-daughter incest in *Little Dorrit* ends in marriage, as the narrative attempts to atone for the unnarrated adultery that is the novel's absent origin. The father does not, however, simply marry the daughter. This central fantasy of marriage occurs, as we have seen, through displacement of relationship and motive, through doubling and disguise, through splitting and twinning of character, through metaphor.[17] William Dorrit, for example, projects his motivations onto his double and brother, Frederick, who displaces him in Amy's affections; Jeremiah Flintwinch's twin brother takes on half the actions of the "stolen will" plot; Clennam displaces his useless love for Pet Meagles onto her dead twin, Lillie; the apparently motiveless Rigaud, alias Blandois, alias Langier, acts out Clennam's hidden motives; Miss Wade mirrors Tattycoram, her self made ripe and rotten. The metaphorical marriage of father and daughter at the novel's conclusion both reveals and attempts to heal the narrative's splits, doubles, and twins.

This metaphorical marriage links not only father and daughter but other family members as well and so creates the genealogically repetitive horrors of incest. The hidden will, Uncle Gilbert's codicil,

[17]Albert D. Hutter applies Freud's mechanism, splitting of the ego, to Dickens' narrative technique in "Nation and Generation in *A Tale of Two Cities*," *PMLA*, 93 (1978), 448–62; " 'The High Tower of His Mind': Psychoanalysis and the Reader of *Bleak House*," *Criticism*, 19 (1977), 296–316; and other articles. See also Elaine Showalter, "Guilt, Authority, and the Shadows of *Little Dorrit*," *Nineteenth-Century Fiction*, 34 (1979), 20–40.

reveals and mediates these substitutions. When the plotless plot unwinds itself, the mistress of Arthur Clennam's father, not Mrs. Clennam, is Arthur's mother. The stolen codicil indicates that Mr. Clennam's mistress' patron's youngest daughter—or niece, if there is no daughter—shall receive recompense for Mrs. Clennam's crime against the mistress, the removal of the mistress' child, Arthur. The patron's youngest niece is Amy. The provisions of the will make no motivational, logical, or legal sense. No relation by blood links the Dorrits to the Clennams, and the lines of descent are absurdly torturous—as is the reader's job of unwinding them.

Yet the two families are motivational and genealogical mirror images. The Clennam family consists primarily of real orphans; the Dorrit family, of metaphorical ones. The Dorrits become a metaphor for Clennam repression, transgression, and punishment. The orphaned mistress links the two genealogies structurally, although she is related by blood to neither: she meets Arthur's orphaned father in Frederick Dorrit's dancing studio, and they later commit adultery. Thus Gilbert Clennam's codicil signifies that an uncle atones for a near-niece's sexual sin and punishment by leaving money to another uncle's niece. By virtue of uncle and niece, Little Dorrit resembles the orphaned mistress. She appears to be Arthur Clennam's metaphorical mother, both by analogy to the Clennam family tree and because his revealed parentage makes him lack a mother. Clennam and Amy are metaphorical son and mother, just as they are father and daughter.

Amy and Clennam also become metaphorical sister and brother through several narrative devices that collapse generation and family desire onto their marriage. Genealogically, the Clennam family in the novel consists of three generations, whose important members are (great-)uncle-father-son. In the Dorrit version of the same structure, Frederick, the uncle, is a brother to the father: uncle-father, by way of brotherhood, collapses the three male generations into two. William Dorrit, who is unable to play the role of father to his children, resembles the absent father of the Clennam family. What appears a difference in generational structure is also a similarity: (great-)uncle-(absent) father-son on one family tree, uncle-(metaphorically absent) father-daughter on the other. This genealogical symmetry of uncles and absent fathers makes Arthur Clennam and Amy Dorrit metaphorical sister and brother. Like Florence Dombey and Walter Gay, like David Copperfield and Agnes Wickfield, like Pip and Estella, they marry.[18]

This substitution of brother and sister for father and daughter also appears in an embedded narrative. When Mr. Dorrit asks Amy to tolerate John Chivery's advances, he tells a metaphorical story, about an ex-collegian and turnkey, that replaces him, as father, with "brother" and Amy, as daughter, with "sister": that brother (who is literally but not narratively a father) wants his sister (who is literally but not narratively a daughter) to coquet with the turnkey in return for prison favors and patronage (p. 271). Dorrit's narrative, like Dickens', generates a confusion that attempts to disguise similarity of situation by reference to difference, all the while admitting similarity and substitution and so creating guilt. Through complex denouement and disguised plotting, then, Dickens achieves in *Little Dorrit* the fantasied marriage of father and daughter, son and mother, brother and sister, all in the persons of Arthur Clennam and Amy Dorrit.

This metaphorical reunion of a family originally split by adultery and illegitimacy is an effort to heal the wound of sexual guilt. Clennam thinks, "If my father had erred, it was my first duty to conceal the fault and to repair it" (p. 787). The narrative conceals the fault through detoured plot and deferred inheritance and also repairs or redeems the fault through incest. The incest proves so metaphorically thorough, so exaggerated a cure that no other relationships can be imagined, no adultery conceived. Amy and Clennam's marriage appears the perfect narcissistic paradise. The entire family genealogy (the space and time of engendering identity and difference) and the entire Oedipal triangle (the structure of desire) collapse on this bride and groom. Mrs. Clennam's house collapses on itself, in the perfect metaphor for such incestuous desire. All other Clennams and Dorrits are now dead (except for Fanny and Tip, who don't count in the linking of Clennams and Dorrits by codicil and who have, through greed and vanity, lost their portions of the inheritance anyway). Clennam and Amy become orphans together, as well as father-daughter, son-mother, brother-sister. They are family and no family, victims and survivors. Their metaphorical

---

[18] See Jacques Lacan's analysis of Judge Schreber's case as resulting from lack of paternal metaphor, "On a Question Preliminary to Any Possible Treatment of Psychosis," in *Écrits: A Selection*, trans. Alan Sheridan (New York: Norton, 1977), pp. 179–225.

incest provides a paradoxical protection against life among the eager, the arrogant, the froward, and the vain.

Does this conclusion, however, undo Dickens' double narrative of a son and a daughter? Let us reconsider some deferred relationships between Oedipal structures and storytelling. Roland Barthes, in the passage I quoted earlier, states that "the pleasure of the text is *not* the pleasure of the corporeal striptease or of narrative suspense," which is an "Oedipal pleasure." The pleasure of reading, as Barthes's own text indicates in its radical structuring of our reading, inheres in the gaps of texts, in the discontinuities of language and narrative. As Barthes's alphabetically arranged fragments demonstrate, textual order is arbitrary yet inevitably linear. *The Pleasure of the Text* discusses and embodies the play of these textual oppositions, the pleasurable paradox of sequence and discontinuity in language and its structures. The "Oedipal pleasure," then, of narrative closure and knowledge that Barthes associates with tracking down the father must, by analogy with Barthes's own demystification of narrative form, appear equivocal at best. Oedipus himself never fully confirms his paternity but assumes it as known because it is prophesied and retold to him by others.[19] If narrative structure metaphorically attempts to confirm paternity, confer authority, and so know end and origin, it also demonstrates that the narrative search for the father and for full knowledge of the son's replacing that father can never be achieved. Limited human perception of the "truth," perhaps itself a metaphor, protects against the roar on the other side of silence. Fredric V. Bogel argues, in fact, that Dickens' melodramatic narrative discoveries (he offers as example Pip's discovery of his real benefactor) derive their intensity from the "striking failures of human knowledge," that patterns of knowledge in Dickens' novels "depend on human error and blindness."[20] *Little Dorrit* more than bears out Bogel's assertions: at the end of the novel, Arthur Clennam's metaphorical blindness repeats and resembles Oedipus' literal, yet dramatically metaphorical and ironic, blindness. The narrative's frequent gaps in motivation,

---

[19]For an examination of Oedipus' guilt from the perspective of René Girard's theories of scapegoating, see Sandor Goodheart, "Oedipus and Laius' Many Murderers," *Diacritics*, 8 (1978), 55–71. See also Girard, *Violence and the Sacred*, trans. Patrick Gregory (Baltimore: Johns Hopkins Univ. Press, 1977), Chs. vii and viii, and Cynthia Chase, "Oedipal Textuality: Reading Freud's Reading of Oedipus," *Diacritics*, 9 (1979), 54–68.

[20]Bogel, "Fables of Knowing: Melodrama and Related Forms," *Genre*, 11 (1978), 97–98.

its doubles, its rhetorical evasions, its pointless plot culminate in the novel's problematic, overdetermined, yet unfulfilled ending.[21]

The novel's final revelation, then, of its complex incestuous and father-seeking structure is also no revelation. Although Arthur Clennam suspects his father has "erred," Dickens keeps Clennam conspicuously absent from the denouement scene; and so Rigaud, Clennam's dark double, learns the secret about Clennam's paternity and birth that Clennam will never—in *this* narrative—know. The child-woman whom Clennam marries knows his secret, but she has equivocally promised to protect him from knowledge of it. In replacing the father, Clennam finds not the purpose and authority he'd hoped for but the lack of it; he finds the incestuous idyll of peace and stasis. Clennam can never know the truth of his Oedipal vocation, never engender the self, transform paternity, and end doubleness. The narrative revelation that originating fathers are corrupt, debased, and inauthentic must be hidden from the narrative's purposeless hero (a paradoxical repetition of his own father) because Oedipus' recognition of sonhood, however fictional, generates tragedy.

If the son fails in *Little Dorrit* to find an authentic vocation and so to replace and acquire knowledge of the father, if the narrative evades full disclosure of paternal secrets, what of the author who attempts to father himself by engendering narrative? Arthur Clennam's search for something stable to cure aimlessness, like David Copperfield's, Richard Carstone's, Sydney Carton's, Pip Pirrip's, and Eugene Wrayburn's, originates in the lack of paternal metaphor. The struggles of these aimless young and not-so-young heroes appear a metaphor for the struggle of the restless Charles Dickens. The later novels, then, disclose and disguise this narrative project: the attempt to write the paternal metaphor, the resemblance between father and son; to discover the failure of metaphor; and so to become one's own father, to create oneself. Clennam's narrative search stands in metaphorical relation to Dickens'. The purpose of this narrative for the

---

[21] See J. Hillis Miller's short meditation on the metaphor of knots and narrative closure, "The Problematic of Ending in Narrative," *Nineteenth-Century Fiction*, 33 (1978), 3–7. See also Alistair M. Duckworth's attempt to wed deconstructive criticism to humanism," *"Little Dorrit* and the Question of Closure," *Nineteenth-Century Fiction* 33 (1978), 110–30. Duckworth's article fails to confront its ambivalent response to its theoretical material; its Derridean terms are in quotes throughout the text and so become attenuated and tentative: "This essay has attempted both to attest to the power of Derrida's deconstructive mode and to restate the merits of a thematic criticism that is willing to become, to an extent, 'grammatological'" (p. 130).

writer, as for his hero, is to confront the guilt of the father. Yet Dickens the writer represses structural and narrative knowledge of the father. Metaphor begets its opposite, its double, catachresis. Narrative sequence, paternal origin as aim and endpoint, becomes attenuated. Full disclosure appears deferred beyond the limits of narrative. Just as Arthur Clennam's will-less father broke out of his religious repression to engender the events of this narrative, however, so Dickens' found fatherhood threatens to break through his repression of it and return to engender more narrative. As Pip's excoriating self-critique will demonstrate, the story of a father must be repeated—like this, yet differently.

# Patterns of Communication
## in *Great Expectations*

### *by Ruth M. Vande Kieft*

Much has been made of the theme of isolation and lack of communication in Dickens's novels. V. S. Prichett says of Dickens's people,

> [Their] distinguishing quality ... is that they are solitaries. They are people caught living in a world of their own. They soliloquize in it. They do not talk to one another; they talk to themselves. ... The people and the things of Dickens are all out of touch and out of hearing of each other, each conducting its own inner monologue, grandiloquent or dismaying. (*The Living Novel*, p. 88)

Dorothy Van Ghent supports this proposition by attempting to show exactly how the characters in *Great Expectations* soliloquize, how their communication fails and occasionally lapses into "the frenzied rotary unintelligibility of an idiot's obsession." Each soul is solitary, an integer, and

> you cannot make "order" with an integer, one thing alone, for order is definitely a relationship among things. Absolute noncommunication is an unthinkable madness for it negates all relationship and therefore all order, and even an ordinary madman has to create a kind of order for himself by illusions of communication. Dickens' soliloquizing characters, for all their funniness, ... suggest a world of isolated integers, terrifyingly alone and unrelated. ... Technique is vision. Dickens' technique is an index of a vision of life that sees human separatedness as the ordinary condition, where speech is speech *to* nobody and where human encounter is mere collision. (*The English Novel*, pp. 125–127)

The sources of these critical judgments are elusive, unless they spring from the assumption that to be successful or meaningful, relationships and ties between humans must be strictly logical, and always accompanied with or expressed by a completely rational process of articulation. The fact is that not only does each character in *Great Expectations* have a "language" sensitive and adaptable to human intercourse, but also the characters are bound together in a highly intricate pattern of relationships which provide for their interaction, communication, and final union with each other. This pattern, both in its comic and tragic effects, is the organizing principle of the novel, is Dickens's "vision" as well as his "technique" in *Great Expectations*.

It is possible first of all to demonstrate that language is not a problem in this novel. One piece of evidence Mrs. Van Ghent uses to illustrate the failure of language is the interview in which Mr. Jaggers discloses to Pip his great expectations, and Joe is offered a compensation for the loss of his apprentice. Shortly before the close of the interview, Joe "swings on [Jaggers]," Mrs. Van Ghent claims, "with unintelligible pugilistic jargon": " 'Which I meantersay . . . that if you come into my place bull-baiting and badgering me, come out! Which I meantersay as sech if you're a man, come on! Which I meantersay, that what I say, I meantersay and stand or fall by!' "

In context, however, this speech seems to me not only completely intelligible, but solidly motivated. Joe has been grossly insulted by Jaggers's implication that he does not keep his word, and is simply challenging Jaggers to a fight involving his honor. Repeatedly, both before and after the great disclosure, Jaggers has pressed Joe about his desire for compensation at the loss of Pip's services. Joe has refused it several times clearly and unequivocally, finally breaking down to the point of saying, " 'If you think as money can make compensation to me for the loss of the little child—what come to the forge—and ever the best of friends!—' " When Jaggers persists in questioning Joe's sincerity, it is too much, and the challenge bursts out of a heart charged with offended love and honor.

Mrs. Van Ghent cites as further evidence the scene in which Joe asserts pleasure in the art of reading when he can find *j*'s and *o*'s, of which he says, "there is no purer expression of solipsism in literature." But when has literacy ever been considered the *sine qua non* of human communication? (By the end of the novel Joe has become more or less literate, but that is irrelevant.) Mrs. Van Ghent says further that in the scene in which Magwitch enjoys hearing Pip read in a foreign language, "the cultivation of the peculiar Dickensian values of language reaches its apogee." This again seems to me a misinterpretation of the context. Magwitch's pleasure is so clearly motivated by his sense of the "prestige value" of knowing foreign languages, that intelligibility is beside the point. Pip's reading would be far less impressive, because far less a sign of accomplishment, if Magwitch *could* understand him. If he wants to speak to "his boy" he can, well enough, and often does at great length. His own language is quite adequate to what he has to express; in fact, at the scene of his sentence in court, it is almost unrealistically noble and profound.

Nor are the verbal "signatures" Dickens supplies for his characters meaningless: such phrases as Mrs. Joe's " 'Be grateful to them which brought you up by hand,' " Pumblechook's mincing " May I?—May I?' " and Wemmick's " 'It's portable property' " do not assume, as Mrs. Van Ghent suggests, "the frenzied rotary unintelligibility of an idiot's obsession": they are rather the clichés which serve as touchstones to the natures and motivations of their characters; meaningful, though not always logically or rationally so, both to those who utter and those who hear them.

Another of the passages Mrs. Van Ghent selects as an illustration of "fantastic private language" is significant as an example of oblique discourse. It is the interview Miss Havisham holds with Joe before Pip leaves her to be apprenticed to Joe as a blacksmith. Of this scene, Mrs. Van Ghent says, "for each question she asks him, Joe persists in addressing his reply to Pip rather than herself, and his replies have not the remotest relation to the questions." It is certainly true that Joe addresses himself to Pip, but it is patently untrue that his replies are irrelevant to the questions Miss Havisham is asking. Each of his statements answers her question exactly, though he talks to her obliquely, through Pip. The conversation goes like this (in brackets I provide dull commonsense paraphrases for Joe's delightfully baroque replies):

> MISS HAVISHAM: You are the husband of the sister of this boy?
> JOE: Which I meantersay, Pip, as I hup and married your sister, and I were at the time what you might call (if youwas any ways inclined) a single man. [Yes, Pip's sister has been my first and only wife.]
> MISS H.: And you have reared the boy, with the intention of taking him for your apprentice?
> JOE: You know, Pip, as you and me were ever friends, and it were looked for'ard to betwixt us, as being calc'lated to lead to larks. Not

but what, Pip, if you had ever made objections to the business—such as it being open to black and sut, or such-like—not but what they would have been attended to. [It wasn't so much that I reared him with the intention of making him my apprentice, as that the two of us have always looked forward to the joy of working together. Of course if Pip had had objections to the trade because of the filth involved, or for other reasons, I shouldn't have tried to force him into it.]

MISS H.: Has the boy ever made any objections? Does he like the trade?

JOE: Which it is well beknown to yourself, Pip, that it were the wish of your own hart. . . . And there weren't no objection on your part, and, Pip, it were the great wish of your hart! [No, he has always seemed to me very eager to do this.]

MISS H: Have you brought your indentures with you?

JOE: Well, Pip, you know, you yourself see me put 'em in my 'at, and therefore you know as they are here. (*Joe produces the indentures and gives them to Pip, who gives them to Miss H., who inspects them.*)

MISS H: You expected no premium with the boy? (*Joe is dumbstruck for an instant, obviously insulted and hurt at the suggestion. Pip remonstrates with Joe, is cut off by—*)

JOE: Pip, which I meantersay that were not a question requiring an answer betwixt yourself and me, and which you know the answer to be full well No. You know it to be No, Pip, and wherefore should I say It? [No, I expected no premium whatever—the idea is preposterous and insulting.] (*At this point the narrator asserts that "Miss Havisham glanced at him as if she understood what he really was, better than I had thought possible, seeing what he was there." She then takes up a small bag from the table beside her, and falling gracefully into the oblique pattern of communication established by Joe, presents the bag to Pip.*)

MISS H: Pip has earned a premium here, and here it is. There are five-and-twenty guineas in this bag. Give it to your master, Pip.

JOE: This is very liberal on your part, Pip, and it is as such received and grateful welcome, though never looked for, far nor near no-wheres. And now, old chap, may we do our duty! May you and me do our duty, both on us by one another, and by them which your liberal present—have—conweyed—to be—for the satisfaction of mind of them as never—(*Here Joe shows he has fallen into frightful difficulties, but he rescues himself triumphantly with the words—*) and from myself far be it! [Thank you for the gift, and you, Pip, for making it possible through your service of Miss Havisham. I certainly never expected it. I hope Pip and I will be worthy of each other, and of your generous interest as evidenced in this gift, which I must again say quite overwhelms me.]

After a final injunction from Miss Havisham that Joe is to expect no further reward but that of a good boy, the interview is terminated.

It is surely evident that there is genuine communication in this scene, that speech is speech *to* somebody, but one may well ask why it should be so circular—or more accurately, in this case, triangular. There is again a quite valid psychological motivation: Joe is in an agony of terror and wonder at this strange and formidable creature in her bizarre setting, and small wonder, considering what she is. What is more natural and human than to approach the unknown and frightening through the known and loved? In this indirect discourse Joe finds a delightfully spontaneous way out of his social and verbal difficulties, saves his dignity, and communicates successfully with Miss Havisham. But there is a further beautiful propriety in this indirect discourse, in that what transpires is essentially a ritual or ceremony, in which the chief participants are Pip and Joe, man and boy already held together by strong bonds of love, now being bound as master and apprentice in fulfillment of their long-cherished desire (though Joe at this point does not know of Pip's growing infidelity). Miss Havisham has a function only comparable to that of the justice of the peace or clergyman in a marriage ceremony: the lovers must make their vows to each other (and to God, in a religious ceremony), not the presiding official. Joe turns this potentially disagreeable business interview into a ceremony of love; he makes vows of duty and affection. It is no wonder he is distressed at the cold suggestion that he has been looking for money to come with the boy: it would be like asking an ardent groom, in the middle of the wedding ceremony, whether he expects his wife to bring him a fortune. He can accept Miss Havisham's money only as a groom might accept a wedding gift, and promptly gives it all to Pip's sister, who spends it on a general celebration.

Beautiful as is Joe's oblique expression, the scene as a whole strikes the reader as comic. This is because obliquity may be related to incongruity, one of the chief sources of comic effect, and there are many incongruities in the scene. Pip is aware of Joe's looking like "an extraordinary bird . . . with his tuft of feathers ruffled." He is standing in the presence of Miss Havisham, herself something grotesque in her fantastic surroundings; his speech seems, to the sniggering Estella, comically misdirected, and Pip is in a sweat of embarrassment. But though among the characters there may be some failure of sympathy, there is surely no failure of language to communicate effectively.

This is one instance of obliquity of discourse, and there are several others in the novel. It is a favorite device of Joe, who frequently speaks of himself or others in the third person, sometimes with a rhetorical flourish, sometimes out of delicacy (as in the scene in chapter lvii in which he prevents Pip from speaking out the painful truth about the history of Magwitch, to save Pip from humiliation). Indirect discourse, evasiveness, or deviation from directness in speech, is also used by Jaggers in relating to Pip the story of Estella and her mother, by Wemmick in his warnings to Pip concerning the safety of Magwitch, and again by Wemmick in his delightfully evasive wedding arrangements with Pip—in each case from a need, real or imaginary, for self-protection. In none of these instances, however, is obliquity of discourse any hindrance to finally successful communication.

If language is an effective agent of communication, the implication is that the persons speaking are in some way related to each other, that individual motives are at least perceived, if not shared, that meanings and assumptions are common, and hence understood. In *Great Expectations* much of this interrelation of the main characters in the novel comes from a common implication in guilt, a common process of suffering because of violation of the moral order, a common process of repentance and regeneration. The sins of parents against children and children against parents, and the sins of social snobbery, are elaborated throughout the novel: not only in the relationships among the principal characters, Joe, Pip, Magwitch, Miss Havisham, and Estella, but tangentially in the aristocratic pretensions of Mrs. Pocket and her abysmal failure as a mother; the false "adoption" of Pip by Pumblechook, and the reactions of the whole town to Pip during the three major stages of his career. And in this guilt, as Edmund Wilson has pointed out, "the highest and the lowest in that English society of shocking contrasts are inextricably tied together" (*The Wound and the Bow*, p. 42). There is a reason why, in Pip's fantasies, the glamorous images of Estella and Miss Havisham are so often strangely blended with the horrible images of convicts and Newgate prison.

The characters are related, then, in their state of shared guilt, which is compounded when the victims of these personal and social crimes take their revenge. But according to the Christian ethical pattern which Dickens follows in the novel, sin must be followed by punishment and repentance, which in turn must be followed by pleas for pardon. The first of the major reconciliation scenes in the novel is that in which Mrs. Joe asks forgiveness of Joe and Pip. Biddy describes the scene as follows:

"She had been in one of her bad states . . . for four days, when she came out of it in the evening, just at tea-time, and said quite plainly, 'Joe.' As she had never said any word for a long while, I ran and fetched in Mr. Gargery from the forge. She made signs to me that she wanted him to sit down close to her, and wanted me to put her arms round his neck. So I put them round his neck, and she laid her head down on his shoulder quite content and satisfied. And so she presently said 'Joe' again, and once 'Pardon,' and once 'Pip.' And so she never lifted her head up any more. . . ."

Her plea for pardon is echoed through the novel: Pip asks it of Joe and Biddy; Miss Havisham asks it of Pip (" 'Take the pencil and write under my name, "I forgive her" ' "); Estella asks it of Pip. But Pip recognizes a still higher point of reference than human forgiveness. Threatened with death at Orlick's hand, he "humbly beseeches pardon . . . of Heaven"; to Estella he says, " 'Oh God bless you, God forgive you' "; and at Magwitch's deathbed he prays, " 'Oh Lord, be merciful to him, a sinner!' "

Among persons so deeply involved with each other morally, so wise with the knowledge of evil and so chastened by suffering, it is not relevant to speak of problems of communication. The characters who share this understanding cannot be considered solitudes. Their language is adequate, and sometimes more than adequate. This final illustration, from Magwitch, riding out on the river toward the sea to meet—he knows not what: freedom, or another, and final, capture:

"We'd be puzzled to be more quiet and easy-going than we are at present. But—it's a-flowing so soft and pleasant through the water, p'raps, as makes me think it—I was a-thinking through my smoke just then, that we can no more see to the bottom the next few hours, than we can see to tne bottom of of this river what I catches hold of. Nor yet we can't no more hold their tide than I can hold this. And it's run through my fingers and gone, you see!" holding up his dripping hand.

"But for your face, I should think you were a little despondent," said I.

"Not a bit on it, dear boy! It comes of flowing so quiet, and of that there rippling at the boat's head making a sort of Sunday tune. Maybe I'm a-growing a trifle old besides."

This seems to me sensitive use of language, a clear sign that the persons communicating are closely in touch with each other's deepest feelings. By his words and his tone Magwitch has told Pip of his resignation, his realistic awareness of what dangers may follow; by the look on his face he has communicated his peace, and even, apparently, a mild hope and cheerfulness.

But though they use language, those two scarcely need it. "The old sound in his throat—softened now, like the rest of him" (Magwitch's inarticulate response to the unfamiliar and strangely moving human pity which first sparked his love for Pip), the pressure of Pip's hand— these are signs of a kind of love and mutual responsiveness which obviate the need for language.

There are in the novel at least two dramatic examples of the fact that language is not indispensable to human communication. One already alluded to is that of Pip's sister after she is struck dumb. Here communication is starkly basic and simple, but it is satisfactory: it is the inarticulate expression of the spirit of penitence and forgiveness. The other example is the case, half-tenderly, half-comically described, of the Aged P., Wemmick's father. He is shut off from human discourse by his deafness, and symbolically, from society, by his position in the little fortress surrounded by the little moat (" 'After I have crossed the bridge,' " says Wemmick, " 'I hoist it up— so—and cut off communication' "). Yet he is in no way really or essentially isolated, simply because he loves and is loved, and out of this wholeness of his being he reaches warmly to the outside world. There is something enormously satisfied and satisfying about this old man: "clean, comfortable, and well cared for." Language is useless, but rituals are important and effective as means of communication in his life: the nightly flag and gun ceremony, the vigorous nodding, the reading of the paper, the little wooden flap which announces names, and above all, the drinking of tea, an occasion at which everybody gets delightfully warm and greasy, and "the Aged especially, might have passed for some clean old chief of a savage tribe, just oiled."

It seems clear that in this novel Dickens does not present human isolation and the failure of communication: rather, his assumption closely resembles that famous one of Donne's, "No man is an island." Yet, though communication among the characters is generally and sometimes even beautifully successful, it has distinct limitations. It is primitive and basic rather than full, complex, or rich in nuance. Its boundaries are determined by the fact that all the characters, with the exception of Pip, are monolithic. Their characters are not really flexible and changing; the large movements of their souls, from sin and hatred to sorrow and repentance, do not serve to make them more complex and subtle in their dealings with others, do not equip them to enter with deep imaginative intelligence into each other's worlds. At the end Pip, who has grown more complex psychologically as well as morally, still seems to be left alone (at least in the first version of the ending), without promise of bliss; and the tone of the book is predominantly melancholy. This is because the narrator is so keenly aware of how life defeats personal happiness, and because he does not, despite the inclusion of Pip's prayers, really know or see beyond this life. Happiness which comes obliquely, through the joy of seeing others happy, is not really enough; the softened heart is left unfulfilled and hungry. Hence, though the ethical pattern of the novel is Christian, the vision is not, finally, religious: there is no real communication between God and man. There is only the basic communication of men who are related in guilt and sorrow, in forgiveness and in love.

It is this kind of communion, and communication, which some of Dickens's modern critics have apparently overlooked. It seems to me that they have rather superimposed a specifically modern problem on this novel of Dickens. It is the problem suggested by T. S. Eliot's description of "the intolerable wrestle with words and meanings": the burdening sense of isolation which comes out of a period in which the conventions of meaning and expression are questioned, because none are widely assumed; a period in which there are no contexts for unity and order. The process of social dissolution had, doubtless, begun by Dickens's time, but Dickens seems to have assumed he knew what "order" was, or ought to be. The narrator of *Great Expectations* states this clearly, though in terms largely negative, in his response to Miss Havisham's agonized cry of epiphany: " 'What have I done? What have I done?' " His response to her outburst is one of pity and tolerance for the sinner, but absolute condemnation of the sin, an attitude he has achieved through his own implication in guilt:

> I knew not how to answer, or how to comfort her. That she had done a grievous thing in taking an impressionable child to mold it into the form that her wild resentment, spurned affection, and wounded pride, found vengeance in, I knew full well. But that, in shutting out the light of day, she had shut out infinitely more; that, in seclusion, she had secluded herself from a thousand natural and healing influences; that, her mind, brooding solitary, had grown diseased, as all minds do and must that reverse the appointed order of their Maker; I knew equally well. And could I look upon her without compassion, seeing her punishment in the ruin she was, in her profound unfitness

for this earth on which she was placed, in the vanity of sorrow which had become a master mania, like the vanity of penitence, the vanity of remorse, the vanity of unworthiness, and other monstrous vanities that have been curses in the world?

"The appointed order of their Maker" is assumed as the norm in this novel, and the terms of that moral order are defined, both negatively and positively, in the lives of the characters. It may be called the metaphysical basis for the communication in this novel.

The kind of communication which Dickens presents in *Great Expectations* is free either to use or dispense with language: if to use it, to do so directly or obliquely, rationally or irrationally: if to be inarticulate, to employ symbolic actions which convey meaning through gesture, ceremony, or ritual. But it is always a kind of communication in which the deepest and most basic moral needs and intents of the human heart have been received by and conveyed to others.

# Communication in *Great Expectations*

## *by George Levine*

In her recent article on *Great Expectations*,[1] Ruth M. Vande Kieft convincingly shows that the characters in Dickens' novel do communicate and that they are not, as Dorothy Van Ghent has argued, "isolated integers." Modern critics, Miss Vande Kieft argues with salutary common sense, in their concentration on the problem of communion and communication, "have superimposed a specifically modern problem on the novels of Dickens." But if the characters in *Great Expectations* are "bound together in a highly intricate pattern of relationships which provide for their interaction, communication, and final union with each other," the plot of the novel nevertheless relies rather heavily on the characters' isolation and misunderstandings. There is even some question about how fully Pip achieves a "final union." It seems to me, therefore, that Miss Vande Kieft has overstated an essentially sound view. Dickens' evangelical conception of the interdependence of all mankind is in large measure undercut by his sense of the way in which contemporary society alienates the individual.

The problem is not entirely the modern one, a matter of what Miss Vande Kieft calls "the burdening sense of isolation which comes out of a period in which the conventions of meaning and expression are questioned"; but that problem is clearly anticipated. This is suggested by the very nature of Miss Vande Kieft's attack on Mrs. Van Ghent's position. The view that Dickens' characters are isolated integers, she asserts, can only spring from "the assumption that to be successful or meaningful, relationships and ties between humans

[1] Ruth M. Vande Kieft, "Patterns of Communication in *Great Expectations*," NCF, XV (March, 1961), 325–334.

must be strictly logical, and always accompanied by a completely rational process of articulation." It is unlikely that Mrs. Van Ghent was making such an unqualified assumption, but if one retreats in time about forty years from *Great Expectations*, one finds this is very much the assumption Jane Austen was making. Not that relationships for her were to be "strictly" logical or "completely" rational; but she required them, at least, to be reasonable. If *Emma*, for example, is full of misunderstandings, they are cleared up in large measure by Mr. Knightley's thoroughly and rationally articulated analysis of them. Moreover, Mr. Knightley is clearly intended to be the value center of the book. The assumption underlying *Emma* is that people are rationally related (although not exclusively so). Emma's position in society imposes on her the responsibility of being kind to Miss Bates and Jane Fairfax. Although she irrationally and selfishly rejects that responsibility, once having learned from her early errors she looks forward to a future when every year would "find her more rational, more acquainted with herself." When she discovers that Harriet is in love with Mr. Knightley, Emma feels for Harriet "with pain and contrition; but no flight of generosity run mad, opposing all that could be probable or reasonable, entered her brain." On the other hand, when one searches for a value center in *Great Expectations*, one finds only Joe Gargery who, if anything, is the embodiment of "generosity run mad." His behavior is never governed by what is reasonable, only by what is instinctively felt. The public and articulable solution has been replaced by the private and irrational one.

This suggests, and his other novels confirm it, that Dickens did not and could not believe in the possibility of rational relationships in Jane Austen's sense. Dickens' assumption is that human relationships are not and *ought not to be* rational. Society, as Miss Vande Kieft concedes, had already begun in Dickens' time its "process of dissolution." But she minimizes the effect of this dissolution on Dickens. J. Hillis Miller has observed, however, that "At the center of Dickens' novels is a recognition of the bankruptcy of the relation of the individual to society as it now exists, the objective structure of given institutions and values."[2] And that this recognition of bankruptcy is present in *Great Expectations* is clear from the way in which our sympathies in the novel lie with criminals, outcasts, and failures.

[2] J. Hillis Miller, *Charles Dickens: The World of His Novels* (Cambridge, Massachusetts, 1958), p. 277.

Moreover, the bankruptcy causes a diminished faith in conventional discursive language so that one finds the important failure of communication coming usually not as a result of the ungrammatical and elliptical language of a Joe Gargery, or the various eccentricities of the other characters, but as a result of perfectly rational and conventional language. Indeed, rationality and conventional knowledge are positive curses throughout the book. Pip's acquisition of literacy is the beginning of his break with everything Joe stands for. The more Pip "learns," as a matter of fact, the less honest and dignified he becomes. He learns to play cards, to despise dirty fingernails, to dress correctly, to talk grammatically. He learns to supply a "margin" when figuring his debts so that he can deceive himself into spending even more money.

The failure of society and language for Pip, as for Dickens, is the outgrowth of a failure of trust. Money is quite literally the root of evil for Pip and for his society. Once having got it (without any sense of meriting it), Pip loses his sense of belonging among the people he had loved. He manages, through a complicated mixture of egotism and guilt feelings, to impute to Joe and Biddy motives of which they are incapable. As Pip tries to assuage his conscience for leaving Joe and offers to send for him, Biddy replies, "Joe is too proud to let any one take him out of a place that he is competent to fill, and fills well and with respect." To this Pip responds self-righteously: "I am very sorry to see this in you. I did not expect to see this in you. You are envious, Biddy, and grudging. You are dissatisfied on account of my rise in fortune, and you can't help showing it." Here, because Pip feels that money has raised him above his original class, he twists and misinterprets perfectly honest, rational, and straightforward language. Without trust language is useless.[3]

All the important misunderstandings in *Great Expectations* can be traced back to a failure of trust. Either the listener distrusts the speaker and refuses to take what is said at face value, or the speaker uses language to deceive (very rarely, however, to lie directly). Except in the case of Joe and Biddy and, to some extent, Herbert Pocket

---

[3]The same kind of thing goes on in many of Dickens' novels. In *Bleak House*, for example, Richard Carstone questions (against his own better knowledge) the motives of Mr. Jarndyce in trying to dissuade him from pursuing the case of Jarndyce vs. Jarndyce. In *Little Dorrit*, Mr. Dorrit, after his release from prison, misinterprets almost everything said to him that is not hypocritically fawning. Like Pip, he turns away from the people who helped him most when he was poor.

and Wemmick, relationships in *Great Expectations* are primarily contractual. They are based on money, not trust and responsibility, and people become objects to be bought and sold. There is no longer any meaningful relation between the classes so that between the powerful and the weak in *Great Expectations* there is an almost insuperable barrier of misunderstandings. The bankruptcy of the aristocracy accounts in part for this brutal and disastrous disintegration of social relationships. What replaced the aristocracy, however, is equally bad. The relation of the middle class to the poor, as Dickens describes it, is based *in principle* on what is legal, and mere legality is dehumanizing (this, of course, is a favorite point of Dickens', one amply illustrated by Jaggers and Wemmick). The legal relationship, moreover, is traditionally based on the assumption that people cannot be trusted; its complex, subtle, and essentially deceitful language helps Pip trap himself in his illusions about Miss Havisham and Stella.

Pip's failure to understand Mr. Jaggers is beautifully symbolic of the dehumanizing effect of contractual relations. When Pip tells Wemmick that he hardly knows what to make of Jaggers, Wemmick replies, "Tell him that, and he'll take it as a compliment. . . . he don't mean that you *should* know what to make of it.—Oh! . . . it's not personal; it's professional: only professional." The dialect of contract is worked out most fully when Pip goes to Jaggers to ask if Magwitch is really his benefactor. When, after some contorted legalisms, Jaggers finally admits the truth, Pip says,

> "I am not so unreasonable, sir, as to think you at all responsible for my mistakes and wrong conclusions; but I always supposed it was Miss Havisham."
>
> "As you say, Pip," returned Mr. Jaggers, turning his eyes upon me coolly, and taking a bite at his forefinger, "I am not at all responsible for that. . . ."
>
> "Not a particle of evidence, Pip," said Mr. Jaggers, shaking his head and gathering up his skirts. "Take nothing on its looks; take everything on evidence. There's no better rule."

Language itself cannot be accepted at face value, for only evidence and facts are credible; and they are the foundation of contractual relationships. The idea recalls what Dickens had done somewhat earlier in *Hard Times*, where Mr. Gradgrind, placing his whole faith in facts, discovers that they have cut him off from understanding his own children.

Facts are only a part, and for Dickens the smaller part, of what ought to be communicated between people. What is primary is sympathy and love, without which even the facts are meaningless. For this reason, Miss Vande Kieft's intelligent and useful analysis of the scene among Miss Havisham, Pip, and Joe is not entirely satisfactory. It is undeniable that Mrs. Van Ghent was wrong in arguing that Joe's answers to Miss Havisham "have not the remotest relation to the questions." But there is also a fundamental misunderstanding in the scene which has nothing to do with the facts being discussed. Miss Havisham speaks in the same kind of legal language which later antagonizes Joe in his interview with Jaggers. Joe really cannot understand—a fact emphasized by the hurt and puzzled tone of his responses—why he should be subjected to such a legalistic inquisition. Miss Havisham's questions, perfectly sensible ones for any legal transaction, seem to Joe to be placing his good faith in doubt. Joe loves Pip and yet finds himself asked, "You expected no premium with the boy?" He will not answer this question until forced to. On the other hand, Miss Havisham cannot understand the essential nature of Joe's answers although she understands fully the facts he is communicating. Joe's answers, as Miss Vande Kieft correctly shows, are expressions of love to Pip. And the language of love, ungrammatical and irrational as it so often is in Dickens, is inaccessible to Miss Havisham.[4]

Full communication in *Great Expectations* comes usually through gestures, inarticulate noises, or ungrammatical and irrational speech. The click in the convict's throat (though it is understood only by regenerated Pip) is a statement of gratitude and love which, for Dickens, no rational speech could duplicate. Herbert Pocket's first long interview with Pip in their grim London rooms is successful not only because Herbert is so cordial but because his "every look and tone" expressed to Pip "a natural incapacity to do anything secret and mean." The relationship between the two is sealed by Herbert's absurd notion of calling Pip "Handel" because Handel had written the "Harmonious Blacksmith." Even Pip's virago of a sister manages

---

[4]The full point of the scene seems to me to be that there is a hopelessly strong barrier between the powerful and the weak. Whatever the literal reasons for Joe's refusal to speak directly to Miss Havisham (and Miss Vande Kieft's suggestions seem to me valid), that refusal suggests that there is no possibility of communication between the rich and the poor. Joe instinctively recognizes this and speaks to someone who, like him, is poor, and who is capable of understanding his expressions of love.

to communicate fully only when she has been struck dumb. She says all that needs to be said in a scene that Miss Vande Kieft quotes. Her last words are "Joe," "Pardon," and "Pip." Joe, of course, is the archetype of the fully communicative man, in this extended sense of term. The illiteracy and absurdity of his language always succeed in communicating honesty, openness, trust, and love. They fail only when others have hardened themselves in distrust.

These examples confirm Miss Vande Kieft's point that there is some kind of communication in the novel and that the specifically modern problem of alienation and misunderstanding is not fully developed in *Great Expectations*. But it is on its way to development. Instead of relying entirely on "strictly logical" and rationally articulated relationships, Dickens seems to reject such relationships entirely. Man's relation to man becomes idiosyncratic, irrational, and inarticulable. Conventional language is debased and conventional knowledge injurious. The disease of contractualism and legalism is only sporadically and infrequently cured. After Pip has been almost universally forgiven and has done all his forgiving, only Joe and Biddy remain unstained with guilt. They, however, are to lead their lives well outside both middle class and aristocratic society. But Mr. Pumblechook remains an unchastened hypocrite. Mr. Trabb keeps selling his wares with oily enthusiasm. Orlick is loose like Cain somewhere on the moors until he is captured for breaking into Pumblechook's house—an act strikingly unconnected to the rest of the plot. In London Mr. Jaggers remains a mystery to his cowering clients and to the death masks on the walls of his office. Wemmick, married though he is, continues his pursuit of "portable property" and refuses to allow one half of his personality to communicate with the other. Most important, however successful Pip has become, he is isolated both from the society of his false expectations (a world well lost) and from the perfect innocence of Joe and Biddy's love. Even if he marries Estella, as Hillis Miller suggests, he marries her with no illusions about society, Estella, or his guilt-stained self.

Thus it seems to me that Miss Vande Kieft distinctly overstates the case when she argues that "Among persons so deeply involved with each other morally, so wise with the knowledge of evil and so chastened by suffering, it is not relevant to speak of problems of communication." Only Pip, and perhaps Estella, is really wise with the knowledge of evil by the time the book ends, and that knowledge cuts both characters off from full assimilation into existing society. The old Christian context of order was still available to Dickens, and

Miss Vande Kieft is correct in suggesting that it underlies the moral development and the complex relationships of *Great Expectations*. But it is undeniably important and revealing that communication in the novel is "primitive and basic rather than full, complex, or rich in nuance." When Joe Gargery becomes a moral hero, the traditional order has failed the novelist. His elevation entails the rejection of the belief in the possibility of dealing intelligently and rationally with the problems of society. The incrustations of civilization which give to Jane Austen's novels this very fullness, complexity, and richness in nuance have fallen away from rot. The characters are thrown more fully and hopelessly back on themselves than ever before, and if they manage to emerge from isolation, it is only in a primitive way. Communication, in a sense that would have been meaninful in any ordered society, is beginning to fail them.

# Our Mutual Friend:
# A Rhetorical Approach to the First Number

*by John M. Robson*

One of the most appropriate words ever used to describe Dickens' special genius is *profusion*,[1] calling up hosts of remembrances of characters, situations, linguistic surprises; suggesting anew the Shakespearian resemblance and also the apparently wastrel character of his art. The kind of detailed reading demanded by a rhetorical approach consistently reinforces this judgment, but it also, especially when applied to a later novel, results in the somewhat contradictory, though now equally accepted, judgment that the loose baggy monsters are held together by vital tissues. The wastrel wants not a rationale for his bounteousness; Dickens' very profusion, rather than denying unity, actually serves it by giving individual details multiple purposes.

This is not the place to expatiate on the uses of classical rhetorical notions in the criticism of fiction, or to try to avoid rejection symptoms by outlining necessary modifications in rhetorical theory when explicating modern fiction. Risking misunderstanding, I shall attempt merely to show how some rhetorical considerations—to which others may well wish to give other names—help in an appreciation of Dickens' aims and achievements in *Our Mutual Friend*.

To begin, I assume that something valuable can be known about the effects Dickens sought; we can form and test hypotheses about his intention to influence his audience through the artistic manipulation of materials, controlled by his imaginative and moral vision, in a

---

[1] See G. M. Young, "Portrait of an Age," in *Early Victorian England* (London: Oxford University Press, 1934), II, 493, where the point is made with reference to *Our Mutual Friend*: " 'I want,' said Bella Rokesmith to her husband, 'to be something so much worthier than the doll in the doll's house.' In the profusion of Dickens, the phrase might pass unnoticed. Twelve years later Ibsen made it the watchword of a revolution."

form available to that audience. An analysis of this sort releases one from reliance on comparative judgments, and enables one to approach a work as unique and as defined by understood personal, historical, and generic parameters.[2] At the very least, Dickens may be seen as attempting, like a rhetor, to change his audience's attitudes and behavior.

It has been said that Demosthenes didn't want his auditors to think, "What a splendid orator!" but to shout, "Let us march against Philip!" Dickens too aimed, through the classical endeavors to please, instruct, and move, to gather a host to strive against the Philippian evil wherever it may be found, internally as well as externally, the private recognition being essential to the public action. Make 'em weep, and make 'em laugh, certainly, but use the tears and laughter to soften hard hearts, and make them pliant and resourceful in, quite simply, the betterment of the human condition.[3]

For the nineteenth-century author, whatever may be true of our contemporaries, fictions had a beginning, middle, and end. In classical rhetoric, this same argumentative necessity is recognized in the division of orations into *exordium*, *narratio*, *confirmatio*, and *peroratio*.[4] Bringing these two descriptions together, one can see the special functions of parts of a novel. Initially one must recognize the intermingling of parts, especially of the *narratio* (the laying out of the case)[5] and the *confirmatio* (the proof—in fictional terms the main thematic development through plot narration). In many Victorian

[2]It should be emphasized that what is here offered is not in any sense a full rhetorical analysis. Such an analysis would involve a consideration of all the rhetorical variables bearing on a particular work, including speaker, audience, occasion, subject, theme, argument, resistance, and materials. One major omission is the consideration of "invention," one of Dickens' great powers; when it is seen in the classical context, as involving intrinsic and extrinsic "proofs," one can bring to bear the biographical evidence. A mere mention of other omissions would bulge this note into another paper.

[3]See, for example, "Heaven knows we need never be ashamed of our tears, for they are rain upon the blinding dust of earth overlying our hard hearts" (*Great Expectations*, ch. xix).

[4]This is the standard division, though some theorists introduced other parts (and used other names) to deal with special cases and refinements. One other part often referred to is *confutatio*, worth mentioning here because Dickens embodies it in his "Postscript, In Lieu of Preface" to *Our Mutual Friend*, which, like his added prefaces to other novels, engages his critics in battle.

[5]In some novelists, for example Scott, the *narratio* is isolated, giving anguish to readers whose expectations have been differently trained.

novels the *peroratio* stands distinct, giving in the final chapter, often through projected plot summary, a satisfying conclusion to individual histories, and embodying, in described or predicted futures, support and recollection of thematic argument.

The *exordium* is a tricky matter. Its function is twofold: to inform the audience, and to capture its attention. These functions combine, for the uncaptured are the uninformed. In fictional terms it may be said that the novelist makes certain attractive promises, and the rest of the novel (mainly *confirmatio*) is a fulfillment of those promises. Surprises there may be—in a great novel there certainly will be—but, at least in retrospect or on rereading, these surprises will be part of the general promise. The *narratio* and *confirmatio* will also be initiated in the *exordium*, for (unless the novelist uses a special kind of preface) there will be a flowing from information about the theme to adumbration of plot elements, and narration (the main component of *confirmatio*) normally begins almost immediately.

Do these notions help in an appreciation of *Our Mutual Friend*? I must here restrict myself for the most part to the *exordium*, which may usefully be seen as comprising the first number part, that is, the first four chapters, and particularly chapters i and ii. Here we find, not unexpectedly, the beginning of the web (the literal meaning of *exordium*). Main settings, time, principal characters, tones, themes, plot: all are brought before us. The sense of mystery and confusion that controls most of the novel is established, for much of the detail as well as the adumbration is shadowy. So much is common in fiction: what is unusual is the amount of adumbration, and, even more strikingly, the ways in which the *narratio*, so painful in inexpert hands, is charged with multiple purposes.

Before turning to analysis and interpretation, it is necessary to call to mind briefly what the first four chapters contain. The short opening chapter, "On the Look Out," presents initially a tableau, set on the Thames between Southwark and London Bridges, of a boat containing two figures, Jesse and Lizzie Hexam, on the lookout for, and eventually finding, a body. A third character, later identified as Rogue Riderhood, comes alongside them just after the body is found, and is rebuffed by Hexam.

The second chapter, "The Man from Somewhere," contains a dinner scene at the Hamilton Veneerings, during which a wide array of Society is displayed and satirized. The desultory dinner conversation turns on a tale told by Mortimer Lightwood about John Harmon, the "Man from Somewhere," who is now returning to

England to inherit from his dead father the wealth represented by great mounds of dust, on the condition that he marry a young woman chosen by his father some fourteen years earlier. The chapter closes with the arrival of a message to Mortimer, who is the solicitor employed in the search for the heir, saying that the drowned body of John Harmon has been found in the Thames.

In Chapter iii, "Another Man," the scene shifts from the Veneerings as Charley Hexam, son of Jesse, takes Lightwood and his friend Eugene Wrayburn to the Hexam home. Then, after a scene in which a bewildered man who gives his name as Julius Handford appears and asks for directions, Jesse takes them, with Handford, to a police station, where the body, unknown by sight to anyone, is identified as Harmon's. There is then a scene in the Hexam home between Lizzie and Charley. The next scene, still in Chapter iii, is set in the Six Jolly Fellowship-Porters, a riverside public house where a coroner's inquest into the death is held. The chapter concludes with the police inspector puzzling over the suspected crime, and an elaborate trope describes the gradual passing of the Harmon murder from society's eyes.

Chapter iv, "The R. Wilfer Family, " moves to a new scene and set of characters: Reginald Wilfer comes from his work in the city, where he is employed by a firm owned by Veneering, to find his wife and two daughters, Bella and Lavinia, the elder of whom is the intended wife of John Harmon. They have just let a room to one John Rokesmith, who is revealed at the end of the chapter, and the number, to be none other than the Julius Handford who appeared and disappeared so mysteriously in the previous chapter.

It is perfectly apparent from this brief summary that Dickens accomplishes a great deal in these chapters: he gives three of the main settings,[6] and introduces all the central characters directly, except for Boffins.[7] The antecedent information necessary for plot development is given, and the plot itself strongly established. But, again, to say this is to say very little, for only a very incompetent novelist would fail to do as much, and many would have the plot more advanced. What is significant is the way in which Dickens

---

[6]There are some seven in all, including "Boffin's Bower," "Our House," Mortimer's and Eugene's chambers in the Temple, and up-river, plus some half-dozen less important ones.

[7]They appear, with Silas Wegg, in the opening chapter of No. II which, like other similarly placed chapters, takes on some of the tasks of an *exordium*. (Others, like the closing chapters of the Numbers, serve in part as transitions.)

rhetorically manages his materials so that every element serves to develop the reader's view of the novel's world, to move him into that world, to engage him in the thematic development, and—let it not be forgotten—to ensure that he will buy the next number, and the next, and the next.

The most comprehensive way to treat the rhetorical development is to raise a billowy spray of marginal commentary beside a thin waterfall of text, but fortunately I cannot do that here. More practicable is a selection of what seem to me important elements in the first chapter, followed by an account of contrasting and reinforcing elements in the second chapter, and to a lesser extent in the third and fourth, with the aim of showing how the *exordium* is confirmed in the rest of the novel.

First, then, the opening words: "In these times of ours, though concerning the exact year there is no need to be precise, a boat of dirty and disreputable appearance, with two figures in it, floated on the Thames, between Southwark Bridge which is of iron, and London Bridge which is of stone, as an autumn evening was closing in." The tense is past, but the time is present: we are in "these times of ours" (with a hint of "hard times for these times"?), and at any and every moment, for "there is no need to be precise." The vague present encompasses the action, and since we (as contemporary readers, that is) are in our own times, we need no historical guide to understand them; we too are engaged in them, caught in the web. In this sense, the novel takes the form of a "History of Our Times" (a popular genre in the nineteenth century), while retaining the force of the eighteenth-century fictional "Histories" to which Dickens owed so much. Less obviously, the opening phrase prepares for a central contrast in the novel: "In these times of ours" stands against "Once upon a time"—more of this later.

Between the iron and stone bridges, forming an initial frame with the banks (though not yet described, known to be slimy with mud and refuse), appears the boat, "dirty and disreputable." A closer view gives us the "two figures" in it, and the autumn evening "closes in"— the concluding *in* finishing what the opening *in* had begun.

A tableau, an engraving: with the second sentence a new paragraph begins, bringing the reader nearer, leaving him still with "figures," but now individualized and given slight characterization: a man (ragged, with grizzled hair) and his daughter (aged nineteen or twenty, dark). The action begins in the next sentence (cinema-conscious, we are likely to see the titles dissolving), as the girl rows and the father sits, eagerly looking out. A series of narrative directions serves to isolate the business he is upon: as we glance about with the narrator, we find no props to prove that he is a fisherman, a waterman, a lighterman, or a river carrier. Not often does a description depend on what isn't there, but here, we are told, there is "no clue to what he looked for"; the only clue, then, is that he looks to the river for something. The tide has returned, and they flow with it; this suggestion, a commonplace of course, is reinforced time and again, especially after the "Harmon Murder" flows on the tide and eventually out to sea at the end of chapter iii. The relation between the two figures gains definition as the girl looks with "a touch of dread or horror" at her father, while he looks only at the river. The dread and horror are transferred to us, for our sympathy goes to the girl: slightly as she has been characterized, she has already become the focus of our human engagement.

The novelist, like the rhetor, needs an appeal to ethos, to personality; this can be established through the understood character of the narrator (and Dickens makes use of this device later on, most markedly in the Social Chorus scenes and when interpreting Betty Higden's terror of the workhouse); but thus far the narrator has confined himself—apart from the "our" in the first sentence—to an impressionistic rendering of what the scene itself most dominantly reveals. (It may be noted that we are not even led to this scene; we simply find ourselves in it.) Dickens is restricted, then, to entering into and forming our judgment through a character. Noticing that this as yet unnamed girl is the focus of our initial sympathy, we may recall, after finishing the novel, that it ends with discussion of her—indeed of her as a "female waterman"—and so be led to establish the center of the novel not in the Belle Wilfer–John Harmon plot, but in the Lizzie Hexam—Eugene Wrayburn plot, which has more loading of social message than the former, and comes to its climax after the former.

Having initiated his appeal to ethos, Dickens begins a major thematic development by devoting a paragraph to establishing that their unexplained and unusual search is not to them rare or inappropriate to their setting. A major thematic note is given the opening place, as the boat is seen (or interpreted) to be "allied to the bottom of the river rather than the surface, by reason of [its] slime and ooze . . . and sodden state." The man and girl are the first of the many in *Our Mutual Friend* to seek to bring up from detritus something of value; the surface is bad enough, it is abundantly made clear, but what lies beneath it, who would habitually search for it, and what evaluatory scale can prize it?

In the next paragraph another narrative element appears, as for the first time the man speaks, giving an order to his daughter and at the same time naming her as Lizzie. He himself remains unnamed until the third character in the scene, also unnamed, identifies him as "Gaffer," then as his "pardner," and finally as "Gaffer Hexam, Esquire." This last naming, coming just after his insinuating attempt to assume a part in the enterprise of another, further serves to characterize him, and, as well as showing his prickly pride, prepares us for the implicit toadyism of his "T'other Governor" and "T'otherest Governor"; we also are prepared for parallel developments in Silas Wegg, with his named hierarchy of imagined social precedence.

The scene is gloomily lit, the brownness of the man's face and arms and the girl's darkness being generally tonal and descriptive, rather than illuminating, until "a slant of light from the setting sun" colors, "as though with diluted blood," a stain in the bottom of the boat that bears a "resemblance to the outline of a muffled human form." Lizzie shivers at the sight, strengthening the impression of her "usage" of horror, while her father merely asks what "ails" her, for he sees "nothing afloat"; the "red light" goes, along with her shudder. In this frankly melodramatic sequence is thus signalled one of the three dominant colors in the novel, which is surprisingly bare of other vivid tones. Red is almost always associated with blood, usually shed blood, though occasionally with its vital force (in contrast with pallor). Black is a common descriptive element, as usual in Dickens, associated with fog, gloom, grief, mystery, and surfaces. The third and predominant color is gold, denoting or connoting money or gilt surfaces.

The thematic force of gold is also brought before us in the opening chapter, when the search proves fruitful. The man, after reaching into the water and securing what he finds there, washes (surely an inadequate cleansing) a coin he holds in his right hand,[8] chinks it, blows and spits on it, "for luck."[9]

[8]At various places in the novel, the right hand is identified as the "business" hand, used for mucky tasks, including insincere handshaking. The most important episode is when Boffin, rudely bidding farewell to the disgusted Bella, offers her his left hand, saying "it's the least used." Also, Sophronia Lammle takes the £100 given to her as "Cashier" in her left hand. The right hand can, however, also be the conveyor of love; Lizzie kisses hers to her father half a page after he washes his.

[9]The words "for luck," appear in quotation marks, followed by "he hoarsely

Money and luck together, brought from the depths. At his point, after the father has chastised the girl for not welcoming what the river, her "meat and drink," the provider of her fuel and of the materials of her cradle, brings, the other man, Rogue Riderhood, appears, strengthening the theme of hazard by saying (and for the first time giving the first man a name): "In luck again, Gaffer?" Rogue is, like a degenerated Pip, a man of great and unearned expectations: the "sweat of his honest brow," emphasized by him time and again, drops only on lucky rewards, turned up by his unending search for the hidden, whether in the pockets of a live sailor (referred to almost immediately, as Gaffer repudiates his "pardnership"), in the coffers of the owners of the steamer that later runs through his boat, almost drowning him, or in the hidden reaches of Bradley Headstone's passion. The quick and the dead are one to him—but not to Gaffer, who indignantly "assert[s] the high moralities," and delivers himself of an angry dissertation on the distinction between taking from a dead man what he can't have or use, and robbing a live one. The narrator's ironic comment about "high moralities" gives this episode a lingering force: Riderhood is morally dismissed, and properly so; Gaffer's position is somewhat equivocal, for Dickens tries to save him from condemnation—he is loved by Lizzie, a "good" character, and hated by his son Charley, a "bad" character—but his trade, Dickens surely avers, is not an honest one.

In any case, the comment comes in the last paragraph, which is marked by a departure from the narrator's stance as merely a percipient observer. To this point, he has given us just what might be seen to have happened; as he concludes his description of the

said," though they come in the midst of the narrator's external description of Gaffer's actions. I here cannot deal with unusual variants on reported and direct speech. Attention should also be drawn to a descriptive term that becomes a thematic signal in the next paragraph of description: "He was a hook-nosed man, and with that and his bright eyes and his ruffled head, bore a certain likeness to a roused bird of prey." The associated symbolic pattern having been so well treated by others, I need refer only to R. D. McMaster's "Birds of Prey: A Study of *Our Mutual Friend*," *Dalhousie Review* 40 (1960–61), 372–81, and Richard A. Lanham's *"Our Mutual Friend:* The Birds of Prey,"*Victorian Newsletter* 24 (Fall 1963), 6–11. Professor McMaster also touches on the question of disguises and roles, treated below, as do Robert Morse, *"Our Mutual Friend,"* *Partisan Review* 16 (1949), 277–89, and Masao Miyoshi, "Resolution of Identity in *Our Mutual Friend*," *Victorian Newsletter* 26 (Fall 1964), 5–9.

Hexams' rowing off, he permits himself a summary comment on the past and a mind's interior, unknown and unknowable to the reader: "A neophyte might have fancied that the ripples passing over it[10] were dreadfully like faint changes of expression on a sightless face; but Gaffer was no neophyte and had no fancies."[11]

Now, to dwell more fully on these matters, using the following chapters as resource:

The world we are invited to enter is a forbidding one, drawn with that realism in detail, but not realism in treatment, noted, I believe by Saintsbury, as habitual to Dickens. The heavy drawing, the loaded mystery and suggestions of unexplored evil, the *outré* quality of the main character, the threat of violence, the dread and terror of the girl: all these suggest not realism but melodrama. But without committing oneself further at this stage, one can see that the melodramatic urge is in the service of genuine emotion: the horror we are invited to share is a legitimate horror, founded in the universal terror of violent death; the stock repugnance at tainted money is fed by the all-too-apparent reality of its attraction; the relation between Gaffer and Lizzie, even as here sketched, is not the hackneyed father-daughter item of the stage. And the contemporary reader, drawn into "these times of ours," would recognize the main setting as starkly but not falsely etched. This is, then, the "real" world, and its actuality is soon made more apparent by contrast.

Chapter ii begins with none of the mystery of chapter i, except in burlesque, including what I here must pass by, burlesque of the narrator's act, especially in the tale told, all unknowingly, of the background to the action of chapter i.[12] Remembering how hesitantly

[10]"It" is, of course, the corpse, never so identified in the chapter. In the Number plan (now in the Pierpont Morgan Library), a note reads: "It in tow," with "It" underlined three times; in the chapter notes, however, Dickens permits himself to write "the body." The Number plans are printed in Ernest Boll's "The Plotting of *Our Mutual Friend*," *Modern Philology* 42 (1944), 96–122; the cited notes are on 102.

[11]In the earlier passage mentioned as dwelling on the habitual behavior of Gaffer and Lizzie, the narrator infers their "usage" from their present behavior; he knows no more than any percipient viewer—the reader—would know.

[12]Some of the phrases used by Mortimer in his tale will, without comment, establish the point: he is "sorry to destroy romance by fixing [John Harmon] with a local habitation"; he sees the story (which obviously has its fascination for him) as "not at all statistical and . . . rather odd"; Old Harmon "lived in a hollow in a hilly country," he says, as he finally launches into the story; he goes on to say that Harmon's daughter was "secretly engaged to that popular character whom the novelists and versifiers call Another," and that they "lived in a humble dwelling,

we are given the histories and names of the two main figures in chapter i (Riderhood isn't named until chapter vi), we cannot but note that the very first words of chapter ii give name and history, such as they are: "Mr. and Mrs. Veneering were bran-new people in a bran-new house in a bran-new quarter of London." The characters and other props are ticketed and listed as soon as the dominant tone has been sounded to full effect. Newness, varnish, stickiness; grandfather, if needed, in storage at the Pantechnicon—not needed, so here is Twemlow, an innocent but convenient piece of dinner-furniture on easy castors.[13] Some time is spent on Twemlow (a signal, in Dickens' uncondemning satire on his ineffectualness, that we are to expect well of him) to establish his confusion over a pressing problem in social relations: is he, or is he not, the oldest friend of the Veneerings? They of course have no friends, and their acquaintants have no characters. This state of nonentity has no importance for the Social Chorus that packs round the Veneerings' dinner table; only a fool like Twemlow would hold his hand to his head over such a triviality.[14]

This Social Chorus is not "real"; apart from those needed in the plot, they have no names, only functions, and even these we take for granted, for we never see them performed.[15] They are slightly differentiated by the shading of opinions that come ready made with their roles; in general, however, they have no color, only glitter,

---

probably possessing a porch ornamented with honeysuckle and woodbine twining"; and, after one of the many interruptions, he continues, "We must now return, as the novelists say, and as we all wish they wouldn't, to the man from Somewhere."

[13]Once again a critic's acuteness makes analysis of a trope unnecessary: see, as a gloss on *Our Mutual Friend*, Dorothy Van Ghent's comments on thing as man and man as thing in "The Dickens World: A View from Todgers's," in *Dickens: A Collection of Critical Essays*, ed. Martin Price (Englewood Cliffs, N.J.: Prentice-Hall, 1967), 24–38 (reprinted from *The Sewanee Review*).

[14]Another character in *Our Mutual Friend* has to give way to puzzled head-holding: Jenny Wren, when she can't distinguish between Fledgeby and Riah as component elements in Pubsey & Co. Like Twemlow, she is unaware of the rules of the game, and so is bewildered by false fronts.

[15]Dickens in fact seldom shows people actually at work; his plots, like those of most novelists, take place in the interstices of the workaday world. Usually only his professional men perform their functions on stage: clergymen, doctors, teachers, lawyers (Mortimer, even, does some of what little work he has to do in front of us), and then the description is normally perfunctory or summary. Exceptions in *Our Mutual Friend*, each of them instructive thematically, include Gaffer, Rogue, Fledgeby, and Jenny Wren.

varnish, powder, and bluff. They are "new": more than once their purposeless chatter is set off by an inquiry as to "news"—and there never is any. Surface dwellers, they make ripples but are carried by the current, and like Riderhood (who is, however, flesh and blood), they look to chance, to speculation, as a lever to raise money and themselves.[16] This impression of evanescence is strengthened by Dickens' use of the present tense in the Chorus scenes;[17] similarly, the emphasis on the impermanence of their dwellings suggests their rootlessness.

Rhetorically, the contrast between the controlling visions of chapters i and ii is a *topos*, a "commonplace," in one of its most frequently used fictional forms, though Dickens goes beyond the normal use by ringing changes on the narrative mode and does not use a single observer to give us a clear basis for comparative judgment. By placing "low" against "high" life, the Newgate threat against the Silver Fork tinkle, he is able to intensify both, as we feel suspenseful and fascinated dread of the first, and take satiric and mordant delight in the second. More, he is able to suggest the life-in-death of the former, and the death-in-life of the latter, while maintaining suspense even about his—or the narrator's—preferences. At the same time, his main purposes—to entice the reader (*exordium*), and to give him sufficient knowledge to follow the plot and enough hints to suggest the theme (*narratio*)—are well served, and the plot development begins (*confirmatio*).

But the *topos* of comparison does not exhaust the angles of vision in these chapters. In what may be viewed as a *topos* of relation, for it connects the two other worlds, being found in both in distorted forms, Dickens employs "once upon a time," the world of romance and childish vision, to suggest that even in "these times of ours" the once may be future, and even present.

In the second chapter, to get Mortimer Lightwood started on what is essential to the *narratio*, the history of the Harmon case, Lady Tippins, in a grotesque parody of coyness, coaxes him (tapping her

[16]Podsnap is marked as at least a partial exception. He starts off with "a fatal freshness" (cf. note 47 below), but is finally seen as, like his plate, solid—and his friends are not the friends of Veneering, though the latter's good table attracts their greed. Is Podsnap, unlike Sydney Smith, who sank by his levity, like Smith's brother, who rose by his gravity? Or is it that his particular speculation, Marine Insurance, is, in the world of the novel, a sound one?

[17]In chapter ii the action begins in what may be called "past-present," but shifts to the present as the Chorus is assembled.

fan on the knuckles of her *left* hand) to tell the story of "the man from Jamaica." The conversation takes a "languid"[18] and surprising course through Eugene Wrayburn's half-remembered jingle about the "man from Tobago," "our friend ['Mutual'?] who long lived on rice-pudding and isinglass, till at length to his something or other, his physician said something else, and a leg of mutton somehow ended in daygo."[19] Lady Tippins chides Eugene for "pretending" not to remember his nursery rhymes, and then cajoles Mortimer with: "Tease! Pay! Man from Tumwhere!"

Now apart from the necessity that the reader know about Harmon, this exchange, in its immediate context, has the force, first, of placing Lady Tippins and the assembled company in a strong satiric light.[20] Second, the exchange of pleasantries deepens the mystery by throwing out half-hints and mistaken assumptions about the main plot, a process furthered by different means in chapter iii. But when seen in the context of the whole novel, it has yet a further force as an exordial opening of a remarkable series of references to nursery rhymes, games, and tales, songs, ballads, adages, and images of childhood, with interspersed references to romances and (usually with strong ironic intent in Chorus scenes) to classical myth.[21]

Just how remarkable the series is could be shown by a complete catalog, not here practicable. Everyone will recall Silas Wegg's ballads and Jenny Wren's songs, and possibly the narrator's "See the

---

[18]The relevant note in the Number plan reads: "Languid story of Harmon the Dust Contractor" (Boll, p. 102).

[19]The source is a limerick from *Anecdotes and Adventures of Fifteen Gentlemen* (London, 1822), possibly by R. S. Sharpe, that first inspired Edward Lear's adoption of the form:

> There was a sick man of Tobago,
> Who liv'd long on rice-gruel and sago;
>   But at last, to his bliss,
>   The physician said this—
> "To a roast leg of mutton you may go."

See William S. Baring-Gould, *The Lure of the Limerick* (London: Panther Books, 1970), 39, 41. I am indebted for the reference to my colleague, Michael Laine.

[20]The four Buffers join in with "You can't resist!" and Mortimer says he feels "immensely embarrass[ed] to have the eyes of Europe" upon him, when his story—a tale of suffering, life, and death—is such a bore.

[21]One may mention—without any intention of upsetting the standard view of Dickens' small Latine, and lesse Greeke—some of the classical references, normally applied by the narrator for satiric purposes: Antinous, Argus, the Colossus at Rhodes, Cupid, Cymon, the Fates, the Graces, Hymen, Jupiter, Mercury, the Muses, Neptune, Pegasus, Priam, Romulus and Remus.

conquering Podsnap comes, Sound the Trumpets, Beat the Drums," and also the book titles: "Cup and Lip," Birds of a Feather," "A Long Lane," and "A Turning." Most of the others are so embedded in the narrative, however, and serve other purposes so immediately and convincingly, that their cumulative effect may, especially on first reading, pass by us. Let me mention some of them of varying significance: the echo in Rogue Riderhood's name is picked up in "little Rogue Riderhood and the wolf" about halfway through the novel, and the tale appears frequently, with variations, in Jenny Wren's view of Pubsey & Co., as Riah changes in her eyes from fairy godmother to wolf and back again. Fledgeby ends as "little eyes," the fox. Tales from the *Arabian Nights*[22] and the *Tales of the Genii*, both of which are explicitly mentioned, are frequently referred to, almost always by the characters themselves, not the narrator: Aladdin's palace, the sultan's tub of water and his buying a slave, speaking fish, ogres, and the genie, for example. Cock Robin, "Bee-Bah, black sheep," Peter Piper, Jack Horner, Mrs. Hubbard's dog, and Jack and the Beanstalk all appear, as do Gulliver, Robinson Crusoe, "the merry greenwood of Jobbery Forest," and Don Quixote. Of games, we see Bella getting her father's foot to the mark, hear the Boffins' narrative go on its way to "Once! Twice! Three times and away!" and listen as Silas Wegg comments, on Noddy Boffin's prowling round the dustheaps, that he's "getting colder and colder! Now he's freezing!" and perhaps most strikingly, we feel distress with Mortimer at Eugene's searching of his motives and identity with the jingle: "Riddle-me-riddle-me-ree, p'raps you can't tell me what this may be?"

Such references are, as has been often noted, a regular feature of Dickens' imaginative projections, but their density in *Our Mutual Friend* suggests more than a habitual recurrence to stock items.[23] In other novels, as here, we have suggestions that fairies bring up nurselings, that there are many orphans deprived of love-cradled visions and adults similarly deprived of imaginative needs by childlessness.[24] Dickens' use of perceptual and imaginative magnification

[22]Dickens often referred to novelists as responsible for a thousand and one tales, in an interesting amalgam of childhood memory and professional duty. See, e.g., Edgar Johnson, *Charles Dickens: His Tragedy and Triumph,* 2 vols. (New York: Simon and Schuster, 1952), 364, 749.

[23]The commentator closest to my view is Robert Morse in *"Our Mutual Friend"*; see pp. 280–81.

[24]This lack is not sentimentally treated in *Our Mutual Friend*, and anyone who feels inclined to sorrow greatly over the Boffins' childlessness might well remember

(another *topos*) as a symbolic device is readily recognized in his other works. But here, it seems to me, the fully developed rhetorical handling of these materials, in connection with two alternate angles of vision (not one, as in *Oliver Twist*) and presented in a common time scale (not in a retrospective one, as in *David Copperfield* and *Great Expectations*), allows Dickens to present the child's vision as more integral with, and hence more effectual in transforming, these times of ours.

To help make the point, let me cite what may seem a strained example. In Chapter ii the Veneerings' guests are moved from reception to dining room when their servant (soon to be finely tagged the Analytical Chemist) announces: "Dinner is on the table!" The narrator interprets the announcement for us: "Thus the melancholy retainer, as who should say, 'Come down and be poisoned, ye unhappy children of men!' "[25] This is apparently a throwaway bit of characterization, which also gives a sardonic, if incomplete, view of society's folly. But the phrase echoes, at least in my mind, to resonate with Jenny Wren's haunting call, later in the novel, to "Come up and be dead!"[26] Her invitation is not offered from the never-stilled dead center of the whirling world, but from a "garden" on top of that microcosm of the speculative chaos, Pubsey & Co., a garden high enough for Jenny at least to be clear of the City's blinding dirt and deafening noise. Here a strong Blakeian note is sounded, with children on slants of light lifting up the suffering to joy in innocence. The "poison" of the Veneerings' table is left below, and a true golden glow surrounds human love and peace.

This is the pure vision, but its broken and reflected lights gleam

---

that Dickens himself was only too aware of the perils of overfecundity. See, for example, his contemporary comment to Lytton: "What a wonderful instance of the general inanity of Kings, that the Kings in the Fairy Tales should have been always wishing for children! If they had but known when they were well off, having none!" (Letter of 16 July, 1866, quoted in Johnson, II, 1065.)

[25]There is no room here to comment on Dickens' use of mock-epic and mock-biblical phrases, especially in conjunction with reported speech. Also worthy of notice, but ignored here, are his hypothetical tropes (in this case, "as who should say"), which are frequent enough (though not so frequent as in, for example, Hawthorne's *Scarlet Letter*) to give a sense that speech and gesture need interpretation, and also that interpretation is likely to be somewhat askew.

[26]Jenny also calls Riah to "come back and be dead!" in the garden, and, dismissing Fledgeby because he is not "dead," tells him to "get down to life!" And when Bradley Headstone wrestles Riderhood into the water and death, he cries, "Come down!"

fitfully for most of the characters, as is seen in the mass of references to the child's world that make up, in my view, much of the *confirmatio*. Even Fascination Fledgeby is caught up, mentioning several times to Jenny her strange "game," though his clouded vision can see in it only a possibility of strategic gain for himself. The most important plot resolution, the Harmon-Wilfer marriage, both in episode and image (the baby's nursery, with birds, flowers, and gold and silver fish)[27] fulfills the fairy tale's promise. Boffin's ludicrous Bower (split between "low" comfort and "high-flying Fashion") is matched by the "golden bower" of Jenny's loosed hair, which startles the worldly and shields confidence and love.

The potential sentimentality of this device is removed by the integration of worlds that is prepared for even in the *exordium*. The child's vision does not exist as an unattainable alternative, as feeble in its true promise as it is strong in appeal. The interlocking of the characters' lives, primarily an element in the *confirmatio*, most obviously provides the needed unity, but the unity is made persuasive by a variety of tropes involving images of ascent and descent that begins, as already noted, in the opening chapters. There is of course irony, inescapable as well as powerful, because the common uses of *up* and *down*, of *surface* and *depth*, refuse easy and constant association with any pair as *good* and *bad*, *healthy* and *diseased*, *life* and *death*, or *truth* and *lies*.

The corpse of the opening chapter, "not *much* worse than Lady Tippins,"[28] rises to be caught, though long battered by the tides; so do all the other bodies found by Gaffer (including that of Jenny Wren's grandfather, who appears on one of the bills on Gaffer's wall in chapter iii). Only Riderhood and Headstone, found "lying under the ooze and scum," do not surface.[29] Eugene floats to be rescued by Lizzie, who "by main strength took him up, and never laid him down until she laid him down in the house." Her actions, as the narrator stresses, and as we know from the opening chapter (and the

---

[27]Another example is the Children's Hospital where Orphan Johnny dies. Its description may be compared, as another example of rhetorical use of materials, with Dickens' comments on the hospital in Great Ormond Street. See K. J. Fielding, ed., *The Speeches of Charles Dickens* (Oxford: Clarendon Press, 1960), p. 251.

[28]This is again apparently a throwaway line, illustrating Eugene's flippant morbidity, but its further importance is indicated by its being on cue from an entry in the Number plan (Boll, p. 102).

[29]Riderhood's "eyes were staring upward"; since they were locked face to face, Headstone's burning gaze must have been relentlessly downward.

number plan), are of "usage,"[30] though this time "it" becomes "he," and she has no horror. It is also usage for her to save, as we have seen in the death of Betty Higden, " 'Bless ye! *Now* lift me, my love.' Lizzie Hexam very softly raised the weather-stained grey head, and lifted her as high as Heaven."

The primary effect of this imagery is not, however, apocalyptic (or, to the cynical, sentimental); the real world of these, our times, is not devoid of transforming, though mundane, promise. The power of love can reconcile depths and surfaces. One of the most effective *topoi* Dickens uses for this effect is the parallel between Lizzie Hexam and Bella Wilfer, approaching finally a doubling. Betty Higden, in the scene last cited, mistakes Lizzie for "the boofer lady," Bella, who has irradiated the dying hours of her great-grandson, Orphan Johnny. The instinctive empathy of Bella and Lizzie is brought out in their confiding together their motives and hopes—an unusual scene for Dickens, showing how differently and more powerfully he is able to treat young women in this novel.[31] As this device is developed later in the novel—Bella and Lizzie do not meet in the first Number—I shall not pursue it here, though it may be mentioned that hints in chapter iii enable us to forecast Bella's hiding her fundamental attractiveness by a glitter of money, which draws the wrong prey; she finally moves upward into joy only by apparently descending socially.

Lizzie's thematic importance, however, is strongly suggested in the early chapters. She is, like her father and their boat, not allied to surfaces, and her drawing is explicitly like a magnet's. In chapter iii, as soon as Charley mentions his sister, Eugene grabs him roughly by the chin; later in the same chapter, Lizzie quietly exits when she finds Eugene staring at her; he is driven by her not only to seductive pursuit, but to pursuit of his own elusive nature, hidden even from himself by his languid, "absurd" surface.[32] This power of Lizzie's is substantiated later in the novel when Eugene's rival, Bradley Headstone (another double), reacts in parallel fashion. His destructive unexplored depths are similarly brought out by Lizzie; he too is

[30]Dickens' notes for the Number include "Back to the opening chapter of the story" [underscored in notes]; for the chapter they include "Back to the opening chapter of the book, Strongly," with "Strongly" underlined three times (Boll, p. 118).

[31]As has been suggested before, this ability may reflect Dickens' new knowledge, gained from his liaison with Ellen Ternan.

[32]Concerning his table manners, it might be noted that, unlike Gaffer, who violently strikes downward at the table with his all-purpose knife, Eugene merely "trifles quite ferociously with his desert-knife."

unaccountably interested in Charley's first mention of his sister; and after his first sight of her he is plunged into schizoid pursuit of incompatible goals. In his schoolmaster's role he is eminently "respectable," though he looks as though he is wearing another man's clothes; in his role as vengeful lover, he descends to the depths of masquerading as Rogue Riderhood, and appears for the first time as though in his own dress.

Charley too is important in these early chapters, as his inchoate attitudes prepare us for further developments in him and also in Lizzie and Bradley. The boy bitterly strives to attain the surface Bradley reflects, angrily rejecting any attempts to cloud his respectability with the mist of human affections. Charley is determined to raise Lizzie so that he will not sink; Bradley is driven to seek a damaging marriage that will lower him (his odd proposal coming in a churchyard in which the dead are raised above the living); Lizzie tries to evade her love for Eugene because he is so far "above" her. One cannot refrain from noting that, in the eyes of Society, Lizzie is right: the Voice of Society says a female waterman can never be a lady. She has not the requisite surface to reflect, as respectable Bradley does even to the Reverend Frank Milvey, what society expects.

Dickens makes splendid use of surface reflections, again introducing the trope in the *exordium*. An important part of the second chapter gives us the gathering around the Veneering's table as in a glass sparkling. Each of the mirrored fragments is introduced by the bare word *Reflects*:[33] the most startling item is Lady Tippins, doubly reflected and distorted into reality. "Reflects charming old Lady Tippins on Veneering's right; with an immense obtuse drab oblong face, like a face in a tablespoon. . . ." Who sees these reflections from the mirror? Not the Chorus itself, confident in its surfaces, and knowing when repairs are necessary, as is witnessed by "the mature young lady's" powder epaulette, Lady Tippins' varnishing, and even poor Twemlow's hair preparation of egg yolks. All the members of Society know that the surfaces they face desire only to reflect other surfaces. It is the reader, through the narrator, who sees what they are too negligent to see.[34]

---

[33]Another example of Dickens' manipulation of syntactic speech structures; in the Chorus scenes the narrator frequently omits initial "It" and "The."

[34]Bella's mirror, which makes its first appearance in chapter iv, is a great trial to her, initially because, having to share it with Lavvy, she has only "one flat candle and a few inches of looking-glass!" Later she tests her upward rise in the world by looking

The gilt surrounds and silvered backing of the mirror indicate that which supports the surface respectability. What the Veneering mirror first reflects are the "new" crest, "in gold and eke in silver, frosted and also thawed, a camel of all work," and the crest's offspring, the table ornaments, a caravan of gold camels, finally and characteristically bearing salt.[35]

The surface, frozen by cold speculation, on which Podsnap's "skaters" cut arabesques, is perilous, even Veneering having, like the Lammies, to flee across the Channel to maintain a fiction; Twemlow keeps his head up over a stable, while Lady Tippins struggles with hers over a milliner's shop.[36]

Dickens makes it clear that genuine support is hard to find, there being a lot of fool's gold about, and true wealth being hidden deep. Actual coins appear but seldom in the novel; three times there are small piles, and these are all in the hands of the poor.[37] Twice money changes hands as part of a bribe, and the drowned corpses, as we see first in the opening chapter, yield a measure from their turned-out pockets. The main center of the frenzied search is, of course, the dust heaps of the Golden Dustman, eventually valuable as material, but hiding in reality nothing but the paper proof of the fluctuating maliciousness of a dead man's will, frustrated finally by living affection. (It is interesting to note that Mortimer tells Society that Old Harmon made certain unspecified conditions to guarantee against his resurrection.) The dead can bury only the dead-in-life, who are numerous, and active enough in helping bury themselves through digging and delving in moral as well as physical refuse.[38] The most assiduous delver, Wegg, appropriately ends with a splash in the

---

into her more commodious and accommodating glass in "Our House," but it never shows her exactly what she wants to see, though it brings out hints of what the reader wants to see.

[35]The Herald's College has "found out" a Crusading ancestor for the Veneerings; their quest is ironically revealed in their "bran-new pilgrims on the wall, going to Canterbury in more gold frame than procession," and fascinating Charley, whose quest is just beginning.

[36]As mentioned above, the "homes" of the members of Society are typically impermanent, just as they themselves are rootless; the search for a true home is a subsidiary theme throughout, seen, for example, in Eugene's attempt to cultivate the goddess of domesticity when Lizzie's magic is working on him.

[37]In chapter xiii we see the "mysterious paper currency" of the streets blown about with the "dust."

[38]Even the boys at Greenwich show a practised willingness to plunge into the mud for sixpences.

scavenger's dust cart, but his dusty-haired former partner, Venus, emerges with a haircut, bringing with him Pleasant Riderhood, whose back hair may cease to tumble down once she is out of Limehouse Hole. More importantly, the attempt by "Sexton Rokesmith" to bury John Harmon's identity leads to a triumphant resurrection through love. The most significant rising, however, is that of the money itself; heaped by the miserly Old Harmon, it comes to be burnished in use by John Harmon and the Boffins, whose benefactions bring "Harmony" finally out of the "Jail."

The working out of this theme needs the full scope of the novel, but the first Number sets it on course. The sinister and false aspects of money-getting have been hinted at in the first two chapters, its real threat of moral distortion is brought before us in the fourth chapter, when Dickens begins his characterization of Bella as petulant, wilful, and self-seeking. Complaining of having been willed away as though she were "a dozen of spoons, with everything cut and dried beforehand, like orange chips," she exclaims: "I love money and want money—want it dreadfully." Dickens carefully hedges this characterization, for the Wilfers are poor, and the disappointment of Bella's expectations contributes, understandably, to her desire. But when she reaches the stage (after for the first time itemizing her secrets)[39] of declaring: "the whole life I placed before myself is money, money, money, and what money can make of life!"[40] the strong medicine of Boffin's pretended miserliness is needed to cure her.

[39]She later happily itemizes secrets for her husband, ending with the "ship" bringing her baby. In itemizing, she is following a characteristic practice of Dickens' characters, who often indulge in inventoried lists (see, for example, Venus in chap. vii, Lady Tippins in chap. x, Rokesmith in chap. xv, Fledgeby and Lammle in Book II, chap. v, and Eugene in Book II, chap. vi).

[40]J. Hillis Miller uses this outburst as the theme-note of his fine "Afterword" to *Our Mutual Friend* in the Signet Classic edition (New York: New American Library, 1964); reprinted in Price, 169–77. His perspective treatment of the theme of money makes it, yet again, unnecessary for me to go into much detail. I do not, however, agree with him if a narrow and literal meaning is to be put upon his opening comment: "*Our Mutual Friend* is about 'money, money, money, and what money can make of life.' " But the rest of his essay makes such an interpretation unlikely. If asked to take one speech as an emblem of *Our Mutual Friend*'s themes, one could do worse than seize on Boffin's explosive riposte—as astonishing, Dickens makes clear, to Boffin and his pretended conspirators as to the reader, and repeated with evident relish—to Rokesmith's effusive but genuine statement that he wishes to "win [Bella's] affections . . . and possess her heart." Boffin bursts out with "Mew says the cat, Quack-quack says the duck, Bow-wow-wow says the dog!"

Boffin's behavior, like Handford-Rokesmith-Harmon's, proves that pretence in itself is not evil. Two linked rhetorical devices, masks and games, have to be examined before the truly damaging pretences connected with status and money can be adequately condemned. In the opening chapter, it will be recalled, we approach only hesitantly the crucial matter of naming characters, while in the second the names are given as a starter. In the fourth chapter the introduction of a new set of characters, the Wilfers, begins with a disquisition on the name of Reginald Wilfer, alias R. Wilfer (to himself), R. W. (to his wife), Rumty (to his fellow clerks and companions), but most commonly (to the narrator) "the cherub."[41] Dickens, of course, is always redolent of nicknames, allegorical suggestions, personal personifications, and metonymies, but surely, as with illusions to the child's world, he outdoes himself in *Our Mutual Friend*, the very title of which is a reaching after an identity.

Hardly a character escapes some transformation through naming. Leaving aside the minor characters, one finds John Harmon not only as Julius Handford and John Rokesmith, but also as "the Man from Somewhere" (as well as from Jamaica and Tobago), the "Secretary" (with the suggestion that he is a piece of furniture), "Our Mutual Friend," "Jack a Manory," "Chokesmith" and "Artichoke," the "Fortune-teller," "Blue Beard," and the "Mendicant"; he also appears in disguise as George Radfoot, the man who actually was murdered.[42] Bella is the "Boofer Lady," the "Mendicant's Wife," the "Home Goddess," the "Cook," "£.s.d.," and, without capitalization, but characteristically, "the lovely lady," and "a certain mercenary person." Not so much is done with the other two lovers, whose tale is less open to play, but Eugene does appear as "Eligible on View," a "lime merchant," and "T'other Governor," and his father is only "M. R. F.," while Lizzie's name (cited by Jenny lovingly as "Lizzie-Mizzie-Wizzie") at least gives the jealous Miss Peecher an opportunity to tell her pupil Mary Anne that "Lizzie" is not "a

[41]This does not exhaust the list: "the facetious habit had arisen in the neighbourhood surrounding Mincing Lane of making christian names for him of adjectives and participles beginning with R. Some of these were more or less appropriate: as Rusty, Retiring, Ruddy, Round, Ripe, Ridiculous, Ruminative; others derived their point from want of application: as Raging, Rattling, Roaring, Raffish." Later, telling Bella of his fellows' playfulness, R. W. exclaims: "What does it matter? I might be Surly, or Sulky, or fifty disagreeable things that I really shouldn't like to be considered. But Rumty! Lor, why not Rumty?"

[42]In chapter viii, as Rokesmith, he seems to catch the sound of his real name imperfectly, trying "Harmoon" and "Harmarn."

Christian name" but a "corruption" of Elizabeth or Eliza, and that it is very doubtful that there were any Lizzies in the early Christian Church.

In this instance one sees obviously what actually goes on throughout: the names are given almost always by characters to themselves and others, with the narrator chiming in only to complete the chorus, as he does with the cherub, Pa (to Bella and Lavvy) Wilfer. So it happens with Nicodemus Boffin: he is "Noddy" or "Nick" to himself; the "Golden Dustman" to most; "Whatshisname," "Spoffin," "Doffin," "Moffin," and "Poffin" to Mrs. Wilfer (who appears as "Ma," "Mrs. R. W.," the "Tragic Muse," and "a Savage Chief") and to Lavinia (who is "Lavvy" or the "Irrepressible").[43] To Wegg, Boffin is the "Worm and Minion of the Hour," the "ursurper," "Dusty Boffin," and "Bof-fin." For a time Noddy is the "Miser" to all but his wife and John Harmon.[44] Even Mortimer Lightwood, who seems to appear *in propria persona* throughout, takes some minor turns: he is first introduced—and he is the only one to be so introduced—in the mirror's reflection as "a certain 'Mortimer,' " with the name in quotation marks, as though assumed;[45] he too is a "lime merchant," and he appears as "Mr. Mortimer Lightwood" in the narrator's pseudo-newspaper police report in chapter iii.[46]

The members of the Social Chorus, being for the most part interchangeable anyway, do not bother much with pseudonyms, their seemingly transparent names being sufficiently opaque to hide the nothingness within. As the *exordium* makes apparent, they do not know, and do not wish to know, one another, beyond the stage of being everyone's "oldest friend."[47] So they have, just as we have,

[43]The Harmon baby becomes the "Inexhaustible"—behind them both is of course the "Inimitable" himself.

[44]His name also appears in an imaginary list of clients (reminiscent of more familiar lists in other novels) prepared by Mortimer's "dismal" clerk ("whose appropriate name was Blight"): "Mr. Aggs, Mr. Baggs, Mr. Caggs, Mr. Faggs, Mr. Gaggs, Mr. Boffin"; and then: "Mr. Alley, Mr. Balley, Mr. Calley, Mr. Dalley, Mr. Falley, Mr. Galley, Mr. Halley, Mr. Lalley, Mr. Malley. And Mr. Boffin."

[45]In the Number plan, the notes for chapter iii (though not for chapter ii, where his name first appears) give Eugene's name in quotation marks (Boll, p. 102).

[46]In view of the recent discovery that T.S. Eliot first thought of "He Do the Police in Different Voices" as a title for *The Waste Land*, it should be noted that this ability of Sloppy (no other name) permits him to pass himself off to Wegg as a "dustman"; this masking is prepared for in chapter xvi.

[47]Dickens hits on a splendid phrase to express their eagerness, as Podsnap, mistaking Twemlow for Veneering, concludes his insincere greeting with "So glad of this opportunity, I am sure!" He expresses the same sentiment on the part of his

Boots and Brewer, who merge with two other Buffers as required, "a Member, an Engineer, a Payer-off of the National Debt, a Poem on Shakespeare, a Grievance, . . . a Public Office" (and their unnamed wives), later to be joined by a "Bank Director," a "Ship Broker," and a "General Officer," and other bathers, and still later by those "Fathers of the Scrip Church," who, "Like astronomical distances, are only to be spoken of in the very largest numbers," a "Contractor" (or "five hundred thousand men"), a wandering "Chairman" (or "three thousand miles a week"), and a financial genius (or "three hundred and seventy-five thousand pounds, no shillings, and no pence"). (One change is made: when Veneering is elected for Pocket Breeches, his wife becomes "W. M. P.")

What this masking and the many disguises suggest,[48] in addition to their functions in immediate contexts, is the extraordinary difficulty of knowing who one is and who others are in relation to one's dreams and expectations. The search is virtually endless. (Will "Jenny Wren"—"The Dolls' Dressmaker," "The Court Dressmaker"— revert to Fanny Cleaver when "He"—Sloppy?—comes along to change her name?) In the absence of inner definition, all fall back on their reflections in the eyes of others, and vanity ensures that "respectability" will make the largest claims. And in a world floated on evanescent golden dreams, the search for defining buoyancy is inevitably without end.

And so the games are played. The children's games, an acting out of fantasies drawn from deep needs, are positively beneficial, shadowing out mythic patterns. But not so the adult games, full of "moves" (that term beloved of modern philosophers), traps, and trains of powder (which tend to "blow up" under their layers). Some favorite games are blackmail (indulged in by Wegg and Riderhood),

---

wife, repeats it to Veneering (still not knowing who he is), and then, when the confusion is dispelled, says to Twemlow: "Ridiculous opportunity—but so glad of it, I am sure!"

[48] They are supported by the orphan theme, and by such mysteries as Silas Wegg's not knowing why Silas, or why Wegg, and the late Mrs. Riderhood's not being able to explain why her daughter is "Pleasant." Riderhood is himself much more fixed (though he objects to Headstone using his name "as if it was a street pump"), insisting on his first name being proper like Jesse Hexam's, just as he insists that he, like Hexam, has a daughter. Also worth mention is Fascination Fledgeby's inability to capture Georgiana Podsnap's first name; he tries "Georgiana" and even (running after echoes of "concertina" and "scarlatina" to "parach—") "Georgeute." Is there here a hint of Christiana Weller? See Johnson, pp. 497–98, and passim.

bribery (Eugene, Fledgeby), betrayal (Mr. Dolls, Riderhood, Sophronia Lammle, and Venus), extortion (Fledgeby, Riderhood), and deception (almost everyone, but most markedly Fledgeby, Riah, Headstone, Radfoot, Boffin, Venus, and, of course, John Harmon). Some of these games (Sophronia's and Venus' betrayals; Boffin's and Harmon's deceptions, for example) are not self-seeking, but these tend to prove the rule. Much could be made of these adult games, with their aim of getting up by putting down, their assessment of human beings as commodities, and their dependence on prey, but, as their development depends largely on secondary characters and situations not introduced in the first number, I shall not dwell on them here.

One child's game that is prepared for, however, justifies mention, the bittersweet game of family, with its inversion of normal roles and abnormal assumption of functions. Lizzie, herself nursed by the river, is a mother-sister to Charley; Podsnap becomes a "new" godfather to the "new" Veneering baby; and the boyish character of Rumty Wilfer being established, his daughter Bella can begin, as early as chapter iv, to play with him as with a child. The most telling inversion comes only with the introduction of Jenny Wren in the first chapter of Book II.[49] The narrator having described the school of Headstone as in a "toy" neighborhood,[50] we are ready for the chapter to move to a dolls' dressmaker, clothing her creatures according to fashion (weddings, not funerals; and not too near the light), and having, for her own child, a disastrously "prodigal father."[51] As *confirmatio* of the early hints, Jenny's games can be seen not only as a compensation for her own twisted existence, but also as properly attracting three characters who lack mothers: Lizzie, who takes her own turn as seer

[49]This is another *exordium*, bringing before us two new settings, the schools and Jenny's house, introducing Bradley Headstone, with Miss Peecher and Mary Anne, adding a new element to the "respectability" theme (the chapter is entitled "Of an Educational Character"), and so reinforcing the *narratio*; by tying loose strands (Jenny as granddaughter of the drowned old drunkard in list slippers, for example), and introducing Eugene's rival-double, it also advances the *confirmatio*.

[50]Edgar Johnson (p. 1023) is slightly misleading on this point, implying that the whole city is toy.

[51]It would be extravagant to add to poor John Dickens' staggering load of identifications that of Mr. Dolls; still, Dickens did think of him as "a prodigal father," e.g., Johnson, pp. 350, 452. The tremulous hands of the drunken Dolls, especially when he is unable to hold the coins Eugene throws at him, suggest yet another biographical gloss; see the reference to Dickens' early experience with the tipsy bookseller in Hampstead Road (Johnson, p. 31).

and fortuneteller looking into the glow of ashes (drawing gold out of red and gray), accommodates easily to Jenny's world, taking up the needle and learning her letters; Eugene, who on his apparent death-bed needs Jenny's vision of children who deliver us from pain, responds to her motherly nursing; and, as already noted, Fledgeby, who is queerly fascinated by her life-in-death call, finally is minis-tered to by Jenny with "vinegar and brown paper"[52]—and pepper.

Though much more remains to be said about the opening number of *Our Mutual Friend* in rhetorical terms, perhaps enough has been outlined to make the main point. If I may chance the image about a novel so much concerned with gold, Dickens literally loads every rift with ore, preparing the attentive reader for his development and resolution from the first words of the novel. His genius is revealed by an analysis of his opening number, which shows, along with the classical requirements for *exordium, narratio*, and the beginnings of *confirmatio*, a marvellous ability to infuse details with multiple pur-poses, so that for him, as for the dolls' dressmaker, there is no waste, and, as in the dust heaps, there is finally found true value in the detritus.

A brief word about the conclusion may help reinforce my ar-gument. In the penultimate chapter, "Persons and Things in Gen-eral," rhetorically the *peroratio*, with the final chapter, "The Voice of Society," an epilogue, the different worlds of the novel are resolved into one. There are darkness and bitterness enough, but surely *Our Mutual Friend* is not, as Edgar Johnson would have it, "the darkest and bitterest of Dickens' novels."[53] The world is swirling, confused, fluid; those who frantically strive to stay afloat at the cost of others sink in their own thrashings, but those who, learning the usage of love and affection, save others, also save themselves. The archetypal force of

---

[52]Brown paper is curiously applied to the human form in two other situations: Miss Peecher cuts out a pattern for herself, and Venus returns Wegg's leg wrapped like a brown-paper truncheon.

[53]*Charles Dickens*, p. 1043. This view is much less misleading, of course, than G. K. Chesterton's strangely contrary opinion, expressed in his introduction to *Our Mutual Friend*: "The opening of a book goes for a great deal. The opening of *Our Mutual Friend* is much more instinctively energetic and light-hearted than that of any of the other novels of his concluding period. . . . Dickens, in his later years, permitted more and more his story to take the cue from its inception. All the more remarkable, therefore, is the real jerk and spurt of good spirits with which he opens *Our Mutual Friend*." *Appreciations and Criticisms of the Works of Charles Dickens* (London: Dent, 1921), pp. 210–11.

the child's vision, seemingly vulnerable in the hard glare of selfishness, triumphs, flooding the "real" world, threatening and labyrinthian in its first view, with promise and even fulfilment. The "Voice of Society" does not triumph. We open in "these times of ours"; we end, with Mortimer, turning our backs on Society and wending our way to the Temple, "gaily."

# The Dying and Undying Voice

*by Edgar Johnson*

The courage that gave Dickens "a true vision of the world" and the kindness that made it predominantly a comic one . . . also account for his gusto in piling up reiterative detail to mountainous heights. . . .

Only in his earlier days, however, was his art one of improvisation; he became a conscientious literary craftsman painstaking to the minutest detail of style and structure. He had, to be sure, no such general theory of the aesthetics of the novel as Flaubert and James agonized to exemplify in their work. But he took his aims with as much earnestness as they did theirs, and strove to perfect a narrative technique that should never call attention to the devices whereby the reader was prepared for each development in the story, but was unobtrusively put in possession of all that he needed to know in order to make every sequence appear spontaneous and inevitable. Only on the surface does he have affinities with naturalism; deep below, he is vibrant with poetic undertones, pregnant with the weighted symbols of allegory, dwelling often within the dark and mysterious region of myth. If he sometimes overworks certain devices of style, like his notorious tendency to fall into iambics in moments of emotion, and his excessive use of rhetorical repetition, at his best he is dazzling in verbal brilliance, coruscating in comedy, and, if anything, exorbitant in his ingenuity of plotting. *Bleak House*, *Little Dorrit*, and *Our Mutual Friend*, all masterpieces of his maturity, are dark and tremendous symphonic structures almost epic in magnitude and impressiveness.

But amid the torrential plenty of Dickens's creation it is almost invidious to single out individual novels for special praise. *Pickwick* is an inspired improvisation almost throughout, and even in the hasty

"The Dying and Undying Voice" by Edgar Johnson. From *Charles Dickens: His Tragedy and Triumph* (New York, 1952, 2 vols.). These last paragraphs of Part Ten, Chapter Four, (pp. 1139–1141) are reprinted by permission of the author.

and sometimes careless work of *The Old Curiosity Shop* there are brilliances that the toil of other writers could not achieve. "He is, by the pure force of genius," Shaw summarized it, "one of the greatest writers of the world. . . . There is no 'greatest book' of Dickens; all his books form one great life-work: a Bible in fact . . . all are magnificent."

Few of the world's great novelists surpass him in vitality and scope. In the thousands of pages of his works he paints the thronging complexity of nineteenth-century society with a range, solidity, and panoramic inclusiveness equaled only by Balzac. He was Dostoevski's master; for *Crime and Punishment* and *The Brothers Karamazov*, though far greater books than *Barnaby Rudge* and *Martin Chuzzlewit*, are tremendously indebted to their studies of murderers and rebels against society. But with John Jasper, in 1870, Dickens was approaching those dark and tangled labyrinths of alienation that Dostoevski explored in Raskolnikov, whose very name means dissenter. And although there is a kind of twisted comedy in Dostoevski, he cannot come within measurable distance of Dickens's high-spirited and irresistible vivacity. There, indeed, even the great humorists, even Rabelais, Voltaire, and Fielding, must bow to him. "We must go back for anything like it to the very greatest comic poets, to Shakespeare or to Aristophanes."

Charles Dickens, said his adoring friend James T. Fields, was "the *cheerfullest* man of his age." But Fields did not see beneath the surface and did not realize that the cheeful demeanor, the courageous faith, were as much achievements as they were the sparkling gifts of temperament. The *Pickwick* sun had risen out of the darkness of the prison and the blacking warehouse, not out of the radiance of a cloudless childhood. And the resolute belief in life and in humanity that Dickens maintained was a banner that he held high in spite of all the evils he saw in society, and in spite of the gathering clouds of personal misery that shadowed his later years. Dickens carried his distresses in his heart, not upon his lips. In middle age, like his middle-aged hero Clennam, he would not be so weak and cowardly as to hold that because a happiness had not come his way or worked well for him, "therefore it was not in the great scheme, but was reducible, when found in appearance, to the basest elements. A disappointed mind he had, but a mind too firm and healthy for such unwholesome air. Leaving himself in the dark, it could rise into the light, seeing it shine on others, and hailing it."

Dickens himself refused to remain in the darkness. Over and over again, though with increasing weariness and difficulty, he beat back the shadows. Out of his sympathy and indignation at men's sufferings, he built up a picture of society and its failures, of the obstacles to the harmonious fulfillment of human needs, that is unsurpassed for clarity and understanding. Out of his own life of struggle and frustration, he wrought a philosophy of dauntless and generous courage that could laugh while it fought and struck its mighty blows for mankind. He was one of the heroes of art, not merely battling the unpastured dragons of life's waste, but enriching and creating a world. When Keats was near the point of death, "Perhaps," he was heard to say, "I may be among the English poets after my death." Matthew Arnold gave the world's reply: "He is; he is with Shakespeare." Of what English novelist can that be said except Charles Dickens?

| | |
|---|---|
| 1812 | February 7. Born at 387 Mile End Terrace, Landport, Portsea. |
| 1824 | Father imprisoned in the Marshalsea for debt. Dickens works several months in a blacking warehouse. |
| 1824–26 | School at Wellington House Academy, London. |
| 1827–28 | Clerk in attorney's office, studies shorthand. |
| 1829–31 | Shorthand-writer (law-reporter) in Doctors' Commons. Reading at the British Museum. |
| 1832 | Reporter for the *True Sun* and the *Mirror of Parliament*. |
| 1833 | First publication in the *Monthly Magazine*, December. |
| 1834 | Reporter for the *Morning Chronicle*. |
| 1836 | February 7. *Sketches by Boz* published in volume illustrated by George Cruikshank. |
| | April. Engaged to undertake *The Pickwick Papers* in monthly numbers. Sales reach 40,000 in later parts (to November 1837). |
| | April 2. Marries Catherine Hogarth. |
| | December 25. Meets John Forster. |
| 1837 | Charles, first of ten children, born January 6. |
| | February. *Oliver Twist* (to March 1839). |
| 1838 | April. *Nicholas Nickleby* (to October 1839). |
| 1840–41 | *The Old Curiosity Shop* and *Barnaby Rudge* appear in weekly parts in *Master Humphrey's Clock*. |
| 1842 | January–June. Tour of the United States. |
| | October. *American Notes*. |

| | |
|---|---|
| 1843 | January. *Martin Chuzzlewit* (to July 1844). |
| 1844–45 | Dickens and family in Genoa; tour of Italy and France. |
| 1846 | *Pictures from Italy.*<br>October. *Dombey and Son* (to April 1848). |
| 1849 | May. *David Copperfield* (to November 1850). |
| 1850 | March. Starts periodical, *Household Words.* |
| 1851 | May. Performs with amateur company of actors before Queen Victoria. |
| 1852 | March. *Bleak House* (to September 1853). |
| 1854 | April 1. *Hard Times* (to August 12). |
| 1855 | December. *Little Dorrit* (to June 1857). |
| 1857 | June 30. First public reading from his works, London. |
| 1858 | June 10. Public declaration of separation from his wife. |
| 1859 | April 20. *A Tale of Two Cities* (to November 26) in new periodical, *All the Year Round.* |
| 1860 | December 1. *Great Expectations* (to August 3, 1861). |
| 1864 | May. *Our Mutual Friend* (to November 1865). |
| 1867 | November 9. Leaves for tour of public readings in the United States (to April 22, 1868). |
| 1869–70 | Public readings in England. |
| 1870 | June 9. Dies at Gad's Hill Place, Rochester. Buried, June 14, in Westminster Abbey. *The Mystery of Edwin Drood* published posthumously. |

# Notes on the Editor and Contributors

WENDELL STACY JOHNSON is author of books on Arnold, Hopkins, and other Victorians; he is Professor of English at Hunter College and the City University Graduate School.

RICHARD BARICKMAN, Assistant Professor of English at Hunter College, has published essays on Dickens and the nineteenth-century novel.

ROBERT A. COLBY is Professor of Library Science at Queens College and author of *Thackeray's Canvass of Humanity*.

GERALD CONIFF has written on D. H. Lawrence and has taught French and English at Columbia, Hunter, and Pennsylvania State University.

GORDON D. HIRSCH is Associate Professor of English at the University of Minnesota.

EDGAR JOHNSON has written widely acclaimed biographical criticism on British novelists and novels, including—along with the standard life of Dickens—*Sir Walter Scott: The Great Unknown*.

GEORGE LEVINE, Professor of English at Livingstone College of Rutgers University, is author of *The Boundaries of Fiction*.

JOHN M. ROBSON, known for his scholarly work on John Stuart Mill, has been for some years Principal of Victoria College, University of Toronto.

DIANNE F. SADOFF is a member of the Colby College English department.

HARRY STONE, Professor of English at California State University, Northridge, is both editor and critic of Dickens.

RUTH M. VANDE KIEFT is Professor of English at Queens College of the City University of New York.

ALEX ZWERDLING, who has published on English prose from Dickens to Orwell, is Professor of English at the University of California, Berkeley.

# Selected Bibliography

There is as yet no complete scholarly edition of Dickens, although his letters have been edited, and various collections of the fiction are available. The New Oxford Illustrated and Nonesuch editions are useful. Some volumes have appeared in the Clarendon Dickens, published by Oxford University Press under the editorship of Kathleen Tillotson, the late John Butt, and, now, James Kinsley; the series is still in progress.

The standard biography, which is also a work of literary criticism, remains that of Edgar Johnson, *Charles Dickens: His Tragedy and Triumph* (New York, 1952, 2 vols.); of some interest, too, is the *Life* by Dickens's friend John Forster (1872–1874, ed. A. J. Hoppe, 1968, 2 vols.).

Critical writing on Dickens adds up to a staggering number of pages, in book and periodical forms. Useful selected lists of some are provided by George H. Ford and Lauriat Lane in *The Dickens Critics* (1961) and Martin Price in his *Charles Dickens: A Collection of Critical Essays* (1967). For a more recent account, with commentary, one can consult the Dickens chapter, by Philip Collins, in *Victorian Fiction: A Second Guide to Research*, ed. George H. Ford (New York, 1978). Several bibliographies appear periodically; a current listing of studies is published in Summer issues of *Victorian Studies*.

The following list includes fifteen books in English written within the past hundred years—most of them during the past twenty-five years—but it excludes more general books in which criticism of Dickens, though significant, is one section. This means that important work by F. R. Leavis, Percy Lubbock, André Maurois, Sylvère Monod, George Orwell, George Saintsbury, George Bernard Shaw, Hippolyte Taine, and Edmund Wilson is arbitrarily omitted.

Axton, William F. *Circle of Fire* (Lexington, Ky., 1966).

Butt, John, and Kathleen Tillotson. *Dickens at Work* (London, 1957).

Chesterton, G. K. *Charles Dickens* (London, 1901).

Cockshut, A. O. J. *The Imagination of Charles Dickens* (London, 1961).

Engel, Monroe. *The Maturity of Dickens* (Cambridge, Mass., 1959).

Fielding, K. J. *Charles Dickens: A Critical Introduction* (Boston, 1965).

Ford, George H. *Dickens and His Reader* (Princeton, 1955).

Garis, Robert. *The Dickens Theatre* (Oxford, 1965).

Gissing, George. *Critical Studies of the Works of Charles Dickens* (London, 1924; first published 1898).

House, Humphry. *The Dickens World* (London, 1941).

Kincaid, James R. *Dickens and the Rhetoric of Laughter* (Oxford, 1971).

Lindsay, Jack. *Charles Dickens: A Biographical and Critical Essay* (London, 1941).

Marcus, Steven. *Dickens from Pickwick to Dombey* (New York, 1968).

Miller, J. Hillis. *Charles Dickens: The World of His Novels* (Cambridge, Mass., 1958).

Stewart, Garrett. *Dickens and the Trials of the Imagination* (Cambridge, Mass., 1974).

# Index